"Masterful, captivating, page-turning
best." —**Nicola Tallis**

"Anne and Elizabeth blazed new trails in queenship, taking new power and influence, and forever altering the roles of women in government and religion. Accessible while academic, Borman's extensively researched work dispels the notion that Elizabeth was ashamed of her mother and enhances our appreciation of England's most extraordinary—and prolifically written-about—queen, examining the life of Queen Elizabeth I through the lens of her mother's life, death, and legacy." —*Booklist*

"Highly recommended for readers interested in British history, royalty, and the Tudor era." —*Library Journal*

"Masterfully corrects the historical record . . . It's in the details Borman shares illustrating the mother-daughter relationship that this book truly shines." —*Washington Independent Review of Books*

"A seminal and groundbreaking work of meticulous, extraordinary, and detailed scholarship." —*Midwest Book Review*

"A fascinating corrective to the historical limbo into which this crucial connection had fallen . . . Through [Borman's] painstaking research for *Anne Boleyn & Elizabeth I*, even the most trivial scraps of information about Anne's life and activities take on vivid importance, becoming pieces of a human mosaic that reveals just how similar mother and daughter were in temperament, intellect, spirituality and appearance . . . Borman argues with heartfelt credibility that, haunted by Anne's demise, her daughter chose to remain single and childless in order to be the monarch Britain needed." —*Bookreporter*

"Respected Tudor scholar Borman makes a case for both women's political and cultural influence, while detailing how they were shaped by the traditions of the day." —**AARP**

Also by Tracy Borman

Crown & Sceptre: A New History of the British Monarchy from William the Conqueror to Charles III

Henry VIII and the Men Who Made Him

The Private Lives of the Tudors: Uncovering the Secrets of Britain's Greatest Dynasty

Thomas Cromwell: The Untold Story of Henry VIII's Most Faithful Servant

Witches: A Tale of Sorcery, Scandal and Seduction

Queen of the Conqueror: The Life of Matilda, Wife of William I

Elizabeth's Women: Friends, Rivals, and Foes Who Shaped the Virgin Queen

King's Mistress, Queen's Servant: The Life and Times of Henrietta Howard

The Story of the Tower of London

The Story of Kensington Palace

Fiction

The King's Witch

The Devil's Slave

The Fallen Angel

ANNE BOLEYN
&
ELIZABETH I

THE MOTHER AND DAUGHTER
WHO FOREVER CHANGED
BRITISH HISTORY

TRACY BORMAN

Grove Press
New York

First published in Great Britain in 2023 by Hodder & Stoughton, an Hachette UK company.

Printed in the United States of America

First Grove Atlantic hardcover edition: June 2023
First Grove Atlantic paperback edition: April 2024

Library of Congress Cataloging-in-Publication data is available for this title.

ISBN 978-0-8021-6331-8
eISBN 978-0-8021-6133-8

Grove Press
an imprint of Grove Atlantic
154 West 14th Street
New York, NY 10011

Distributed by Publishers Group West

groveatlantic.com

24 25 26 27   10 9 8 7 6 5 4 3 2 1

To Owen Emmerson and James Peacock, with heartfelt thanks

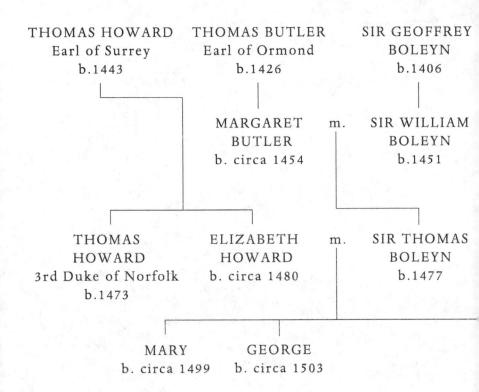

THOMAS HOWARD
Earl of Surrey
b.1443

THOMAS BUTLER
Earl of Ormond
b.1426

SIR GEOFFREY
BOLEYN
b.1406

MARGARET
BUTLER
b. circa 1454

m.

SIR WILLIAM
BOLEYN
b.1451

THOMAS
HOWARD
3rd Duke of Norfolk
b.1473

ELIZABETH
HOWARD
b. circa 1480

m.

SIR THOMAS
BOLEYN
b.1477

MARY
b. circa 1499

GEORGE
b. circa 1503

THE BOLEYNS

FAMILY TREE

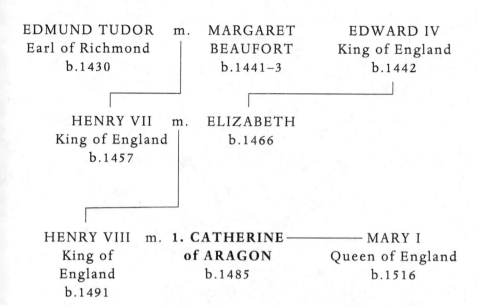

EDMUND TUDOR   m.   MARGARET   EDWARD IV
Earl of Richmond   BEAUFORT   King of England
b.1430   b.1441–3   b.1442

HENRY VII   m.   ELIZABETH
King of England   b.1466
b.1457

HENRY VIII   m.   **1. CATHERINE** ———— MARY I
King of   **of ARAGON**   Queen of England
England   b.1485   b.1516
b.1491

2. ANNE BOLEYN —— ELIZABETH I
b. circa 1501   Queen of England
     b.1533

3. JANE SEYMOUR —— EDWARD VI
b. circa 1508   King of England
     b.1537

4. ANNE of CLEVES
b.1515

5. CATHERINE HOWARD
b. circa 1521–5

6. KATHERINE PARR
b.1512

THE TUDORS

CONTENTS

'Born of an infamous woman'

ONE OF THE oldest and most precious items in the collection of Chequers House, the country residence of Britain's prime ministers, is a tiny, exquisitely crafted ring, fashioned from mother-of-pearl and embossed with rubies and diamonds. The bezel carries an intertwined 'E' in diamonds and 'R' in blue enamel, for 'Elizabeth Regina', which gives a clue both to its status and its age. But the most fascinating part of the ring is hidden from view. It opens to reveal two portraits: one is of Elizabeth I; the other is thought to be of her mother, Anne Boleyn, the most famous – and controversial – of Henry VIII's wives. When closed, the two portraits almost touch: face to face, mother to daughter. The Virgin Queen was well known for her love of expensive and elaborate jewellery, yet this comparatively simple piece was her most cherished possession and she kept it with her until the day she died. It is a poignant symbol of the private reverence in which she held her late mother throughout her long life.

Anne Boleyn and Elizabeth I. Two of the most famous women in British history. Their stories are as familiar as they are compelling. Henry VIII's obsessive love for Anne turning to bitter disappointment when she failed to give him a son, and to her bloody death on the scaffold barely three years after being crowned queen. Her daughter Elizabeth's turbulent path to the throne, her long and glorious reign – a 'Golden Age' for England, with over-seas adventurers, Shakespeare and Spenser, royal favourites, the vanquishing of the Armada – all presided over by the self-styled Virgin Queen.

And yet, Anne and Elizabeth's stories have never been told together: the nature of their relationship, the impact it had on their own lives and those around them, and its enduring legacy. In part, this is understandable. Elizabeth was less than three years old when the Calais swordsman severed her mother's head at the Tower of London on 19 May 1536. Even while Anne had lived, Elizabeth had seen little of her and had followed the traditional upbringing for a royal infant, established in a separate household, far removed from her parents at court. And then there is the impression that Elizabeth herself gave. 'She prides herself on her father and glories in him,' observed Giovanni Michiel, the Venetian ambassador to England during the reign of Elizabeth's sister Mary. The many references that Elizabeth made to her 'dearest father', and the way in which she apparently tried to emulate his style of monarchy when she became queen, all support this view.[1]

By contrast, Elizabeth is commonly (but inaccurately) said to have referred directly to Anne only twice throughout her long life. She made no attempt to overturn the annulment of her mother's marriage or to have her reburied in more fitting surrounds than the Tower of London chapel. The obvious conclu-sion is that Elizabeth was at best indifferent towards, and at worst ashamed of, Anne. But the truth is both more complex and more fascinating. Exploring Elizabeth's actions both before and after she became queen reveals so much more than her words.

Both women broke the mould that Tudor society had created for queens – and, indeed, for women in general. Elizabeth became a ruler of whom Anne would have been inordinately proud – indeed, the sort of queen she herself might have become if her life had not been cut so brutally short. There is a delicious irony in the fact that the child who had been the bitterest disappointment to Henry VIII would go on to become by far the longest-reigning and most successful of his heirs. Her legacy would reverberate down the centuries and can still be felt today. And it was a legacy that derived primarily from her mother.

This book is not a joint biography but will piece together the intertwining threads of Anne and Elizabeth's stories. In so doing, it will shed new light on both women: the private desires, hopes and fears that lay behind their dazzling public personas. It will also consider the surprising influence that each had on the other – both during and after their lifetimes.

When it comes to the Tudors, we have been obsessed with the story of Henry VIII and his six wives and debate endlessly the question of whether Elizabeth I really was the Virgin Queen. Along the way, we have missed the most fascinating relationship of all: that between a mother and daughter who changed the course of British history.

CHAPTER I

'Fettered with chains of gold'

IN CONTRAST TO many other prominent families in Tudor England, the Boleyns could boast neither royal blood nor aristocratic pedigree. They were likely of northern French descent, one of numerous Norman families to settle in England after the conquest of 1066. The first known reference to the Boleyns is found in the deed for a small plot of land close to Norwich in 1188. The family remained in Norfolk for the next three centuries and settled in the prosperous village of Salle, nineteen miles north-west of Norwich, which made much of its wealth from the wool trade. Working as tenant farmers, by the 1400s they had risen to sufficient prominence to be accorded a lavish memorial brass in the local church of St Peter and St Paul.[1] It was commissioned by Geoffrey Boleyn (c.1380–1440), whose son and namesake, a hatter, established the family's fortune. In 1454, the younger Geoffrey became Master of the Worshipful Company of Mercers and was elected Lord Mayor of London three years later. To signal his prestige, he purchased several properties, including the manors of Blickling in north Norfolk and Hever in Kent. By 1451, he was so wealthy that he loaned King Henry VI money for an expedition to France.[2]

The younger of Geoffrey's sons, William, inherited his ambition. As well as continuing to expand his father's various mercantile businesses, he secured employment in the service of King Richard III, who made him a knight of the Order of the

Bath at his coronation in 1483. William also made an extremely advantageous marriage, to Margaret Butler, daughter and co-heiress of the seventh Earl of Ormond, a prominent Irish nobleman. With a deftness that characterised the Boleyns' rise to power, when Richard was defeated by Henry Tudor at the Battle of Bosworth in 1485, they were quick to prove their allegiance to the new king. In the tense early years of the dynasty, during which Henry VII was plagued by plots and pretenders, he gave William Boleyn responsibility for raising the alarm in the event of an attack on England's east coast. Boleyn was subsequently appointed High Sheriff of Norfolk, Suffolk and Kent.

With an eye to the future, William invested heavily in the education of his eldest son and heir, Thomas. Aged about eight when the Tudors came to power, he was fluent in Latin and French, the languages of diplomacy and the court, and grew into a charming and cultured young man. He proved his military prowess, too, by helping to defeat the Cornish rebels in 1497, when he was about twenty years old. Rising rapidly in royal favour, Thomas Boleyn was among the guests at the wedding of Henry VII's eldest son Arthur to Catherine of Aragon in 1501. Arthur died a few months later, which meant that the king had only one surviving son: the ten-year-old Prince Henry. In the summer of 1503, Thomas Boleyn accompanied Henry VII's eldest daughter Margaret to Scotland for her marriage to James IV – a union that linked the houses of Tudor and Stuart for the first time, which would have far-reaching implications for Henry's successors. Boleyn conducted himself so well that he was entrusted with other important diplomatic assignments.

Upon the death of his father in 1505, Thomas became the head of the family and he would take the Boleyns to the apogee of their power and prestige. When Henry VII died in April 1509, his seventeen-year-old son ascended the throne. Thomas was quick to win favour with the new king. He was created a Knight of the Garter (the most senior order of knighthood) and an esquire of Henry VIII's inner sanctum, the privy chamber. Now in his mid-thirties, Thomas Boleyn was almost twice the age of Henry and his boisterous favourites. But he was highly personable and his knowledge of horses, hounds and bowls made him an irresistible companion to a young king more interested in sport than statecraft. Like most of his fellow courtiers, Thomas was so ambitious for promotion that he was content to dedicate his life to royal service – or, as the poet Thomas Wyatt put it, to be 'fettered with chains of gold'.[3]

By the time of Henry VIII's accession, Thomas Boleyn was a married man with a growing family. He had secured one of the most prestigious brides on the marriage market. Elizabeth Howard was the eldest daughter of Thomas Howard, later second Duke of Norfolk, and was appointed to serve Catherine of Aragon, the widow of Prince Arthur, whom Henry had married soon after becoming king. 'She brought me every year a child,' Thomas noted, although only three survived to adulthood: George, Mary and Anne.[4]

The Boleyn children were raised at Blickling Hall and Hever Castle, but the latter soon became the principal Boleyn seat thanks to its proximity to court. Scant details of their upbringing survive. Judging from the date of his entry at court, George seems to have been the youngest, and Mary was later referred to as the elder of the two daughters, although there is some doubt about this.[5] Estimates of Anne's date of birth range from 1501 to 1507. Although it was sons that counted, daughters were useful for forging advantageous marriages. From a young age, Anne and Mary were schooled in the accomplishments expected of young women at the time, including music and dancing, embroidery and religion. They were also taught literature and languages – the latter being something that Anne excelled in. Her Elizabethan biographer, George Wyatt, praised her intellectual gifts and her father proudly noted that she was exceptionally 'toward'.[6]

Thomas Boleyn was soon presented with the perfect opportunity to broaden his daughter Anne's education. Henry VIII was a young king with warlike ambitions that were directed towards England's traditional enemy, France. To bolster his position, he sought an alliance with the Holy Roman Emperor, Maximilian. In 1512, Henry sent Thomas to the Habsburg court in Brabant to treat with Maximilian's daughter, Margaret of Austria, who was regent of the Low Countries for her young nephew, the future Charles V. Boleyn soon won Margaret's trust and favour – to the extent that he helped to secure not only a treaty but also a position for his daughter Anne in Margaret's service. Her court was a vibrant centre of culture and learning that attracted some of the leading intellectual and artistic talents of the age, including the renowned humanist scholar, Erasmus of Rotterdam. For a young woman of Anne's ability it was a glittering opportunity, and she grasped it with both hands.

Anne arrived in Mechelen in the summer of 1513, when she was at most about twelve years old. She quickly won favour with Margaret, who wrote to Thomas Boleyn: 'I find her so bright and pleasant for her young age that I am more beholden to you for sending her to me than you are to me.'[7] With the aid of a tutor assigned to her by Margaret, Anne's command of French improved dramatically, as she was at pains to tell her father in a letter that he treasured for the rest of his life. It is clear from this that Thomas intended his daughter's time in Brabant to be a mere stepping stone to a career at court, as Anne reflected: 'You desire me to be a woman of good reputation when I come to the Court.'[8] He had impressed upon her the importance of becoming fluent in French so that she could converse with Margaret's sister-in-law and Henry VIII's queen,

Catherine of Aragon, who had also been taught the language by Margaret.

The court at Mechelen refined Anne's cultural tastes, too. Margaret was a passionate collector of art and her palaces were filled with masterpieces by the likes of Jan van Eyck and Hieronymus Bosch. She was also an active patron of music and favoured Franco-Flemish composers such as Pierre de la Rue and Johannes Ockeghem. But it was the vibrant intellectual atmosphere that influenced Anne the most. Margaret's court attracted some of the leading lights of the Renaissance and she owned numerous works by female scholars, notably Christine de Pizan.

Born in Venice in 1364, Christine gained renown as a poet and author at the court of Charles VI of France. Her most celebrated work was *The Book of the City of Ladies*, first published in 1405, which has cemented her reputation as an early feminist before that term was even invented. In this, she countered the commonly held idea that women were intellectually inferior to men and pointed to examples of successful female scholars and rulers from the past to bolster the case for female education. 'If it were customary to send little girls to school and teach them the same subjects as are taught to boys, they would learn just as fully and would understand the subtleties of all arts and sciences,' she argued.[9] Margaret, who was living proof of Christine's argument, had at least two copies of *The Book of the City of Ladies* by the time of Anne's arrival at Mechelen. It is likely that Anne read it or at least discussed the ideas it advocated because these would define her approach as queen – and, later, that of her daughter Elizabeth. She would also have seen the set of six tapestries depicting scenes from the book that were presented to Margaret by the city of Tournai. Anne had accompanied Margaret there to meet Henry VIII shortly after his victorious siege in August 1513.

For Anne, the palace of Mechelen was a finishing school like no other, but thanks to a shift in the diplomatic situation it came to an abrupt end in the summer of 1514, when Henry VIII abandoned his Habsburg alliance in favour of France. As part of the bargain, he pledged his sister Mary in marriage to the aged Catholic Louis XII. Both of Thomas Boleyn's daughters were required to join Mary's entourage in France. Anne's stay there lasted longer than the marriage: Louis died just three months later and Mary Tudor returned to England, after secretly marrying Charles Brandon, Duke of Suffolk – a close favourite of her brother Henry – who had been sent to escort her home. Anne subsequently transferred her service to Claude, the young consort of the new French king, Francis I.

Just as she had in Mechelen, Anne – who was probably now in her early teens – quickly became a favourite with her new mistress, who was close to her in age. By contrast, Anne's sister Mary gained a dubious reputation and was rumoured to have been the French king's mistress for a time (he was said to have nicknamed her his 'English mare' and 'hackney'). At some point, Mary Boleyn returned to England, where she entered Catherine of Aragon's service. Soon afterwards, she married William Carey, a close attendant of Henry VIII, and became the king's mistress.

The cultural tastes that Anne had begun to develop in Margaret's court found full expression in France. 'She knew perfectly how to sing and dance . . . to play the lute and other instruments,' reflected the French court poet, Lancelot de Carles.[10] Anne also became 'very expert in the French tongue' and was a voracious reader of French literature.[11] She developed a love of lively conversation – something that set her apart from the quieter, more placid ladies of the court. She had an impeccable sense of style, too, and was described as 'the fairest and most bewitching of all the lovely dames of the French court'. De Carles was full of admiration: 'She became so graceful that no one would ever have taken her to be English by her manners, but a native-born Frenchwoman.'[12]

The greatest influence on Anne during her years in France was her close friendship with Francis I's sister, Marguerite of Navarre, who was twenty-two years old at the time of Anne's arrival – about ten years her senior. Marguerite was an outstanding figure of the French Renaissance. She embraced the radical religious ideas that were sweeping across Europe and led a group of noble ladies who tried to change the Catholic Church from within. She passionately believed that people from all backgrounds should have direct access to the word of God through the translation of the scriptures and had connections with such leading reformers as Jacques Lefèvre d'Etaples, Guillaume Briçonnet, Bishop of Meaux, and the courtier-poet Clément Marot, who entered her service in 1519. As such ideas began to gather ground, Marguerite was able to import banned religious texts through her network of reformist connections. She was also profoundly influenced by Martin Luther, the German theologian whose *Ninety-five Theses*, a blistering attack on the abuses of the Roman Catholic Church in 1517, signalled the beginning of the Reformation and resulted in his excommunication by Pope Leo X in 1521. The ideas that Luther promoted – notably salvation by faith alone, rather than through the authority of the pope and his representatives – later became known as Protestantism.[13]

To the precocious young Anne, all of this was both exciting and inspiring. The seventeenth-century historian Sir Roger Twysden, who wrote a history of the Church of England, credited Marguerite with being the first to spark and nurture Anne's interest in reform, although the fact that Anne's brother George also grew up to be a reformist suggests that the influence may have begun at their home of Hever.[14] Given that Anne was at the peak of her impressionable teenage years, though, Marguerite's influence must have been profound. It is telling that in later years, many of the reformist texts that Anne read and commissioned were in French.[15] The Bible that she used was a French translation by Jacques Lefèvre d'Etaples.

Giving ordinary people direct access to the word of God through such translations was something that Anne would passionately support in later years. Although it would be both anachronistic and inaccurate to describe her as a Protestant – she was an evangelical who sought to change the Church from within – she was fully conversant with Lutheran theology and embraced the idea of justification by faith.

Anne's new companion was the author of numerous texts, notably *Le miroir de l'âme pécheresse* (*The Mirror of the Sinful Soul*). Incest was a dominant theme in the poem, which shocked contemporaries, particularly as Marguerite was known for her love of her brother. Her writings delved beneath the veneer of courtly love and exposed the dangers of sexual violence, betrayal and deception. Anne absorbed Marguerite's lessons with all the eagerness of a precocious young student. Marguerite was living proof that a woman could openly express opinions and wield dominion in every sphere of life, rather than being the submissive vassal of men. Anne never forgot the experience. Twenty years later, when Queen of England, she wrote to her former mentor in tones of affection and admiration that she never expressed towards any of her other acquaintances – the king included.

Marguerite's mother, Louise of Savoy, was another dominant force in the French court. According to one source, she 'lays claim to managing everything' on behalf of her son, Francis I.[16] This was a world in which women exerted power skilfully and effectively, flouting the conventional view that they were the weaker sex, entirely subject to the will of husbands, fathers and brothers. It gave the young Anne Boleyn an entirely different worldview to most of her contemporaries in England and would profoundly influence her queenship.

A recent discovery hints at the status that Anne came to enjoy at the French court. An exquisite, throne-like chair made from walnut was purchased at auction in 2022 by a specialist in Tudor antiques. The intricately-carved decorations, with the Tudor rose entwined around the dolphins of France, symbolises a union between the two countries – possibly the Treaty of Eternal Peace in 1518, which pledged Henry VIII's daughter Mary in marriage to the baby son of Francis I and Queen Claude. At the centre of the decoration are the initials 'AB', which are strikingly similar to those found at Hampton Court and other places associated with Anne. A further clue to its owner is the presence of 'eavesdroppers' close to where the sitter's ears would have been – perhaps a reference to Anne's role as an interpreter at the French court. As ambassador to France, Anne's father would have been instrumental in the negotiation of this alliance and was probably present at the ceremonies and celebrations that accompanied it. Here was a man who took pride in his family and never missed an opportunity to push his children into the limelight. If his daughter Anne had been seated on a chair of such status and presence, it would have been impossible not to notice her. Thomas may have even commissioned it himself, or it could have been a gift from Claude or Marguerite.[17] Either way, it is testament to her exhalted position in the French queen's service.

Anne's time in France came to a sudden end in 1521, when a shift in the diplomatic situation prompted her recall to England. There was another reason: her uncle, Thomas Howard, later third Duke of Norfolk, wanted to marry her into the Irish Butler family, who were contesting the Boleyns' right to the earldom of Ormond. The match fell through, but Anne soon attracted a host of other suitors – notably the poet Thomas Wyatt, who shared her interest in religious reform, and Henry Percy, later sixth Earl of Northumberland. George Cavendish, a servant of Henry VIII's chief adviser Cardinal Thomas Wolsey, claimed that there was such 'secret love' between Anne and Percy that they planned to marry.[18]

Anne's father had secured her a position in Catherine of Aragon's household, where she joined her sister Mary. The first recorded mention of her is at a court pageant organised by Cardinal Wolsey for Henry VIII on Shrove Tuesday (4 March) 1522. Anne, now in her late teens or early twenties, played the part of Perseverance – a role that would prove fitting in the years to come. The chronicler Edward Hall describes how she and her fellow ladies were clad in gowns of white satin with the name of their character embroidered in gold, and on their heads they wore 'bonnets of gold, with jewels'.[19] Anne made quite an impression. 'Coming to be planted in the Court, she drew all men's thoughts to set upon her the highest and dearest prince of worthiness,' recorded George Wyatt.[20]

In the eyes of her contemporaries, Anne's allure derived more from her personality than the way she looked. 'Madam Anne is not one of the handsomest women in the world,' sneered the Venetian ambassador. Hers was not the fashionably pale beauty admired at Henry VIII's court. Her complexion was 'swarthy', 'rather dark' or 'sallow . . . as if troubled with jaundice', her hair raven-black, her bosom 'not much raised'. But her eyes – 'black and beautiful' – took 'great effect' on those whom she fixed with her gaze. 'Truth to tell,' observed de Carles, 'such was their power that many surrendered to their obedience.'[21]

The years spent in France had given Anne an irresistible *je ne sais quoi*. Her continental sophistication and polish made the English ladies with whom she vied for attention seem dull and provincial. Her skill at singing, dancing and playing instruments excelled theirs; her style and fashion were striking and unique. Even the hostile Catholic writer Nicholas Sander admitted: 'She was always well dressed, and every day made some change in the fashion of her garments.'[22] Anne did not just love fashion for its own sake, but rightly judged that in order to act the part, she must dress the part. George Wyatt noted that Anne's looks 'appeared much more excellent by her favour passing sweet and cheerful; and . . . also increased by her noble presence of shape and fashion, representing both mildness and majesty more than can be expressed'. While he admitted that she could be 'very haughty', he concluded: 'For behaviour, manners, attire and tongue she excelled them all.'[23]

Little else is recorded of Anne during the early years of her service at court. Only when she caught the notice of the king did this model of French sophistication set tongues wagging. The first notable occasion was another Shrove Tuesday, in 1526. On that day, Henry VIII jousted in the guise of a tortured lover, clad in cloth of gold and silver embroidered with 'a man's heart in a press, with flames about it' and the slogan: 'Declare I dare not'.[24] Proof that he was referring to Anne is found in a letter he wrote to her the following year, in which he admitted to 'having been now above one whole year struck with the dart of love'.[25] The affair appears to have developed gradually out of a charade of courtly love. By late 1526, all the court knew that Lady Anne was the king's latest *inamorata*.

This was very different to Henry's previous infidelities, though, for Anne proved to be the most unyielding of mistresses. Perhaps having learned from the example of her sister Mary, who had been quickly discarded after the king had grown bored, Anne refused to sleep with him. Perhaps, too, she had her eyes on the far greater prize of being queen. According to George Wyatt, Catherine of Aragon soon had the measure of her rival and told her: 'You are not like others, you will have all or none.'[26] The idea that the king might set aside his faithful and popular wife and marry Thomas Boleyn's daughter would have been unthinkable to most of his subjects – and, perhaps at this stage, to Henry himself. This was not an age when divorce was commonplace, particularly among kings. But Anne knew that he was tiring of a wife who, at forty, was five years his senior and apparently already past childbearing.

Anne played her hand perfectly. The stridently self-confident king was not used to rejection and there was a growing sense of insecurity in his letters. He lamented that he was 'not yet sure whether I shall fail or find a place in your affection', and begged Anne to 'give yourself, body and heart, to me'.[27] He even promised that if she assented, he would make her his 'sole mistress', a privilege that he had granted no other woman before. But Anne was determined to hold out for more and told him: 'I would rather lose my life than my honesty . . . Your mistress I will not be.' She proceeded to play the king with all the skill that she had learned at the French court, giving him just enough encouragement to keep him interested and admonishing him if he tried to overstep the mark. Thus, one moment Henry was writing with gleeful anticipation at the prospect of kissing Anne's 'pretty duggs [breasts]', and the next he was lamenting how far he was from the 'sun', adding mischievously, 'yet the heat is all the greater'.[28] For a king who admitted to finding writing 'tedious and painful', the fact that seventeen of his letters to Anne survive testifies to his passion for her.[29]

This charismatic and accomplished young émigré from the French court was unlike any other woman Henry had met. He was captivated by her sharp mind and quick wit, her unshakeable self-confidence. But Anne also held out the promise of giving Henry the thing he desired most in the world: a son. Despite numerous pregnancies, Catherine of Aragon only had one surviving child, the Princess Mary. The Tudors were still a fledgling dynasty and Henry was painfully aware that he needed to secure its future with a male heir. He made much of his illegitimate son, Henry FitzRoy, born in 1519 (the result of an affair with a lady-in-waiting named Bessie Blount), as if to prove that the problem with siring sons lay not with him but with his wife. A contemporary scholar in the king's service listed among Anne's attractions the fact that she was 'young, good-looking . . . and likely enough to have children'.[30]

As Henry's obsession with Anne grew, so did her influence at court. The Imperial ambassador, Eustace Chapuys, warned Princess Mary that her mother's rival 'is the person who governs everything, and whom the King is unable to control'.[31] A Venetian envoy reported: 'There is now living with him [the king] a young woman of noble birth, though many say of bad character, whose will is law to him.'[32] Another visitor to court was shocked at how Henry 'caresses her [Anne] openly and in public as if she were his wife'.[33] Anne was constantly in the king's presence – far more so than his consort. Her behaviour towards Catherine of Aragon grew ever more insolent. She remarked to her fellow ladies-in-waiting that 'she did not care anything for the Queen, and would rather see her hanged than acknowledge her as mistress'.[34] The building accounts for Hampton Court show that in June 1529, Anne employed glaziers to get rid of her royal mistress's emblems from the windows of her apartments. She also treated Catherine's daughter with disdain, boasting 'that she will have the said Princess for her lady's maid . . . or to marry her to some varlet'.[35] As a show of support for her mother, Mary, who was ten years old when her father's interest in Anne first came to notice, began to strongly identify herself with the Spanish cause, throwing in her lot with Chapuys and his Imperial master, Charles V. She also fervently embraced her mother's Roman Catholic faith.

Growing sympathy for the queen and resentment towards her rival, both at court and across the kingdom, worked little effect on Henry, who began to contemplate the shocking step of setting aside Catherine so that he could marry her lady-in-waiting. In 1527, he promised marriage to Anne, little knowing either how long he would have to battle for it or how tumultuous the result would be. Given that England was part of Roman Catholic Europe, the king required the pope's permission to secure an annulment, but this was made tortuously complex by international politics and war. In May 1527, Rome had been sacked by troops loyal to the Holy Roman Emperor, Charles V, and Pope Clement VII had been made a prisoner in his own citadel. Catherine of Aragon was Charles's aunt so Clement was understandably reluctant to antagonise him. But he also kept Henry in play by making conciliatory moves, including sending his legate, Cardinal Campeggio, to hear the case in England.

After years of protracted negotiations and frustrations, Anne and her supporters advocated a change of strategy that would have far-reaching implications. A group of leading theologians, including Anne's chaplain, Thomas Cranmer, and another of her close associates, Hugh Latimer, collected a body of evidence from ancient texts (known as the *Collectanea satis copiosa*), which advocated the radical notion that royal power was superior to the pope's. This was supported by a number of universities in Europe, whose collective opinions were published under the patronage of Anne's father in April 1531. All of this chimed with the growing criticism of the Roman Catholic Church that was sweeping across Europe and would become known as the Reformation.

Anne had long been interested in religious reform. Her time in France – particularly that spent with Marguerite of Navarre – had instilled in her a desire to rid the Church of abuses and corruption. One of the most notorious was the sale of 'indulgences', which lessened the time a person would spend in purgatory after their death. Fierce criticism was also levelled at the monasteries, those great symbols of the Roman Catholic faith, many of which had grown rich from the profits of their vast estates and neglected the charitable function they were supposed to fulfil. The martyrologist John Foxe claimed that Anne was sent a copy of *Supplication for the Beggars* by the radical Protestant exile and propagandist Simon Fish in 1528, the year it was published. The pamphlet was a stinging attack on the abuses of the Roman Catholic Church, which Fish accused of everything from greed to murder and even treason. According to Foxe, Anne showed this to the king, who was so impressed that he offered immunity to Fish and his wife so that they could return to England.[36]

Two years later, a Frenchman named Loys de Brun presented Anne with a French treatise on letter-writing as a New Year's gift. The text makes it clear that she was already known for her reformist beliefs because it refers to her habit of reading French books 'for the teaching and discovering of the true and straight path of all virtue: such as approved translations from holy scripture, filled with all good doctrines; or equally, other good books by erudite men, giving salutary remedies for this mortal life and consolation to the immortal soul'.[37] Anne also commissioned a manuscript volume of 'The Epistles and Gospels' from her sister-in-law's father, Henry Parker, Lord Morley, in which the scriptural texts were written in French.

Inspired by Marguerite's example of a woman who could wield influence over a male-dominated court, Anne now began passionately to champion religious reform. John Foxe listed her at the head of a group of reformers who shaped the religious views of the king himself: 'So long as Queen Anne, Thomas Cromwell, Archbishop Cranmer, Master Denny, Doctor Butts with such like were about him and could prevail with him, what organ of Christ's glory did more good in the church than he?'[38]

Anne owned a specially illuminated copy of William Tyndale's illegal translation of the New Testament, which carried the proud inscription 'Anna Regina Angliæ', and left an open copy of it in her apartments for her ladies to read. She also gave them each a book of devotions for their personal use. A cornerstone of the reformist beliefs was that the Bible should be translated into English so that everyone should have direct access to the word of God. One of Anne's own books of devotions that survived into the nineteenth century argued strongly that for too many years people had been 'oppressed with the tyranny of thy adversary of Rome . . . and kept close under his Latin letters' and referred to Henry as 'thy supreme power our prince'.[39] Such ideas were deeply subversive and had previously been confined largely to academic circles. But, thanks to Anne's exalted position, they now began to circulate throughout the court and polite society.

The notion of the pope as a tyrant was most forcefully expressed in Tyndale's controversial work, *Obedience of a Christian Man*. As well as arguing that people should experience God through the scriptures, rather than through the intercession of priests and other trappings of the Church, it also advocated the radical idea that kings ought to exert supreme authority over their states, unfettered by the church in Rome. Both John Strype and George Wyatt recount that Anne put a copy into the king's hands, having marked certain passages for his attention, and 'besought his grace most tenderly to read the book'. This was an extremely risky move. Earlier in his reign, Henry had publicly denounced the teachings of Martin Luther and defended the supremacy of the pope, earning him the title '*Fidei Defensor*' (Defender of the Faith) from Leo X. But thanks to the long and bitterly frustrating campaign for an annulment, much had changed since then. Tyndale's work had a profound impact on Henry, who upon first consulting it was said to have exclaimed: 'This is a book for me and all kings to read.'[40] Thenceforth, he became increasingly fixated with the idea of creating a church over which he, not the pope, wielded dominion.

Henry might have aligned himself with such beliefs more for political expediency than a genuine zeal for reform, but the same was not true of the woman whom he was intent upon marrying. Since arriving in England in 1522, Anne had befriended a number of leading reformers at court – among them the king's personal physician, William Butts, who introduced her to a group of evangelicals at Cambridge University. Through Anne's influence her reformist contacts were later appointed to powerful bishoprics – positions that they held throughout Henry's reign and, in some cases, that of his successor. It was said that men such as Hugh Latimer, Nicholas Shaxton, Thomas Goodrich, Edward Fox, William Barlow and even Thomas Cranmer, who was appointed Archbishop of Canterbury in 1533, owed their positions to her. The latter would later remark: 'I loved her not a little for the love which I judged her to bear towards God and the Gospel.'[41] Anne also chose the outspoken reformist Thomas Burgh of Gainsborough Old Hall in Lincolnshire as her Lord Chamberlain.

Among the other reformers who benefited from her influence was the Cambridge scholar Edward Crome. He had been interrogated in the king's presence for radical preaching in 1530 and forced to recant. But he did not relinquish his beliefs and had several more brushes with the law in the years to come. It is a testament to the strength of Anne's own reformist principles that she did not shrink from being associated with such a controversial character but nominated him to the rectory of St Mary Aldermary in London – a post that he retained until his death in 1562, by which time Anne's daughter Elizabeth was on the throne.

Anne's patronage of reformers extended beyond England. She was in touch with French reformers such as Clément Marot, to whom she had been introduced by Marguerite of Navarre. The evangelical clergyman William Latymer referred to a French gentlewoman named Mrs Marye who 'fled out of France into England for religion' and was so well treated by Anne that she said she preferred banishment to being at home with her friends. Anne secured the king's agreement to bring another evangelical, John Sturmius, from Paris to England, although by the time Henry's letters arrived, Sturmius had already escaped to Germany. She had more success in providing sanctuary to the French evangelical Nicholas Bourbon, 'a learned young man, and very zealous in the scriptures'. Upon his arrival in England, she had him installed at her expense in the household of the king's physician, William Butts, and appointed him tutor to her nephew Henry Carey, as well as the son and namesake of the king's favourite, Henry Norris and Thomas Howard.[42]

Latymer described Anne as 'well read in the scriptures' and 'a patron of Protestants'. He recalled that she told her chaplains: 'I have carefully chosen you to be the lanterns and light of my court' and that she wished them to teach her household 'above all things to embrace the wholesome doctrine and infallible knowledge of Christ's gospel'.[43] She sent Latymer to Flanders to buy radical religious texts on her behalf and he was seized by the English authorities on his return, along with the books. In the early seventeenth century, the daughter of Sir William Locke, who supplied velvet for bindings, recalled: 'I have heard my father say that when he was a young merchant and used to go beyond sea, Queen Anne Boleyn that was mother to our late Queen Elizabeth caused him to get her the gospels and epistles written in parchment in French together with the psalms.'[44] Anne was also known for the protection she offered to importers of illegal English scriptures. A man named George Joye once sent her a sample sheet of the book of Genesis translated into English.

Anne specially commissioned a number of French evangelical

texts. Her brother George produced hybrid versions of reformist works for her, with the Bible text in French (which was legal) but the far more subversive commentary in English. One of these was by Jacques Lefèvre d'Etaples, whose works Anne had long been influenced by. Writing in 1541, a religious radical named Richard Hilles included Anne and her brother in a list of the most influential patrons of reform. One of Anne's associates later told her daughter Elizabeth: 'True religion in England had its commencement and its end with your mother.'[45]

Anne's personal piety is attested by her protection and advancement of religious radicals who might otherwise have been condemned for heresy. In 1528, she intervened in a controversy that had erupted at Wolsey's foundation, Cardinal College, Oxford. Thomas Garret, curate of the nearby All Hallows, Honey Lane, was arrested for selling heretical books to scholars at the college. 'I beseech your grace with all my heart to remember the parson of Honey Lane for my sake shortly,' Anne pleaded with Wolsey. Garret was spared and enjoyed a flourishing career for the next few years.[46] William Betts and Nicholas Udall, who had also been implicated in the scandal, went on to enjoy Anne's patronage, Betts becoming her chaplain and Udall writing verses for her coronation pageants.

In around 1530, an evangelical called Thomas Alwaye petitioned her to help release him from his 'miserable thraldom' after he had been persecuted by Wolsey and other senior bishops for buying copies of the New Testament in English, along with other prohibited texts. His letter makes it clear that he was by no means the first reformer on whose behalf Anne had interceded:

> I remembered how many deeds of pity your goodness had done within these few years . . . whereof some looking for no redemption were by your gracious means not only freely

delivered out of costly and very long imprisoning, but also by your charity largely rewarded and all thing restored to the uttermost, so that every man may perceive that your gracious and Christian mind is everywhere ready to help, succour and comfort them that be afflicted, troubled and vexed.[47]

In espousing the reformist religion, Anne bolstered the annulment campaign but also made some dangerous enemies at court. The religious conservatives were in no doubt that the king's increasingly radical reforms could be laid at her door – and that of her brother, George. Chapuys reported to his master, Charles V, that 'the concubine' had told the king: 'He is more bound to her than man can be to woman, for she extricated him from a state of sin . . . and that without her he would not have reformed the Church to his own great profit and that of all the people.' He later described her as 'the principal cause of the spread of Lutheranism in this country'.[48] An anonymous sketch that was delivered to Anne's chambers reveals the depth of hatred towards her. Alongside a male figure labelled 'H' were two females labelled 'K' and 'A' – the latter having no head. She showed it to one of her ladies, who remarked in horror that if she thought it might come true, she would not marry the king 'though he were an emperor'. But Anne calmly replied: 'For the hope I have that the realm may be happy by my issue, I am resolved to have him whatsoever might become of me.'[49]

In February 1531, Anne's brother played a key role in persuading senior members of the English church of the scriptural justification for the king's supremacy over Rome. Convocation, the church's ruling body, granted Henry the title of 'singular protector, supreme lord, and even, so far as the law of Christ allows, supreme head of the English church and clergy'. It was a major victory for the Boleyn faction – and the first step towards a sweeping reformation of England's religious life. The same year, Queen Catherine was banished from court and her rooms given to Anne. Thenceforth, she was referred to as the 'Dowager Princess' to emphasise Henry's assertion that her marriage to his late brother Arthur had been consummated, which meant that their own was invalid. Edward Hall noted that by the beginning of 1532, 'the Lady Anne Boleyn was so much in the king's favour, that the common people which knew not the king's true intent, said and thought that the absence of the queen was only for her [Anne's] sake'. The chronicler, who was always at pains to present Henry in as positive a light as possible, claimed that the only reason he had sent Catherine of Aragon from court was because he had been rebuked by members of the Church 'for keeping company with his brother's wife'.⁵⁰ The assertion must have sounded weak, even to Hall's ears.

On 1 September 1532, Henry personally invested Anne with the Marquessate of Pembroke. This seemed to be the clearest signal yet that he meant to make her his queen, since the only other marquesses at that time were members of the royal family. A contemporary account describes how she wore 'her hair loose hanging about her shoulders' – a symbol of virginity.⁵¹ Flanked by a large entourage of 'great ladies', she dressed in crimson velvet and ermine, wore a coronet of gold and was 'completely covered with the most costly jewels', according to the Venetian envoy.⁵² The letters patent, issued early the following year, which confirmed her elevation to the peerage, included the first known use of the falcon as Anne's official badge.⁵³ But they also sounded a note of uncertainty about the king's intentions because the wording stipulated that the title would descend to her son even if he was born outside lawful marriage.⁵⁴

A month after her ennoblement, Anne escorted the king to

Calais, where he hoped to enlist the support of his rival, Francis I, for his intended marriage. Back on familiar territory, Anne revelled in the occasion. She hoped to see Francis's sister and her former companion, but Marguerite failed to attend. Undeterred, Anne made the most of the visit and was shown great courtesy by Francis, which she and Henry were quick to interpret as approval for their union. Bolstered by this, and now certain that the marriage was within her grasp, Anne at last consented to sleep with Henry.

According to Hall, soon after disembarking at Dover in November 1532, the couple went through a secret ceremony of betrothal. Upon their return to court, the sharp-eyed Chapuys noticed that 'the King cannot leave her for an hour'.[55] By December, Anne was pregnant. That Henry was aware of her condition is suggested by the fact that he transferred to her a sizeable gift of gilt plate and, in the second week of December, went with her to inspect new building works at the Tower. Then, on 24 January, it became common knowledge that Anne's chaplain, Thomas Cranmer, would be the next Archbishop of Canterbury. Lancelot de Carles remarked that Anne's pregnancy:

> . . . brought very great joy to her heart
> For she believed that it was a guarantee
> Of love and of the sure and certain hope
> That the future would continue in this way.[56]

The king now had to act quickly if the baby was to be born legitimate. Even though his wrangling with the Church was ongoing and he had not yet secured an annulment from Catherine, he married Anne on 25 January 1533 in his private chapel at Westminster.

CHAPTER 2

'A virgin is now born'

EVEN THOUGH HER marriage to the king was still under wraps, Anne could not resist dropping heavy hints that she was expecting his child. As ever, it was Chapuys who was the first to pick up on them. On 15 February, he reported to Charles V that Anne had told her uncle the Duke of Norfolk that she would go on pilgrimage to pray to the Virgin Mary if she was not pregnant by Easter. The following week, she loudly declared a craving for apples, then went back to her apartments, her laughter echoing along the corridors. The king himself gave several signs that something important had changed in their relationship. In March, he arranged for preachers at court to proclaim the invalidity of his marriage to Catherine and 'the virtues and secret merits' of Anne.[1] Cranmer was consecrated as Archbishop of Canterbury at the end of the month and a few days later convocation, the parliament of the English church, pronounced the king's first marriage invalid.

Easter Saturday, 12 April 1533, was an important day for Anne. In his chronicle, Edward Hall noted that the king 'perceiving his new wife Queen Anne, to be great with child', appointed all necessary officials to attend her, after which 'she went to her closet openly as queen, with all solemnity'.[2] Now that she had safely passed the uncertain weeks of early pregnancy, Henry was content that she should at last be openly acknowledged as his queen, with her own household, even though his marriage to Catherine of Aragon had not yet been formally ended. Around the same time, the king ordered Parliament 'to corroborate and confirm the king's marriage and establish the succession of the same'.[3]

The event sent shockwaves across the court and caused a flurry of ambassadorial dispatches. 'This morning of Easter Eve, the Marchioness Anne went with the King to high mass, as Queen,' reported the Venetian ambassador, 'and with all the pomp of a Queen, clad in cloth of gold, and loaded with the richest jewels; and she dined in public; although they have not yet proclaimed the decision of the Parliament.' Chapuys was even more scandalised: 'She has changed her name from Marchioness to Queen, and the preachers offered prayers for her by name. All the world is astonished at it for it looks like a dream, and even those who take her part know not whether to laugh or to cry.' For all Henry's defiance in taking a new wife before freeing himself of the old, Chapuys noted that he was 'very watchful of the countenance of the people' and that he had secretly instructed his new Archbishop of Canterbury to 'declare that he was at liberty to marry as he has done without waiting for a dispensation or sentence of any kind'.[4]

Henry was right to be nervous. Even his greatest apologist, Edward Hall, admitted: 'Many wise men said that the king was not well counselled to marry the lady Anne Boleyn before the divorce was adjudged, for by marrying before the first marriage was dissolved, they said, that the second marriage might be brought in question, and verily they said true.' He reported rumours that the pope would put a curse on all Englishmen and that he and Charles V would 'invade the realm and destroy the people'. He added, though, that other 'wise men' thought the marriage was 'Godly and honourably done . . . and that God loved this marriage, considering that the new Queen was . . . with child.'⁵ There was the incontrovertible fact, though, that the child had been conceived outside of wedlock. Even before it had drawn breath, its legitimacy had been called into question. It was a stain that no amount of propaganda would ever entirely erase.

Anne's pregnancy was formally announced in May, although there could have been few people at court who were not already aware of it. An extra panel had been added to her skirts to accommodate her growing belly. On 23 May, Archbishop Cranmer, presiding over a special court at Dunstable Priory, ruled that the king's first marriage was unlawful. Five days later, he declared Henry's new marriage valid. By then, preparations were already underway for Anne's coronation. Despite the speed with which they were made ready, the festivities surrounding the event were so ostentatious that they far eclipsed those for Catherine of Aragon's coronation in 1501.

No detail was overlooked in the planning, as the original twenty-page document outlining the procedures testifies.⁶ The overarching theme was the assumption of the blessed Virgin Mary and the symbolism was carefully designed to emphasise the legitimacy of Anne's position and her suitability as queen. The fact that she had recently been created Marquess of Pembroke had done little to enhance her status in the eyes of Henry's subjects. Compared to the king's first wife, she was little more than a commoner – only the second such queen since 1066.⁷ Confident that Anne would be the mother of his heir, Henry knew it was vital to erase any doubt among his people that she was the rightful queen in order to safeguard the future of the Tudor dynasty.

On 29 May 1533, a flotilla of barges 'garnished with banners and streamers' and cloth of gold conveyed Anne and her new husband from Greenwich to the Tower, ahead of which was 'a great red dragon continually moving and casting off wild fire' that was in turn surrounded by 'terrible monsters and wild men'.[8] The whole effect was 'a right sumptuous and triumphant sight to see and hear . . . a thing of another world'.[9] It was not without controversy, though. The new queen's Lord Chamberlain, Thomas Burgh, had sparked outrage among the citizens of London by seizing Catherine of Aragon's royal barge and ripping her coat of arms off it so that it could be replaced with those of the new queen. He was honoured with a place in the barge, close to his mistress.

Upon arriving at the Tower, Anne ascended the stone steps that led from the river to the wharf and walked the short distance to the Byward postern gate, where Henry was waiting to greet her with a kiss. The couple then made their way to the royal apartments, which had been lavishly refurbished for the occasion. A new great chamber and dining room had been built, together with a bridge across the moat that provided access from the new queen's private garden into the city. The preponderance of yellow ochre would have made the apartments dazzling to behold. The same colour was used for Anne's apartments at Greenwich and Eltham, which suggests it was either a favourite with her or symbolised the bright new beginning that she represented. At the Tower, the finishing touch was the addition of the onion domes atop the White Tower, creating the iconic silhouette that is still recognised the world over.[10]

During the royal couple's two-day stay, eighteen Knights of the Bath were created – a tradition established by Henry IV at his coronation in 1399 and continued ever since. They included a young man called Francis Weston, the king's former page and sporting partner. Most of those honoured were connected to the new queen, though – such as Henry Parker, her brother George's father-in-law, and Edward Stanley, Earl of Derby, who was married to Anne's cousin, Katherine. Fifty Knights Bachelor were also created, among them Henry Norris and William Brereton – names that, like Weston's, would become notorious in a little under three years' time.

For her ceremonial entry into the city, Anne had chosen a classical theme, with scenes designed by Holbein representing Apollo and the Muses, the Three Graces and the Fountain of Helicon. The overarching message was one of renewal, expressed through the transformation of London's monuments and streets. The new queen's white falcon was on prominent display throughout the pageant, resting on a bed of Tudor roses.[11] Although it is now synonymous with Anne and the Boleyns in general, Henry had only granted it to her on her elevation to the marquessate of Pembroke. It was a fitting choice because the same bird had long been an emblem of Anne's Irish ancestors, the Butlers, earls of Ormond. It also had strong royal associations and had been used as an emblem by the celebrated warrior king Edward III, as well as by Henry's maternal grandfather, Edward IV, with whom he strongly identified.[12] Perhaps, too, the fact that the falcon is a bird of prey of which the female is larger than the male appealed to a woman known for her domineering nature.

One of the falcon's earliest and most glorious appearances had been at Hampton Court, where Henry had ordered extensive redecorations in Anne's honour, stripping away the initials and emblems of his first wife and replacing them with Anne's. Even though Anne was probably not then queen, each beautifully carved oak falcon wore an imperial crown (a testament to the king's ambition to set himself above the pope) and carried a sceptre. Painted gold and silver so that they would catch the light, they rested on a bed of red and white Tudor roses atop a tree stump – a centuries-old royal badge. Roses were synonymous with fertility, and the colours with which these were painted symbolised the union of Lancaster and York in the Tudor dynasty. The speed with which they were put up is suggested by the slipshod painting.

The falcons in the coronation pageant were also crowned. In one spectacular scene, a temporary castle had been built with a hill in the background. As Anne's procession passed by, a stump on the hill poured out a mass of red and white roses, then a painted cloud opened up to release a white falcon, which swooped down onto the flowers. As a final touch, an angel descended from the same cloud and placed an imperial crown upon the head of a white falcon, declaring: 'It cometh from God, and not of man.'[13] The message was clear: with the accession of Anne, already pregnant, new life would burst forth from the Tudor stock.

As the queen moved past the pageant, 'The White Falcon', a ballad by the contemporary playwright Nicholas Udall, was read out:

> Of body small.
> Of power regal,
> She is, and sharp of sight;
> Of courage hault
> No manner fault
> Is in this Falcon White,
>
> In chastity,
> Excelleth she,
> Most like a virgin bright:
> And worthy is
> To live in bliss
> Always this Falcon White.[14]

Throughout the procession, the city of London was displayed as a kind of celestial Jerusalem, with Anne as the Virgin. Much was made of the fact that she shared her name with the Virgin's mother and a contemporary account of the coronation extolled Anne as a 'splendid image of chastity'.[15] The new queen's purity was emphasised by the fact that she wore 'her hair hanging down' and was dressed all in white. Her litter was of white cloth of gold, led by two palfreys 'clad in white damask down to the ground, head and all'.[16] By contrast, her ladies were dressed in crimson velvet.

The new queen's swollen belly gave a lie to all of this, particularly as her pregnancy appeared more advanced than might be expected, given that she had only married Henry a little over four months earlier. A pageant at the corner of Gracechurch Street made a direct reference to her condition. The character of Urania, one of nine Muses portrayed, sang in Latin:

Indeed if the stars keep faith,
And are neither too false nor vain,
Already for a long time Anne's womb has been swelling,
And soon a sweet prince will appear.[17]

Anne may have triumphed in her pregnancy but she was all too well aware that many of her new husband's subjects viewed her unborn child as a bastard growing within a usurper's belly. As the author of an anonymous Spanish chronicle observed: 'It is a thing to note that the common people always disliked her.'[18] A month after her coronation, a Lancashire parson ranted against the proclamation of Queen Anne: 'I will none for queen but Queen Catherine; who the devil made Nan Bullen, that whore, queen?' Others called the new queen a 'goggle-eyed whore', a 'whore and harlot' who 'should be burned in Smithfield'.[19] But Anne knew their vicious words would count for nothing if she carried a son. Along the processional route were numerous symbols of fertility, including an image of the 'fruitful' Saint Anne, 'with all her issue beneath her'.[20] The fact that Saint Anne had produced only daughters was quietly ignored. At the coronation ceremony itself, the crown of St Edward was used. This was usually reserved for the reigning monarch alone so was a great honour – intended, perhaps, to further legitimise the new queen and the heir she carried.

The coronation ceremonies went on for four days, each of which was celebrated with great pomp and attended by all of the senior dignitaries and churchmen in the kingdom. There were some notable absentees, though, including the king's sister Mary, who was bitterly opposed to her new sister-in-law and used the (admittedly valid) excuse of poor health to avoid attending. The former lord chancellor and royal favourite, Thomas More, was also absent, which helped seal his fate two years later. Many of those who did attend were motivated more by a desire to stay in favour with the king than to honour his new queen. Chapuys concluded that the coronation had been 'a cold, meagre and uncomfortable thing, to the great dissatisfaction, not only of the common people, but also of the rest'.[21] Dissatisfaction soon turned to open mockery. Everywhere along the processional route were Henry and Anne's initials intertwined. But this cipher was turned to parody as the new queen passed and cries of 'HA HA' could be heard among the disdainful crowds.

It had been a long and exhausting event. On the day of the coronation itself, Anne had been on show for nine hours without respite. The fact that she was six months pregnant added significantly to her fatigue. It is an indication of how anxious Henry was to have his new wife crowned – and therefore validated in the eyes of the world – that he risked the health of their unborn child by putting her through this ordeal, magnificent though it was. Although in public Anne appeared to have suffered no ill effects, in private there was concern that all was not well. Henry was reported to be frantic with worry and even expressed a hope that she would miscarry if it would save her life. He cancelled the customary summer progress and went with his new queen to

Windsor, where they could live more quietly. While this worked the desired effect, Anne did not seem to enjoy the late stages of her pregnancy and complained about the loss of her famously slender figure. Around the time of her coronation, Archbishop Cranmer had observed her to be 'somewhat big with child'.[22] This had been echoed by Sir William Kingston, Constable of the Tower and a frequent visitor to court, who on 24 June wrote to Lady Lisle: 'The Queen's Grace is in good health . . . and has a fair belly as I have seen.'[23] Anne's distress was perhaps due to more than just vanity. The Tudors believed that pregnant women were 'not so fit for dalliance [sex]' because it was harmful to the unborn child, so Anne may have feared that the king's notoriously fickle affections might soon be diverted by one of the many attractive young women at his court.[24]

Sure enough, in August 1533, as Anne entered the eighth month of her pregnancy, rumours of a secret liaison between the king and a 'very beautiful' woman began to spread throughout the court. Chapuys noted with evident satisfaction that the new queen was 'very jealous of the King, and not without legitimate cause'. He reported that when Anne confronted Henry about it, he bluntly told her she must 'shut her eyes and endure as well as more worthy persons', by whom he meant his first wife, Catherine of Aragon. This may have just been vicious gossip, put about by Anne's enemies. But if true, it was the first hint that all was not well in the marriage. The qualities that had made Anne so alluring as a mistress – her 'wilful', passionate nature, her obstinacy and outspokenness – had quickly become irksome in a wife. The suggestion that Henry was already comparing her unfavourably to her predecessor was ominous, as was his remark 'that she ought to know that it was in his power to humble her again in a moment more than he had exalted her'.[25]

To the outside world, all appeared well. The courtier John

Russell wrote to Lord Lisle in Calais that he 'never saw the King merrier'. This was corroborated by Queen Anne's Receiver General, George Taylor, who reported: 'The King's grace and the Queen is in good health and as merry as ever I saw them in my life.'[26] On 21 August, the royal couple moved from Windsor to Whitehall and then to Greenwich a few days later. Henry's favourite palace and the place of his birth had been appointed for his wife's 'confinement' – the period when an expectant royal mother went into complete seclusion to await the birth.

There had been a flurry of activity at Greenwich since early August, as everything was made ready for the birth. Detailed instructions for an expectant queen's 'lying-in' still survive among the manuscripts of the British Library.[27] These were based on an elaborate set of conventions – part-religious, part-medical – that stretched back for centuries. They had been refined in the fifteenth century by Lady Margaret Beaufort, who had drawn up strict ordinances for 'the deliverance of a queen'. The royal wife would be secluded in her chamber, which was actually a suite of rooms based upon the privy chamber apartments usually found at court, with certain modifications. For example, an oratory would be installed, including an altar laden with 'images of gold and many great relics', so that prayers could add necessary succour in an age when knowledge of obstetrics was limited, together with a font to provide a quick baptism for a sickly baby.

The instructions specified that a queen's confinement must begin six weeks or at least one month before the child was due. The expectant queen would select the room in which she wished to give birth. Not surprisingly, this received the greatest attention. Lady Margaret's ordinances dictated that the floor should be carpeted and the chamber hung with heavy tapestries – 'sides, roof, windows and all' – depicting scenes from romances or other pleasant subjects so as not to upset mother or child. The

theme for the tapestries in Anne's chamber was the story of
Saint Ursula and her 11,000 virgins, which would prove fitting.
Once the tapestries had been hung, the floor was 'laid all over
with thick carpets' and even the keyholes were blocked up to
keep out any glimmer of light from the world beyond. There
were more practical touches, too, such as two specially made
folding tables decorated in the 'antique' work that Anne favoured
– one 'for a breakfast table' and the other 'for her grace to play
upon' at cards.[28]

The centrepiece was a 'rich Bed of Estate', with a mattress
stuffed with wool and covered with sheets of the finest linen, and
two large pillows filled with down. It was bedecked with an elaborate counterpane, 'richly embossed upon crimson velvet', lined
with ermine, edged with gold and 'decorated with trees and other
embroidery of Venice gold'. Described as 'one of the richest and
most triumphant beds', it was said to have formed part of the
ransom of the Duke of Alençon, who had been captured at
Verneuil in 1424 – possibly a nod to Anne's connections with the
French court.[29] A crimson satin tester and curtains embroidered
with gold crowns completed the ensemble, with the queen's arms
being added as another reminder of her lineage (and, therefore,
her right to the throne). The final touch was the installation of
two cradles – one a 'great cradle of estate', richly upholstered
with crimson cloth of gold and an ermine-lined counterpane to
match that of the queen's bed; the other a more modest carved
wooden cradle painted with gold.

Even by the standards of Henry's court, when completed this
richly arrayed birthing chamber must have been dazzling. It would
also have been stifling and oppressive for those within, with its
heavy tapestries that shut out all light, and the thick velvet fabrics
that smothered the bed – especially since it was the height of
summer. This was made worse still by the braziers, which had

been lit for some days before the queen entered her chamber, as well as by the heady perfumes that filled the air.

While these preparations were underway, Anne made a request of her own regarding the birth of her child. She asked her husband to procure from his former wife the 'rich triumphal cloth' that Catherine of Aragon had brought with her from Spain for the baptism of her future children. This cloth, a painful reminder of all her children who had been stillborn or died in infancy, was one of the few possessions that Catherine had left, and she was aghast when she heard of Anne's request. As a public relations exercise by Anne, aimed at emphasising the legitimacy of her unborn child, it backfired spectacularly. Public sympathy was firmly with the ousted queen, and the woman who had supplanted her was now viewed with even greater resentment. Having had ample evidence of her predecessor's strong will during the protracted battle over the annulment, Anne should have known better. Catherine held firm and the new queen was forced to relent.

On 26 August, Anne formally took to her chamber. As custom dictated, she went in procession to the Chapel Royal to hear mass, then hosted a banquet for all the lords and ladies of the court in her great chamber, which had been richly decorated for the occasion. There, 'a goodly spice plate . . . of spice and comfits' was served to the queen and her guests, and the Lord Mayor of London offered her a drink from a gold cup.[30] Soon afterwards, she was escorted to the door of her bedchamber by two high-ranking ladies, beneath a canopy of state. Her Lord Chamberlain, Thomas, Lord Burgh, called for all present to pray for the safe delivery of her child, then Anne took formal leave not just of the king, but of all the male courtiers, officials and servants.

As she stepped into her bedchamber, the queen entered an exclusively female world. A group of 'ladies and great gentlewomen' were appointed to attend their royal mistress's every need.[31] Among them, at the king's request, was his daughter Mary. This was very far from being an honour. Thanks to Anne, she was no longer a princess, but simply 'Lady Mary', the king's bastard daughter. And now she was forced to witness the birth of a new heir who would push her even further from the throne. She and the other ladies of Anne's chamber performed every duty, even those usually allocated to male servants. As Lady Margaret Beaufort's ordinances prescribed: 'Women were to be made all manner of officers, as butlers, panters, sewers.'[32] Any provisions or other necessary items would be brought to the door of the Great Chamber and passed to one of the female attendants within. Even the king was refused entry. All this was intended to emphasise that childbirth was a purely female mystery. In a male-dominated society, this was the only sphere in which women held precedence. But there was a price to pay for this temporary superiority: at the end of the elaborate, exclusively female ritual, the queen must produce a male heir.

Anne herself seemed confident enough of this. A letter had already been drafted thanking God for sending her 'good speed, in the deliverance and bringing forth of a prince'.[33] The king shared his wife's optimism and had decided that the boy would be chris-tened Henry or Edward. He and Anne had also invited the French king to stand as godfather. Francis I's ambassador in England, Jean de Dinteville, told his master that he had been asked to 'hold at the font the child of which the Queen is pregnant, if it is a boy'.[34] Henry had also ordered a splendid joust to mark the safe delivery of his son. One courtier remarked that he had never seen His Majesty so 'merry'. If the astrologers and soothsayers were to be believed, then he had good reason, for all bar one had predicted the birth of a prince. The exception was the renowned 'seer', William Glover, who wrote to the new queen that 'a messenger of Christ' had commanded him to tell her that she would have a 'woman [child] which should be a princess of the land . . . also that your Grace should be delivered of your burden at Greenwich'. Little wonder that, as he himself admitted, he had been 'loth' to pass on the message.[35]

Quite apart from the sex of her child, there must have been some concern about its chances of survival. Childbirth was fraught with danger in Tudor times. Around a quarter of children died at birth, and the same number again died in infancy. The risk of post-partum infection and other complications made it just as perilous for the mother and accounted for the shockingly low life expectancy among women at this time. Anne's own mother had lost several babies in infancy and her sister Mary had borne a son with disabilities who Anne would not suffer to be at court. As her husband's courtiers waited for news, wild rumours began to circulate abroad. It was reported in Flanders that Anne had given birth to a monster. Another tale had it that her child had been stillborn. Few people wished Anne a happy hour. But her health was generally good and as one observer remarked, she seemed 'likely enough to bear children'.[36] It was also promising that she had fallen pregnant almost immediately after first having sex with the king.

Just twelve days after entering her confinement, on the eve of the Feast of the Virgin (7 September), Anne's labour began. This was much earlier than anticipated, which suggests that the baby was premature or that Anne had miscalculated her due date – perhaps deliberately. Painfully aware that her child's legitimacy was already in doubt, she had no wish to draw attention to the fact that it was conceived out of wedlock. The labour, which, according to Anne's earliest biographer, William Latymer, was 'particularly painful', progressed throughout the morning and early afternoon. Then, shortly after three o'clock in the afternoon, the baby was born. Just as Anne had hoped, this child would be the triumph of the Tudor dynasty, its name echoing down the centuries as one of the greatest monarchs that ever lived. But this was not a moment to rejoice because the child, though healthy, was a girl.

'The seventh day of September, being Sunday, between three and four of the clock after noon, the Queen was delivered of a fair lady,' reported Edward Hall. He made no comment on the crushing disappointment at the child's sex but noted that the *Te Deum* was sung for the queen's safe deliverance and went on to the safer topic of the christening, for which 'great preparation' was made.[37] Written during Elizabeth's reign, George Wyatt's account was just as selective. He claimed that the king 'expressed his joy for that fruit sprung of himself, and his yet more confirmed love towards her [Anne]' and 'caused her child openly and publicly to be proclaimed Princess Elizabeth'. He went on to describe the 'great joy' felt by the people 'that the king had now issue legitimate of his own body', adding the revealing line: 'and for the hope of more after'.[38]

But there can be no doubt that after all the turmoil the king had put his country through to rid himself of Catherine and marry Anne, it was a humiliating disappointment. Only a son would secure the Tudor dynasty and silence his critics. The notion of female sovereignty was abhorrent to Henry and his subjects. England had only had one queen regnant, the Empress Matilda, whose brief and bloody reign four hundred years earlier had plunged the country into civil war.[39] Daughters were only useful as pawns in the international marriage market, and the king already had one of those.

The new queen betrayed no hint that anything was amiss. 'Henceforth they may with reason call this room the Chamber of Virgins,' she was reported as saying, 'for a virgin is now born in it on the vigil of that auspicious day when the church commemorates the nativity of our blessed lady the Virgin

Mary.'[40] Even if this quote is erroneous, it would have been entirely in character for Anne to have brazened it out. But her reaction may have been genuine. From the very beginning, maternal instinct seemed to win out over any disappointment at her baby's sex and she doted on the child. It is only hindsight that lends the birth such ominous significance. As far as Anne was concerned, both she and her daughter had emerged unscathed from the ordeal and there was little reason to doubt that she might bear the king many more children.

In the public court beyond, a herald announced the birth of a healthy princess. The letters that had been prepared were hastily amended with an additional 's' after 'prince'. Headed 'By the Queen', they declared: 'It hath pleased the goodness of Almighty God, of his infinite mercy and grace, to send unto us, at this time, good speed, in the deliverance and bringing forth of a Princes, to the great joy, rejoicing, and inward comfort of my Lord, us, and all his good and loving subjects of this his realm.'[41]

The king, on the surface at least, showed little of the fury that historians have since assigned to him upon hearing that his long quest for a male heir was still not over. When he visited his new-born daughter for the first time, he remarked to Anne with a similar sanguinity to her own: 'You and I are both young, and by God's grace, boys will follow.'[42] He also offered his wife an assurance that he would not forsake her, which was surely more ominous than comforting. He then announced that the girl would be named Elizabeth, after both his mother and Anne's. The author of a contemporary Spanish chronicle claimed: 'The King could not be more delighted than he was. He made many grants, and gave many favours' to mark his daughter's birth.[43] But the celebratory jousts and fireworks were quietly cancelled, and the French king was no longer expected to stand as godfather to a mere princess.

On the day of the christening, a gleeful Chapuys wrote to his Imperial master, Charles V:

The King's mistress was delivered of a daughter, to the great regret both of him and the lady, and to the great reproach of physicians, astrologers, sorcerers, and sorceresses, who affirmed that it would be a male child. But the people are doubly glad that it is a daughter rather than a son, and delight to mock those who put faith in such divinations, and to see them so full of shame.[44]

He later added that the new queen had shown 'great disappointment and anger' at the birth of her daughter. He could not resist opining: 'Misfortune manages well; and God has forgotten him [Henry] entirely, hardening him in his obstinacy to punish and ruin him.'[45]

Whether temporary setback or unmitigated disaster, there is very little contemporary evidence to suggest that giving birth to a girl irrevocably damaged the relationship between Henry and Anne or set the seal on her doom. Yet Elizabeth's arrival had significantly weakened her mother's position. Having a son would have made her virtually invincible, certainly in the eyes of the king, who would never have forsaken the mother of his legitimate heir. It would also have silenced Anne's critics and taken the sting out of Catherine of Aragon's Catholic supporters – and those of her daughter, Mary, whose claim to the throne would have withered away against that of a boy. Although her claim was still superseded by that of Anne's new daughter, most people still viewed the elder Tudor princess as the rightful heir.

With a mere daughter, Anne was no better than Henry's rejected first wife: indeed, in the eyes of Catholic Europe and most of Henry's English subjects, she was a good deal worse. The child that should have been her security threatened to be her undoing, and Anne was plunged back into a world of uncertainty and hostility. Her enemies at court and abroad now had even more ammunition against this pretender to the throne. Even her husband was hedging his bets. Within weeks of Elizabeth's birth, he had summoned his illegitimate son, Henry FitzRoy (now Duke of Richmond), home from France, where he was living as a guest of Francis I. Either Henry wanted to remind his people that he could father sons or, more worryingly for Anne, he planned to keep the boy in reserve in case she failed in her duty.

The Chapel of the Observant Friars, where Henry himself had been baptised, was prepared for the christening of his new daughter. This took place on 10 September and was observed with as much solemnity as if the child had been a boy. The contemporary chronicler, Edward Hall, who had a keen eye for court ceremony, has left behind a vivid account:

> All the walls between the king's palace [of Placentia] and the [Church of Observant] Friars were hanged with Arras, and all the ways strawed with green rushes: the Friars Church was also hanged with Arras. The font was of silver and stood in the midst of the church, three steps high, which was covered with a fine cloth, and divers gentlemen with aprons and towels about their necks gave attendance about it, that no filth should come in the font, over it hung a square canopy of crimson satin, fringed with gold . . . between the quire and the body of the church, was a close place with a pan of fire, to make the child ready in. When all these things were ordered the child was brought to the hall, and then every man set forward.[46]

Despite all these careful preparations, Anne was painfully aware that her new daughter was being unfavourably compared to her stepdaughter. She therefore resolved to do everything in her power to undermine Mary's position by taking what was hers and giving it to Elizabeth. According to Chapuys, this even included her name. Anne had argued fiercely that her new-born daughter should be christened Mary, claiming that it was entirely appropriate considering that she had been born in the 'Chamber of the Virgins' and on the eve of the Virgin Mary's nativity. Her true motive was clear to the ambassador, however, who claimed that she wanted to give the people a new Mary so that the old one would be forgotten.[47] More sensitive than Anne to the hostility that this would spark among his subjects, the king refused.

'Many lords, knights and gentlemen' assembled at Greenwich to see Henry and Anne's daughter christened in great state – although, as tradition dictated, the royal couple themselves were not present. Hall made a point of noting that the Duke of Suffolk, who was still in mourning for his wife Mary, the king's sister, had been summoned to attend. This was significant: the duke had privately opposed the annulment of the king's first marriage and had only reluctantly attended the coronation festivities. Another hostile guest was Gertrude Courtenay, Marchioness of Exeter, one of Catherine of Aragon's closest friends. She was accorded the honour of being one of the godmothers but made little secret of the fact that 'she really wanted to have nothing to do with this' and only agreed 'so as not to displease the king'.[48] Henry's eldest daughter Mary, now aged seventeen, was also in attendance, but it was Anne's family who were most prominent. Her step-grandmother, the dowager duchess of Norfolk, was given the honour of carrying the infant princess, accompanied by Anne's uncle, the Duke of Norfolk. Her brother George, Lord Rochford, carried the canopy, along with two Howard relatives. Anne's former chaplain and one of her greatest advocates, Thomas

Cranmer, Archbishop of Canterbury, was one of the godparents. All eyes were on the tiny princess, who was swathed in a purple mantle with a long train edged with ermine. 'The child was named Elizabeth, and then the trumpets blew, then the child was brought up to the altar, and the Gospel said over it.'[49]

Immediately after the ceremony, the godparents presented the infant princess with gifts, including 'standing cups of gold'. Hippocras (spiced wine), comfits and wafers were then served to the guests 'in such plenty that every man had as much as he would desire'. Afterwards, in a procession lit by five hundred torches, 'they brought the princess to the Queen's chamber'. Anne was bedecked in magnificent robes and lay in the bed where she had given birth three days before, with Henry by her side. The couple showed every sign of joy when they saw their little daughter and celebrated heartily with their guests. Hall noted: 'The Mayor and the Aldermen tarried there a while, and at the last the Dukes of Norfolk and Suffolk came out from the king, thanking them heartily, and said the king commanded them to give them thanks in his name: and from thence they were had to the cellar to drink, and so went to their barges.'[50]

As a public relations exercise, it was faultless. But cracks had already begun to appear. Although the christening was observed with all due ceremony, Chapuys claimed that it was 'like her mother's coronation, very cold and disagreeable both to the Court and to the city, and there has been no thought of having the bonfires and rejoicings usual in such cases'.[51] Young though she was, Elizabeth herself became the focus of hatred, just like her mother. Two friars were arrested for saying that the princess had been christened in hot water, 'but it was not hot enough'.[52] Meanwhile the Spanish court referred to the 'concubine's daughter' as the 'little whore' or 'little bastard' and viewed her as a just punishment by God for the English king's rejection of papal authority.

Aware of the hostile gossip, Anne protected her daughter as fiercely as a lioness her cub – even against members of her own family. She accused her uncle, the Duke of Norfolk, of showing 'too great familiarity' towards Chapuys, and forbade him from having any further conference with him. She was right to be suspicious: the ambassador claimed that Norfolk 'had spoken to me about the legitimacy of the Princess [Mary], and the right of succession belonging to her even if there were 1,000 daughters from this new marriage'.[53]

While Anne strove to protect and promote her daughter's interests, she was painfully aware that there were few who would do the same. Even with the backing of her powerful Habsburg connections, Catherine of Aragon had been unable to stop Henry from ending their marriage and banishing her to a miserable exile. With only a handful of allies, most of them of dubious loyalty, Elizabeth's mother was left dangerously exposed.

CHAPTER 3

'No other Princess in England'

ANNE BOLEYN WAS not an obviously maternal woman. Her forthright, ambitious and occasionally vicious nature was more suited to the political arena than the royal nursery. True, she had once told Henry that she longed for children because they were 'the greatest consolation in the world', but she knew full well that they were also the surest means of securing her own place within it.[1] But Elizabeth's birth seemed to change all of that. From the beginning, Anne lavished affection upon her new-born daughter and could hardly bear to be apart from her. A contemporary made a point of observing how fair-skinned Elizabeth was at the time of her birth, as if to draw a deliberate contrast with her 'swarthy' mother. Only her dark eyes marked her out as Anne's daughter. Lancelot de Carles agreed that Elizabeth 'quite resembled her father in her features, certainly more so than she did her mother, the queen'.[2] But the bond between Anne and her baby daughter was obvious to all.

Flying in the face of royal convention, when the queen returned to court after being 'churched' (a ceremony of thanksgiving for the safe delivery of her child), she brought her daughter with her rather than leaving her in the nursery, superintended by wet-nurses and other attendants. Far from hiding the child away like the unwanted daughter that most courtiers viewed her as, Anne caused a stir by keeping Elizabeth close to her at court.

'Day and night she would not let this daughter of hers out of her sight,' observed the author of the Spanish chronicle. 'Whenever the Queen came out in the royal palace where the canopy was, she had a cushion placed underneath for her child to sit upon.' At a time when royal tradition dictated that children be kept closeted away in nurseries, attended by wet-nurses and an army of other servants, this was both unconventional and shocking – even more so because the new queen had failed to produce the male heir that the king so desperately desired. Yet there was no sense of shame or disappointment; rather, Anne seemed proud to show off her tiny, flame-haired princess to courtiers, ambassadors and other dignitaries.

More shocking still was Anne's professed desire to breastfeed her daughter. For a royal wife, this was unheard of. As soon as they were out of the womb, their new-born would be suckled by a wet-nurse. Breastfeeding was thought to hinder conception – an important consideration, given that a royal wife's primary duty was to fill the royal nursery with heirs. Moreover, Anne was now in her early thirties, which was considered late in her childbearing cycle, so time was of the essence. When he heard of it, the king, whose patience with his new wife was already wearing thin, ruled against such a notion. A woman named Mrs Pendred was swiftly assigned as wet-nurse to the princess.

Anne knew that she was powerless to prevent another, far greater sacrifice. Tradition dictated that a royal infant could only remain at court for the first few weeks of its life. Thereafter, it would be established in a separate household where the nurse-maids, governesses and other attendants would become its surrogate family and its parents would be virtual strangers. Elizabeth would grow to know the truth of this and, in her teenage years, repeated the following observation by Saint Gregory: 'We are more bound to them that bringeth us up well than to our parents, for our parents do that which is natural for them, that is bringeth us into this world but our bringers up are a cause to make us live well in it.'[3]

Henry had chosen his palace at Hatfield, some twenty miles from London, as the most suitable place for his new daughter's upbringing, which he and Anne were 'very particular' about, according to one contemporary.[4] This pleasant retreat in Hertfordshire comprised a handsome red-brick palace built by Cardinal John Morton in the late fifteenth century (of which only the western range, including the great hall, survives today), surrounded by beautiful gardens and a deer park that stretched for several miles.[5] Its location was considered ideal because although it was only a few hours' ride from London's royal residences, it was a safe distance from the unhealthy, plague-ridden air of the capital. This latter consideration prompted the move to take place. On 2 December 1533, the privy council met to consider, among other pressing items, 'a full conclusion and determination for my Lady Princess's house'.[6] With Christmas approaching, it was agreed that the risk of infection at Greenwich was too high because people from across the city and country would come to court.

But there was one important detail that Anne was determined to personally superintend: the appointment of her daughter's household. As a princess, Elizabeth was to be served primarily by women. There was a wet-nurse to suckle her and four 'rockers' to attend her in her cradle, as well as numerous other ladies to nurse, bath, amuse and protect her. It was a premise of Tudor childhood that infants would be marked for life with the character of the women who nursed them. Their attendants would therefore be subject to the utmost scrutiny, particularly if they were appointed to care for royal children.

Knowing that she was widely despised and that Elizabeth's birth had dangerously weakened her position, Anne could trust few women. In selecting her daughter's household, she therefore gave precedence to her Boleyn relatives. These included her uncle by marriage, Sir John Shelton, who was appointed comptroller of Elizabeth's household, and his wife Anne and her sister Alice Clere (both sisters of the queen's father, Thomas Boleyn), who took general charge of the household.

The place of honour – that of Princess Elizabeth's 'Lady Mistress' – was entrusted to Lady Margaret Bryan, the half-sister of Queen Anne's mother. By the time she entered Elizabeth's service, Lady Margaret was aged about sixty-five and had been married three times and widowed at least twice.[7] Her son, Sir Francis Bryan, was one of the king's closest companions and his wild behaviour had earned him the nickname 'Vicar of Hell'. Lady Margaret herself was a woman of excellent pedigree. Her mother, Elizabeth Tilney, had been a favoured servant to Edward IV's queen, Elizabeth Woodville, and their eldest daughter, Elizabeth of York, consort of the first Tudor king, Henry VII. Lady Margaret was one of the children from Elizabeth Tilney's first marriage to Sir Humphrey Bourchier, while her second, to Thomas Howard, second Duke of Norfolk, produced numerous children, including Anne Boleyn's mother Elizabeth and her uncle Thomas, third Duke of Norfolk. This tie of kinship must have been reassuring to Anne, given that Lady Margaret was one of the only appointees chosen by the king. She strengthened their association by taking a financial bond from her daughter's new Lady Mistress and by keeping in regular contact with her.

Lady Margaret had already proved her worth as a royal governess by caring for Henry VIII's elder daughter, Mary, for six years and had performed the task so competently that Henry had rewarded her with the title of baroness. Having been accustomed to treating Mary as heiress to the throne since her birth seventeen years earlier, she must have, with some sympathy, witnessed the girl suffer the humiliation of being declared a bastard and ordered to yield precedence to the baby Elizabeth. But Lady Margaret, who had formerly served Catherine of Aragon, was a seasoned enough courtier to know that loyalties must shift with the times. It is to her credit that she subsequently encouraged Mary to look with affection upon her younger sister, despite all the reasons she had to despise her.

Two other members of Princess Elizabeth's new household with connections to her mother were Blanche Milborne, Lady Troy, and her niece Blanche Parry. Through her second marriage, Lady Troy was connected to Elizabeth Somerset, Countess of Worcester, one of Anne Boleyn's closest companions, whom Lady Troy had attended. She had formerly served in the household of Henry VIII's elder daughter, Mary, when the princess had been moved to Ludlow as a child. Lady Troy evidently proved her worth there because she was subsequently entrusted with the important task of choosing a wet-nurse for Elizabeth and later helped the younger Tudor princess learn her letters.

Lady Troy's niece, Blanche Parry, was in her mid-twenties and unmarried at the time that she was chosen to serve Princess Elizabeth. The Parrys were an ancient and distinguished Welsh family with a long history of service to the crown, and Blanche also benefited from her aunt's association with Lady Worcester. She was put in charge of the four 'rockers' of Elizabeth's cradle – an important task because it helped keep the child quiet and amenable, and thus ensure that favourable reports of her could be sent back to court. Blanche's character was ideally suited to such a trusted position. She was quietly assiduous, had impeccable morals and was entirely devoted to Elizabeth's service. She quickly struck up a close relationship with the young princess and always set her needs above her own – something that Elizabeth would come to expect of her other ladies, with mixed results. It has been suggested that Blanche sang her to sleep with Welsh lullabies and taught her the rudiments of that language as she grew older. Blanche's love of Wales was well known, and one contemporary praised her as a 'singular well willer and furtherer of the weal public' of that country.[8]

Through these ties of kinship and acquaintance, Anne sought to ensure that her daughter was surrounded by positive influences and that she would grow up a Boleyn, not just a Tudor. These influences would endure well beyond Elizabeth's childhood and would remain with her throughout her long life. But one of the most prominent members of the new household may have been selected for an altogether different reason. Upon the annulment of her parents' marriage, Henry's elder daughter Mary had been commanded to 'lay aside the name and dignity of Princess'. But she continued to insist that she was 'the King's true and lawful daughter and heir'.[9] This 'pernicious' behaviour earned a stinging rebuke from her father, who admonished her for 'forgetting her filial duty'. Undeterred, she repeated that she was his 'lawful daughter, born in true matrimony', but assured him that 'in all other things you shall find me an obedient daughter'.[10] Determined to bring Mary to heel, her father announced that he intended to disband her establishment and merge it with that of his new daughter – with the latter being superior.[11]

Mary's allies were aghast. 'The King, not satisfied with having taken away the name and title of Princess, has just given out that, in order to subdue the spirit of the Princess, he will deprive her of all her people . . . and that she should come and live as lady's maid with this new bastard,' reported Chapuys, adding that Mary was 'mightily dismayed' by this turn of events. Like Mary, he was convinced that Anne was behind it. 'I do not understand why the King is in such haste to treat the princess in this way, if it were not for the importunity and malignity of the Lady.'[12] It would have been entirely in character for Anne to have inspired the appointment, given the callous way that she had treated Mary and her mother up to now. But while Anne's enemies interpreted this as pure spite, it also smacked of insecurity. Forcing Mary to relinquish her independence and join a new, combined household with her half-sister may have been a deliberate and very visible attempt to bolster Elizabeth's legitimacy.

Mary had no choice but to obey her father's command and make her way to Hatfield. It was clear from the start that she would be treated with all the indignity and disgrace of a bastard. The three-month-old Elizabeth was conveyed to her new home in a velvet litter, escorted by the dukes of Norfolk and Suffolk, together with a large retinue of ladies and gentlemen. She was clothed in sumptuous materials, her hands warmed by a black fur muffler trimmed with white satin ribbon and her head covered with a cap of purple satin and taffeta. Awaiting her at Hatfield was a luxurious suite of rooms that included a bed covered with russet damask, and satin cloths of estate beneath which she would receive guests. Visitors to Hatfield would be left in no doubt as to which of the king's daughters was his true, legitimate heir. To emphasise the point, on her way to her new establishment, Elizabeth was paraded in front of the people of London on an unnecessarily circuitous route through the capital. 'There was a shorter and better road,' complained Chapuys, 'yet for greater solemnity, and to insinuate to the people that she is the true Princess, she was taken through this town.' By contrast, her half-sister Mary was forced to travel in a humble litter of leather, not royal velvet, and was accompanied by 'a very small suite'.[13]

The king had drastically reduced his elder daughter's allowance, and within weeks she was described as 'nearly destitute of clothes and other necessaries'.[14] Worse still, Mary was forced to leave behind almost all of the ladies who had been her constant companions since childhood, including Margaret Pole, Countess of Salisbury, who had first been appointed to her household fourteen years earlier. They had forged a close bond since that time and the countess had begged to be allowed to accompany her. Chapuys observed that it was 'out of the question that this would be accepted; for in that case they would have no power over the Princess'.[15] Instead, Mary would be surrounded by hostile Boleyn relatives and associates. Anne encouraged her aunt, Lady Anne Shelton, to treat Mary as harshly as she herself would have done in the same position.

For all her defiance, Anne must have felt her daughter's absence keenly. Young as she was, Elizabeth was a vital ally against her mother's enemies at court because she symbolised Anne's fertility and thus the hope of future children. She was also the king's only legitimate heir. On a more personal level, it was clear to everyone who saw them together that Anne adored her daughter. It is easy to assume that because, at least among the upper classes, Tudor children were raised largely at a distance from their mothers, the maternal bond was weaker. To support this, the fact that women generally had a higher number of children and that infant mortality was commonplace is often cited. But it does not follow that Tudor mothers felt any less love for their offspring than their modern counterparts. Approaches to child-rearing might have changed dramatically over the past five centuries, along with longer life expectancies, but human nature has not.

But could the same be said of Elizabeth? Had three months been enough for her to form an instinctive attachment to her mother – one that would survive beyond infancy? That was something over which Anne had little control, but in selecting her daughter's attendants from among her own kin, she had at least ensured that Elizabeth would have regular – and positive – reminders of her mother. Anne also strengthened her ties with her infant daughter by sending regular tokens to Hatfield. From the moment of Elizabeth's birth, she had lavished expensive presents upon her. Anne had always had a great sense of style and was highly skilled at using clothes to project her royal status. Aware that at least half the kingdom viewed her as a usurper and her new-born daughter as illegitimate, she made sure to dress Elizabeth in the same regal style, creating a miniature version of herself. The royal household accounts reveal that no expense – or trouble – was spared. One entry cites: 'Boat hire from Greenwich to London and back to take measure of caps for my lady princess and again to fetch the princess's purple satin cap to mend it.'[16] It took no fewer than three journeys to Greenwich and back before the queen was satisfied that the cap was a perfect fit.

Anne's influence over her daughter's wardrobe continued after Elizabeth had been established in her own household. The best account of the many gifts of clothing she sent to her daughter is provided by a memorandum of 'Materials Furnished for the use of Queen Anne Boleyn and the Princess Elizabeth', between January and February 1535, when Elizabeth had been at Hatfield for just over a year.[17] Every detail of the child's costume was considered by her mother: from the collar of a dress made from 'russet velvet' to some purple sarsenet 'for lining of a sleeve of purple satin embroidered for my Lady princess'. The records show that Anne was spending some £40 per month on clothes and accessories for herself and her young daughter (equivalent to around £18,000 today) – a considerable sum compared to her other expenses. The total annual bill for Elizabeth's household was around £2,000 – far higher than her half-sister Mary's had been.

The love of fashion that her mother had inspired would stay with Elizabeth for life, finding expression in a sumptuous array of gowns, gloves, shoes and other accessories, all worked in the finest fabrics and the most vivid colours. The Venetian secretary to England estimated that Elizabeth owned more than six thousand dresses.[18] This may have been an exaggeration, but the inventory taken at her death listed 1,900 dresses in the royal wardrobe – more than any other queen before her.

Anne's influence over her daughter's upbringing extended to her education. She wanted Elizabeth to be raised in the reformist faith and shaped by the same humanist beliefs that had influenced her own early years. The queen's chaplain, Matthew Parker, one of the most committed reformers at court, visited her daughter's household to deliver sermons.[19] Another of her chaplains, William Latymer, later told Elizabeth that Anne:

Vowed to almighty God that if it would please him to prolong her days to see the training up of her young and tender babe prince Elizabeth, she would endue her with the knowledge of all tongues, as Hebrew, Greek, Latin, Italian, Spanish, French, in such sort that she might in after time be able sufficiently to judge of all matters and embassages, and as occasion might serve sufficient knowledge to administer the estate.[20]

Anne would have her wish. Elizabeth inherited her mother's gift for languages and by the age of just ten, she was translating French, Italian and Latin texts with ease. A Venetian envoy later claimed that she 'possessed nine languages so thoroughly that each appeared to be her native tongue'.[21]

Once Elizabeth had been settled at Hatfield, Lady Margaret soon supplied the place of her absent mother. The sources imply a highly organised, no-nonsense approach to her duties, and a formidable will that would brook no challenge to her authority from the rest of the household. But towards her young charge, she was tender and affectionate. She referred to herself as

Elizabeth's 'mother', and the tone of her letters to the queen attests to the fondness that she felt towards this pretty, red-headed child. Margaret was effectively an extension of Anne and carried out her orders with such care that Elizabeth came to view her as a second mother. Given that Anne was seldom able to see her daughter, this could have made her jealous, but instead it brought the two women closer together, united by their affection for the child. By the end of Lady Margaret's first year in charge of the royal nursery, she was known to have such influence with the queen that courtiers sought her advice when trying to win favour. A former attendant of Anne, Honor Grenville, Viscountess Lisle, who had moved to Calais when her husband was made lord deputy in the year of Elizabeth's birth, consulted Lady Margaret about the choice of a New Year's gift for the queen in 1534. Following her advice, she sent Anne a little dog to add to her collection of pets. Anne liked it so much that she immediately snatched the dog from the messenger's arms without waiting for him to utter the customary request to accept it.[22]

Lady Margaret may have been a welcome source of stability during the early days of Elizabeth's new life at Hatfield, but the same could not be said of the princess's half-sister. Upon her arrival, Mary had been ordered to go and pay her respects to Princess Elizabeth. She retorted that she 'knew no other Princess in England except herself, and that the daughter of Madame de Penebroke [Pembroke] had no such title'. The most that she would concede was to call Elizabeth 'sister', considering that her father had acknowledged her to be his, just as she called the Duke of Richmond (the king's bastard son, Henry FitzRoy) 'brother'.[23] Anne was furious when she heard of this and ordered her aunt, Lady Anne Shelton, to box Mary's ears 'as the cursed bastard she was'.[24] Further indignities were heaped upon the elder princess. At mealtimes, she was forced to sit at a lower table while her infant half-sister was given the place of honour. Mary therefore took to eating her meals in her room. This was reported to Anne, who duly ordered her stepdaughter back to the dining room.

Increasingly troubled by the news of his eldest daughter's behaviour, in January 1534 the king decided to go in person and force her to see the error of her ways. When the queen heard of this, she urged her husband not to bestow such an honour upon the ungrateful girl and suggested that he should send his able adviser Thomas Cromwell instead. Chapuys shrewdly observed that this was born of insecurity on Anne's part and that she feared 'the beauty, virtue and prudence of the Princess might assuage his wrath and cause him to treat her better'. Anne knew that many still persisted in referring to Mary by her former title – Chapuys among them. In reporting the king's visit to Hatfield, he told Charles V: 'The King went lately to see his bastard daughter [Elizabeth], who is twenty miles away, and the Princess [Mary] with her.'[25] In April 1534, one of the spies working for the king's newly created principal secretary, Thomas Cromwell, overheard a man declare that 'he would bestow his life and all he had upon my lady Mary's title against the issue that shall come of the Queen'.[26]

Although Henry went ahead with the visit, as a concession to Anne he sent orders that Mary was to be kept from him and took Cromwell along so that he might speak to her on his royal master's behalf. But even the most powerful man in her father's court failed to intimidate the eighteen-year-old Mary, who was made of the same mettle as her mother. She refused to acknowledge the new queen and her daughter, insisting that she had 'already given a decided answer and it was labour wasted to press her'.[27] As her father was preparing to mount his horse for the ride back to London, she suddenly appeared on a terrace at the top of the house and knelt down in reverence. Disarmed by such a touching display of filial affection, Henry bowed to her and put his hand to his hat. All present followed suit and 'saluted her reverently with signs of good will and compassion'. It was a small but significant victory for Mary, who took it as proof that her father still loved her, despite all the persuasions of her despised stepmother. By the time Henry arrived back at court, though, he seemed to have resumed his former stance and complained to Chapuys of Mary's obstinacy, 'which came from her Spanish blood'. But when he was reminded by another ambassador present that his elder daughter had been well brought up, 'tears came into his eyes, and he could not refrain from praising her'.[28]

Anne was enraged. Chapuys reported a conversation with an acquaintance, who 'knew for certain that she [Anne] had determined to poison the Princess'. He was later told by another informant that Anne had boasted she would 'use her authority and put the said Princess to death, either by hunger or otherwise', adding that she 'did not care even if she were burned alive for it after'. Mary herself seemed to fear that this might happen but told Cromwell that her enemies at Hatfield 'were deceived if they thought that bad treatment or rudeness, or even the chance of death, would make her change her determination'.[29]

At the heart of Anne's cruelty towards Mary lay a growing insecurity. Rumours that the king was beginning to tire of his new wife had started almost immediately after Elizabeth's birth. As early as November 1533, the French ambassador noticed that 'the King's regard for the Queen is less' and added: 'There is little love for the one who is queen now, or any of her race' – which, of course, included her daughter Elizabeth.[30] The queen was all too well aware that her only hope of winning back her husband's love and esteem was by giving him a son.

Three months after Elizabeth's birth, in December 1533, Anne's cousin, Lord William Howard, was sent on an embassy to Rome and while there announced that she was pregnant again, which means she must have conceived in November at the latest. Her pregnancy was confirmed by Chapuys in a letter to Charles V on 28 January 1534. It had an immediate and transformative effect on the king's attitude towards his wife. In March, he made two very public demonstrations of his newly restored esteem. The first was to provide for her to be regent and 'absolute governess of her children and kingdom' if he died before these children reached their maturity. More significantly, on 23 March Parliament passed the Act of Succession, which bestowed 'the imperial crown of England' on the children of Henry's marriage to Anne, rather than those from his (now unlawful) union with Catherine of Aragon. This confirmed that Elizabeth was heir presumptive and her elder sister Mary was illegitimate. The Act also stipulated that if any of the king's subjects expressed anything 'to the prejudice, slander or derogation of the lawful matrimony' between him and 'his most dear and entirely beloved wife Queen Anne' or against their heirs, they would be guilty of high treason. To make sure of their obedience, every subject was required, if asked, to swear an oath recognising the king as supreme head of the Church.[31]

Emboldened by this new Act, Anne paid a visit to Hatfield shortly afterwards. While she was no doubt eager to see Elizabeth, who was now six months old, her visit was at least equally motivated by a determination to bring Mary to heel. Aware that cruelty and intimidation had worked little effect, she changed tack. Upon arriving at Hatfield, she sent a message to Mary, inviting her to come and honour her as queen. If she proved compliant, then Anne would ensure that she was 'as well received [at court] as she could wish' and would regain the king's 'good pleasure and favour' for her. Mary replied tartly that she 'knew not of any other queen in England, than madam, her mother', but that if 'Madam Boleyn' wished to intercede for her with the king, she would be most grateful.[32] Anne was outraged and left for court vowing to do Mary as much harm as she could. With neither side willing to concede even an inch, stalemate ensued.

Mary refused to accompany her sister to Eltham Palace in March 1534 and 'was put by force by certain gentlemen into a litter with the aunt of the king's mistress, and thus compelled to make court to the said Bastard'. As a further punishment, she had all her royal jewels confiscated. Lady Anne Shelton heaped more misery on her by telling her that the king 'would make her lose her head for violating the laws of his realm'.[33] In desperation, Mary and her Spanish allies began hatching plans for an escape to the continent.

In April 1534, an excited Henry ordered a beautiful silver cradle decorated with precious stones and Tudor roses from his gold-smith, Cornelius Hayes. The same month, he and Anne went to see Elizabeth at Eltham, where preparations were underway 'against the coming of the Prince'.[34] With the prospect of a son looming ever larger, the king was prepared to be magnanimous towards his daughter. On 18 April, Sir William Kingston reported that Elizabeth was: 'As goodly child as hath been seen, and her Grace is much in the King's favour, as a goodly child should be, God save her.' On 27 April, Anne's Receiver General, George Taylor, reported: 'The Queen is merry and in good health . . . and the Queen hath a goodly belly: praying our Lord to send us a prince.'[35]

Three months later, Anne's brother was sent to France to ask that the planned meeting between Henry and Francis be postponed because the queen was 'so far gone with child she could not cross the sea with the King'.[36] But after the end of July, there was no further reference to the pregnancy or to Anne having 'taken her chamber', so she had either miscarried or the child had been stillborn. It is also possible that Anne, under intense pressure to conceive a son, had experienced a phantom pregnancy.[37] Just two months later, the queen thought she was pregnant again, but in late September Chapuys reported: 'The Lady is not to have a child after all.' A few days later, he added the ominous news: 'Since the King began to doubt whether his lady was enceinte or not, he has renewed and increased the love he formerly had for a beautiful damsel of the court.'[38]

After a time, Mary's dignified behaviour and her refusal to be cowed by threats or cruelty won her the respect of the other members of Elizabeth's household. Even Anne Shelton was admonished by the queen's uncle and brother for 'behaving to the princess with too much respect and kindness, saying that she ought only to be treated as a bastard'. Likewise, it was reported that 'one of the principal officers of the Bastard [Elizabeth] has been removed because he showed some affection to the Princess [Mary] and did her some service'. When Mary was seen walking along a gallery at Hatfield, the 'country people . . . saluted her as their princess'. This resulted in her being kept in much closer confinement, her windows being 'nailed up through which she might have been seen'.[39]

But when the household moved to Greenwich in August 1534, these instructions were flouted. As usual, Mary was obliged to give precedence to her half-sister, but as soon as Elizabeth's litter had set off and Mary had mounted her horse in readiness to follow, the comptroller of the household whispered to her that she might 'go before or after, as she pleased'. She seized her chance to assert what she saw as her rightful position and 'suddenly pushed forward', overtaking Elizabeth's litter and arriving at Greenwich about an hour before her. Later, when the party prepared to enter the barge to the palace, Mary 'took care to secure the most honourable place'.[40] Her act of defiance was reported to Anne, who made sure that her stepdaughter was given an inferior place in the procession that accompanied Elizabeth's move to a different residence the following month. Mary was already in poor health and this apparently 'increased her illness'.[41]

As well as trying to enforce her daughter's superiority over Mary in their combined household, Anne also promoted Elizabeth's interests in the international marriage market. She was dismayed when, in the summer of 1534, there was talk of a settlement between Charles V and Francis I that involved the marriage of Henry's daughter Mary to the dauphin. Worse still, when Henry made a counter-proposal of a marriage between his younger daughter Elizabeth and Charles, the French king's third son, it met with a lukewarm response. Undaunted, Anne used all her energy and resolve to champion the match, knowing that allying her daughter with a scion of the ancient Valois lineage would greatly enhance Elizabeth's legitimacy in the eyes of the world. The idea of her daughter marrying a French prince was personally pleasing to Anne, too, given her own close affinity to the country. She entertained the most senior of the French envoys at a great banquet and they were also invited to visit her daughter's household. Anne must have been gratified to hear that they were impressed by the richness of Elizabeth's apparel – something that she had always paid particular attention to – as well as the splendour of her surroundings.[42] Anne's public confidence belied her private insecurity. Only once did the mask slip. One of the French diplomats confided to his master: 'By what I can make out, she is not at her ease.'[43]

Towards the end of October 1534, Anne paid a visit to her daughter and stepdaughter at Richmond Palace, accompanied by her uncle Norfolk and the Duke of Suffolk. To her dismay, while she was with Elizabeth, her uncle and Suffolk went to pay their respects to Mary. It was an ominous sign of how quickly court loyalties could shift, even among members of her own family. 'She is my death, or I am hers,' Anne lamented.[44] Worse still, Henry's attitude towards his eldest daughter began to change. There were even rumours that he would restore her to the succession and oust the 'little bastard' Elizabeth. The same month as Anne's visit to Richmond, Chapuys gleefully reported that the king had said that he 'loved the Princess [Mary] more than the last born, and that he would not be long in giving clear evidence of it to the world'. During the first few months of 1535, he sent Mary gifts of money amounting to some 'sixty or eighty ducats'.[45] But he was also heard to denounce her 'for the bastard she is, and he will have no other heir but the Princess [Elizabeth]'.[46] Anne might have derived some comfort from this, but it was also an indication of how dangerously fickle her husband could be. Probably at her instigation, Elizabeth came to stay at court for five weeks in the early months of 1535 – her most prolonged spell there since being established in her own household.[47]

Anne's vulnerability was exposed again in May 1535, when her brother George went to Calais in hopes of concluding the marriage alliance between his niece Elizabeth and Francis I's son, Charles. He soon returned to England empty-handed and went at once to find his sister, rather than reporting to the king. It was clear that Elizabeth had been rejected by the French. After a long discussion, Anne emerged in a fury and pointedly excluded the French envoys from an entertainment held at Hanworth shortly afterwards. Even though she had cherished a close affinity with France since her youth, her anger and resentment knew no bounds.

Elizabeth's rejection by the French did little to tarnish the joy and pride that her mother felt towards her. The princess was clearly thriving and had sailed through the anxious first weeks and months of infancy. Her precociousness was widely praised.

'When she was two years old she talked and walked like any other child of four,' claimed one chronicler. Anne spent as much time with Elizabeth as her duties at court allowed and derived intense satisfaction from the obvious delight that her husband took in their daughter. 'Her grace is much in the King's favour,' observed one courtier present. When Elizabeth came to stay at Eltham, close to the royal court, the king and queen visited her there. Anne ensured that the princess would have a constant reminder of her mother by ordering her emblem to be installed in the stained-glass windows of the gallery where she played, at a cost of a shilling each.[48]

Elizabeth's early childhood was as peripatetic as that of her royal parents. As well as Hatfield and Eltham, she and her household stayed at Hunsdon and the More in Hertfordshire, Langley in Berkshire, and Richmond in Surrey. For the most part, her mother was obliged to keep track of her wellbeing by letter rather than in person because her duties as queen – not to mention the pressure to produce a male heir – required her attendance at court. Anne was a more active and influential consort than many of her predecessors in the long history of the crown. As queen, she was a major landholder, which carried substantial responsibilities and authority. Elizabeth's birth might have weakened the hold that she had had over Henry since the beginning of their courtship, but she still wielded an unusual degree of public influence. She had furthered the careers of such religious and political heavyweights as Cromwell and Cranmer, as well as Thomas Audley, who became Lord Chancellor in 1533, and Henry Norris, groom of the stool and chief gentleman of the king's privy chamber. Each of these men were eager to do her bidding – at least, for as long as her star was in the ascendant. Her brother, George, meanwhile, whose support was unconditional, was prominent in both the privy chamber and privy council. Anne's network stretched overseas, too. A known Francophile, she worked tirelessly to promote an Anglo-French alliance and was close to several of François I's ambassadors, notably Jean du Bellay and Jean de Dinteville. The latter had played a prominent role in her coronation procession.

As queen, Anne also gave full expression to her ideas for educational and social reform. As well as supporting individual scholars such as William Barker and even the bastard son of her old adversary, Thomas Wolsey, she provided generous grants to both Oxford and Cambridge and interceded with Henry to secure them tax exemptions. Anne also took a keen interest in the problem of poverty. She became known for the extent of her personal charity and strove to alleviate the living conditions of the poor by providing opportunities for work. Anne found a willing ally in Cromwell, whose ideas for social reform were – like his royal mistress's – way ahead of his time. In 1535 the religious reformer William Marshall (who was known to Anne) drew up plans for poor relief at Cromwell's behest. He supported these by dedicating to the queen an account of the way poor relief was set up at Ypres and encouraging her to persuade Henry to set up a similar system in England. It was clear that, having waited so long to be queen, Anne was determined to exploit her position to the full.

Given the scale of the queen's activities, it is not surprising that she was rarely able to visit her daughter. But her correspondence reveals that Elizabeth was never far from her thoughts. She regularly exchanged letters with Lady Bryan to ensure that her daughter had everything necessary for her proper upbringing. In the autumn of 1535, the queen and Lady Margaret conferred over the weaning of Elizabeth. This generally happened when a child reached the age of two – much later than today. Lady Margaret confirmed that her young charge was able to drink from a cup and no longer needed a wet-nurse. The matter was then referred to the king and his council, who agreed that 'my lady princess' should be weaned 'with all diligence'.[49] Lady Bryan was put in charge of the task, but Anne sent her a private letter, possibly with her own maternal instructions about how this should be done. According to Tudor custom, once weaned a child's diet would still largely comprise milk, and only gradually would poultry and other white meats be introduced. Rich food was considered unsuitable, even for royal offspring, and the records show that Elizabeth was granted no exception to this rule.

Her regular correspondence with Lady Bryan must have been a welcome distraction for Anne from the troubles at court. Not only was her marriage becoming increasingly strained, but she also alienated her most powerful ally, Thomas Cromwell. Their commitment to religious reform had previously united them, but Anne grew concerned by Cromwell's increasingly radical actions and suspected that they were driven more by greed than a genuine commitment to reform. Matters came to a head in June 1535 when they quarrelled over plans to begin a dissolution of England's monasteries.

The monasteries had long been the subject of vociferous criticism by religious reformers both in England and across Europe and now Cromwell had them in his sights. In January 1535, Henry had appointed him Visitor-General of the Monasteries and Vicar General of the entire kingdom, which gave him immense power over the Church. Cromwell wasted no time in planning a wholesale dissolution of these great religious houses. To justify it, he and his extensive network of agents began gathering evidence of corruption and abuses, carefully ignoring the genuine piety and good works that many monasteries still embodied. At the same time, he secured the king's support for the scheme by making it clear how much wealth he stood to gain by it, given that the monasteries were second only to the crown in property and riches. It was well judged. The French ambassador, Charles de Marillac, denounced Henry as 'so covetous that all the riches in the world would not satisfy him'.[50]

All of this set Anne on a dangerous collision course with the king and his chief adviser. She was in favour of rooting out corruption in the monasteries: in 1535 she had the famous relic of 'the blood of Hailes' investigated and campaigned to get the nuns of Syon Abbey to accept the royal supremacy. But, crucially, Anne was staunchly opposed to abolishing the religious houses altogether and wanted to see them converted to educational purposes instead. She even established a pilot for this by appointing Matthew Parker dean of a re-founded collegiate church of Stoke by Clare, in Suffolk. As well as providing regular religious instruction taught in English and Latin, this prepared boys to take up bursaries at Cambridge. Anne also argued fiercely that any profits from the repurposed monasteries should go to charitable causes, rather than the royal coffers, as Cromwell advocated. She was encouraged in this view by one of her chaplains, John Skip, who as almoner was responsible for distributing money to the poor. She told Cromwell in no uncertain terms: 'That she would like to see his head off his shoulders.'[51]

Making an enemy of Cromwell was a dangerous move, particularly as Anne's once unassailable influence with the king was slipping rapidly away. But her reformist zeal was too strong to be suppressed. In September that year, she agreed to a request from her chaplain, Matthew Parker, that she might advance the cause of William Bill, an evangelical scholar of St John's, Cambridge, who was too poor to take up a fellowship. Thanks to her generosity, Bill was soon in post and went on to a prestigious career in the Church.

But Anne's influence was on the wane. The Venetian ambassador observed that Henry seemed 'tired to satiety with her'. Anne's famed self-confidence, which had proved so irresistible to any man who crossed her path, was replaced by fear and self-doubt. Chapuys remarked with satisfaction that the queen's diminishing authority 'has already abated a good deal of her insolence'. Another scornful courtier observed how she took to following the king about 'like a dog its master'. It was obvious to everyone, not least Anne herself, how much the balance of power between them had shifted. She even made conciliatory moves towards her stepdaughter, Mary, but they were scornfully rejected. The stress was beginning to take its toll on Anne's appearance. One courtier scathingly referred to her as 'that thin old woman', even though she was still only in her mid-thirties.[52]

Worse still, Anne had a rival. Although he was discreet about it, she knew that her husband had strayed from the marital bed. By now resigned to his infidelity, she tried to limit the damage by putting one of her cousins – either Mary or Madge Shelton – in his path. After all, she had first-hand knowledge of how a mistress might unseat a queen. But another of her ladies had caught Henry's eye. Ambassador Chapuys had first noted the king's attentions towards Jane Seymour in October 1534.[53] The fact that the following year's summer progress included a visit to the Seymour home of Wolf Hall in Wiltshire may have been an indication of Henry's favour towards this modest and rather plain young woman – and to her brother Edward, who was rapidly rising in his service. Even though Chapuys was inclined to favour Jane because of the threat she posed to Anne and the 'great love and reverence' she showed towards Henry's daughter Mary, he was at a loss to explain the king's interest in her. According to his account, she was 'of middle stature and no great beauty, so fair that one would call her rather pale than otherwise'. Jane certainly had none of Anne's charisma and was 'not a woman of great wit', although like her she was inclined to be 'proud and haughty'. Chapuys concluded that she must have a fine *'enigme'*, meaning 'riddle' or 'secret', which in Tudor times referred to the female genitalia.[54]

Perhaps Jane's greatest attraction for Henry, though, lay in the fact that she was Anne's opposite. The queen's feisty, outspoken nature had made her irresistible to the king as a mistress, but they were irksome qualities in a wife. Henry praised Jane as 'gentle and inclined to peace' and she would adopt the motto 'Bound to obey and to serve'.[55] But Jane did take one lesson from her rival and refused to become Henry's mistress. Just as it had with Anne, this stoked his desire.

The king's growing interest in Jane Seymour intensified the pressure on Anne to conceive an heir. Being under such strain was hardly conducive to this, but she fell pregnant during the summer progress of 1535. It is an indication of how much Anne's confidence had been damaged by the uncertainties and betrayals of the past two years that, rather than triumphing in her condition, she was plunged into a depression, plagued by an intense fear of what might happen if she failed. She was also tormented by jealousy at her husband's attentions towards Jane Seymour, particularly as her condition prevented her from luring him back into her own bed. Although the king was delighted about his wife's pregnancy and outwardly solicitous of her every need, it was noted that in private he 'shrank from her . . . at this time when most she was to have been cherished'. Chapuys concurred with evident satisfaction: 'For more than three months this King has not spoken ten times to the Concubine.'[56]

CHAPTER 4

'Of corrupt seed'

THE NEW YEAR brought welcome news for Anne. On 7 January 1536, Catherine of Aragon died. For as long as she had lived, the majority of Henry's subjects had viewed her as the rightful queen; his second wife as a 'concubine' and usurper. Now Anne was the uncontested Queen of England. 'You could not conceive the joy that the King and those who favour this concubinage have shown at the death of the good Queen,' remarked a dismayed Chapuys, 'especially the earl of Wiltshire and his son [Thomas and George Boleyn], who said it was a pity the Princess did not keep company with her.' While Mary was reported to be 'inconsolable' as she retreated to the seclusion of Hunsdon, her father and stepmother appeared at court 'clad all over in yellow from top to toe'. Although this was the colour of mourning in Spain, it was also strongly associated with Anne. Princess Elizabeth was invited to share in her mother's triumph. 'The Little Bastard was conducted to mass with trumpets and other great triumphs,' the ambassador reported. 'After dinner the King entered the room in which the ladies danced, and there did several things like one transported with joy. At last he sent for his Little Bastard, and carrying her in his arms he showed her first to one and then to another. He has done the like on other days since.'[1]

Anne appeared triumphant as she watched her husband proudly parading their daughter before the court, but she was still plagued by anxiety. The ever-vigilant Chapuys confided to his master:

'Notwithstanding the joy shown by the concubine at the news of the good Queen's death . . . she had frequently wept, fearing that they might do with her as with the good Queen.' The ambassador went on to report that he had heard via one of the principal persons at court that:

> This King had said to some one in great confidence, and as it were in confession, that he had made this marriage, seduced by witchcraft, and for this reason he considered it null; and that this was evident because God did not permit them to have any male issue, and that he believed that he might take another wife, which he gave to understand that he had some wish to do.[2]

This was deeply ominous. Anne's reputation had already been tarnished by her long and unpopular courtship with the king and by her flirtatious relationships with his courtiers. It was a commonly held belief that witches were sexually promiscuous and indulged in such perversions as incest. It was also a capital crime, punishable by death. With Catherine of Aragon dead, if the king got rid of his second wife he would no longer be expected to take back his first, so he would be free to marry a woman of his choosing.

Events now spiralled rapidly out of control. On 24 January, the king was knocked from his horse at a joust in Greenwich and 'fell so heavily that every one thought it a miracle he was not killed'.[3] Five days later, as Catherine of Aragon was laid to rest in Peterborough Cathedral, Queen Anne suffered a miscarriage, 'to her greater and most extreme grief'.[4] Chapuys claimed that the foetus 'seemed to be a male child which she had not borne 3½ months, at which the King has shown great distress'. Anne laid the blame on her uncle, the Duke of

Norfolk, for frightening her with the news of the king's accident. Few believed her. 'Some think it was owing to her own incapacity to bear children, others to a fear that the King would treat her like the late Queen, especially considering the treatment shown to a lady of the Court, named Mistress Semel [Seymour], to whom, as many say, he has lately made great presents.'[5] It is doubtful whether the sex of Anne's child could have been identified with any degree of certainty, given that this is usually only possible after seventeen weeks' gestation. But her enemies seized on the rumour that it had been a boy, knowing it would help to damn her in the king's eyes. 'I see that God will not give me male children,' Henry remarked bitterly.[6]

What little affection the king still bore towards his second wife now slipped rapidly away. Visiting her after the miscarriage, 'he told her, as if for spite, that he would not speak to her after she had returned to court'.[7] Upon hearing that Anne partly blamed the misfortune on loving him more than his first wife had and therefore being heartbroken at the knowledge that he 'loved others', Henry was 'much grieved' and spent as much time apart from her as possible, 'when formerly he could not leave her for an hour'.[8]

As Anne Boleyn's star was falling, Jane Seymour's was on a seemingly inexorable rise. The king showered her with 'great presents', such as in April 1536, when he sent her a purse of money with an accompanying declaration of love. Jane's reaction was the epitome of maidenly modesty: she reverently kissed the letter before sending it back unopened, begging Henry to consider that there was 'no treasure in the world that she valued as much as her honour, and on no account would she lose it, even if she were to die a thousand deaths'. She slyly added that if the king wished to send her such a present in future, then he should wait 'for such a time as God would be pleased to send her some advantageous marriage'.[9]

Seeing history repeat itself, but with another woman as the protagonist, must have been torture for Anne and she occasionally lashed out at her rival with slaps and curses. During the bleak early months of 1536, with the king barely speaking to her and the vultures at court circling over their prey, she busied herself with ordering pretty new clothes for her infant daughter. These appear in a list of her expenses that still survives in The National Archives and provide a poignant glimpse into the care that Anne took over her daughter's attire. Among the garments and accessories she ordered 'for my lady Princess' was a gown of orange velvet, a yellow satin kirtle and a black muffler. Anne's impeccable taste is shown in the choice of colours, all of which would have set off Elizabeth's bright red hair to dazzling effect. Purple was also prominent among her choices, which was very deliberate since the colour was the preserve of royalty. As she fought to stabilise her own fragile position at court, Anne was also trying desperately to protect her daughter's.

The beleaguered queen's maternal care is also revealed by the provision of a fringed crimson satin cover for the head of her daughter's cradle, a russet damask bedspread, 'fine pieces of needle ribbon to roll her Grace's hair' and a pair of 'pyrwykes', a device to straighten the fingers – something that Anne was particularly concerned about, given that her own were long and slender. The last item that she ordered as queen was for her daughter: a cap of taffeta covered with a caul of damask gold.[10]

In April, the two-and-a-half-year-old Elizabeth was invited to join the court at Greenwich. Her mother spent a great deal of time playing with her and dressing her in the new velvet frocks and made-to-measure satin caps. Elizabeth's presence was a welcome distraction for Anne from the rising tensions at court.

The simmering hostility between the queen and Cromwell had boiled over into open aggression on Passion Sunday (2 April) 1536, two weeks after the Act for the Suppression of the Lesser Monasteries had been passed, signalling the beginning of the piecemeal destruction of these symbols of Roman Catholicism and the diversion of their riches to the crown – something that Anne had always argued fiercely against.[11] In retaliation, she instructed her almoner, the Cambridge evangelical John Skip, to preach a sermon at a service attended by the king and his court. This was a thinly veiled attack on the 'immoderate zeal' of Cromwell, who in Anne's eyes had exceeded their once mutual desire for rooting out the abuses of the Catholic Church and had descended into greed and corruption. Skip 'insisted on the need of a king being wise in himself and resisting evil counsellors who tempted him to ignoble actions'. He went on to tell the story of Haman, the wicked and greedy enemy of Queen Esther in the Old Testament, who persecutes the Jews and tries to divert their riches to the royal treasury. The story ends with Haman facing death on the scaffold.[12]

Both Henry and Cromwell left the chapel in a rage and Skip was swiftly arrested.[13] Undaunted, Anne made the most of one of her only remaining allies. Relations between Cromwell and his once close associate Cranmer had been strained for some time. In November 1535, Cranmer had written to defend himself after Cromwell had accused him of looking 'upon the king's business through my fingers, doing nothing in that matter [regarding the royal supremacy] . . . and I marvel not that you do so think, which knoweth not what I have done'.[14] Anne now exploited the faltering alliance between the two men. A little under three weeks after Skip's sermon, Cranmer wrote to Cromwell, making it clear that he shared the queen's disapproval of the destruction of the monasteries.

Cromwell struck the next blow, and it would prove decisive. The king appeared to forgive his wife for the Skip controversy, but Cromwell knew that his master was desperate to rid himself of her. Whether Henry instructed Cromwell to find the means or whether the latter did so on his own initiative has been the subject of intense debate ever since. Cromwell later boasted to Chapuys that he 'had planned and brought about the whole affair'.[15] If this was true, then he knew that he was acting with the king's blessing.

Although his royal master had started muttering that the marriage was against the wishes of God, it would have exposed him to ridicule if he had used that as the basis for another annulment. Instead, Cromwell drew inspiration from Anne herself. From the moment of her arrival at Henry's court fourteen years earlier, she had delighted in surrounding herself with a coterie of male admirers. It is highly unlikely that her relationship with them had ever strayed beyond the realms of innocent flirtation: she was too shrewd and self-disciplined to have risked her hard-won position on a thoughtless affair. But Cromwell now began discreetly gathering evidence of adultery. For the most part, this comprised scraps of gossip and overheard conversations from Anne's ladies – mostly those hostile to their mistress. The king himself had also been heard to remark that his second wife seemed more experienced than a virgin ought to be when they had first slept together.

While most accounts suggest that Anne was entirely in the dark about Henry's intentions, on 26 April 1536 she had a telling exchange with her chaplain, Matthew Parker. According to his later testimony, she commended her daughter to his spiritual care and shared her hopes for Elizabeth's education. Anne had judged well: Parker would honour the promise he made that day for the rest of his life. The fact that the beleaguered queen was making provision for her daughter's future suggests that she considered her own to be in doubt.

The queen's fears were heightened when, on 30 April, she returned from walking her dogs in Greenwich Park to find the court abuzz with the news that an urgent meeting of the council had been called that evening. Convinced that this involved her or Elizabeth in some way, Anne gathered up her daughter in her arms and rushed to find the king. The ensuing scene was later described to Elizabeth by Alexander Ales (or Alesius), a Scotsman and Cambridge theologian who had been among the courtiers at Greenwich:

> Never shall I forget the sorrow which I felt when I saw the most serene Queen, your most religious mother, carrying you, still a baby, in her arms and entreating the most serene king your father, in Greenwich Palace, from the open window of which he was looking into the courtyard, when she brought you to him. I did not perfectly understand what had been going on, but the faces and gestures of the speakers plainly showed that the king was angry, although he could conceal his anger wonderfully well. Yet from the protracted conference of the council (for whom the crowd was waiting until it was quite dark, expecting that they would return to London), it was most obvious to everyone that some deep and difficult question was being discussed.[16]

Quite what that question was is not certain, but that night the king and queen's upcoming visit to Calais was cancelled and arrangements were made for Henry to travel there alone a week later. On May Day, 'solemn jousts' were held at Greenwich, according to Henry's annual custom. But it was soon apparent that all was far from well. 'Suddenly from the jousts the king departed, having not above six persons with him, and came in the evening from Greenwich to his palace at Westminster,' Edward Hall reported. 'Of this sudden departing many men mused, but most chiefly the queen.'[17]

Anne was not kept in the dark for long. The following morning, she was watching a game of tennis when a messenger arrived with ominous news: she was to present herself before the council. Among the members waiting to greet her was her uncle, the Duke of Norfolk. Anxious to avoid being tainted by their kinship, he was the first to upbraid his niece, who later recounted she had been 'cruelly handled' by him. To her horror and dismay, Anne was told that she faced charges of adultery. To these were later added incest with her brother George and treason. The latter charge arose from a throwaway remark that Anne made to Henry Norris on 29 April. When she asked him why he had not yet married her cousin, Madge Shelton, and he gave a noncommittal answer, she teased: 'You look for dead men's shoes, for if aught came to the King but good, you would look to have me.'[18] This was twisted into a plot to kill her husband, marry Norris or one of her other lovers and rule as regent for her daughter Elizabeth.

The evidence was little more than gossip and hearsay and would not have been sufficient to even bring a case to trial in a modern-day court of law.[19] Anne was almost certainly innocent: she had neither the means nor, probably, the will to conduct a string of illicit affairs. Privacy was a rare commodity at the Tudor court, particularly for the sovereign and their consort. As Elizabeth later remarked: 'I do not live in a corner. A thousand eyes see all I do.'[20] Even Anne's enemy, Chapuys, admitted that she and her alleged accomplices had been 'condemned on presumption and certain indications, without valid proof or confession'.[21] But Henry was not interested in the justice of her case, only in freeing himself to marry Jane Seymour. With bewildering speed, Anne went from Queen of

England to wicked seductress. John Husee reported to Lady Lisle that Anne's crimes were 'so abominable and detestable that I am ashamed that any good woman should give ear thereunto'.[22]

Deaf to Anne's protestations of innocence, the council told her to make ready for her journey to the Tower. She was given little time to gather her belongings and none at all to say goodbye to her daughter. A short while later, the citizens of London heard the thunder of cannon, by which, as one eyewitness recorded, 'we understood that some persons of high rank had been committed to prison within the Tower of London'.[23] Bewildered and terrified, Anne's composure collapsed when she arrived at the fortress and alighted from the barge. Sinking to her knees, she wailed that she 'was not guilty of her accusement'. In terror, she turned to the Constable of the Tower and cried: 'Master Kingston, shall I die without justice?' He assured her: 'The poorest subject the king hath, had justice,' at which Anne laughed. When he proceeded to lead her to the same apartments she had stayed in before her coronation, it prompted another hysterical outburst. 'It is too good for me,' she cried, before bursting into fits of hysterical weeping and laughing.[24]

A group of carefully selected women were waiting to attend Anne – and, more importantly, to gather any information that might bolster the case against her. They included two of her aunts: Elizabeth, wife of Sir James Boleyn, and Lady Anne Shelton, who had attended Anne's daughter and the Lady Mary. By now, the beleaguered queen could not even trust her own family and complained that it was 'a great unkindness in the King to set such about me as I have never loved'.[25]

Among the manuscripts of the British Library is a letter to the king dated 6 May 1536 and signed: 'Your most loyal and ever faithful wife, Anne Bullen. From my doleful prison the Tower.' Whether it really was written by Anne has been the subject of lengthy debate among historians ever since. Doubt has been cast by the fact that the handwriting is different to that of Anne's other surviving letters. Some of the content does not ring true either, particularly the implied criticism of the king – something that a woman of Anne's political guile would hardly have risked at such a time. The letter does, though, assure Henry: 'Never prince had a wife more loyal in all her duty, and in all true affection, than ever you have found in Anne Bullen.' It also expresses gratitude for his having raised her from 'a low estate to be your Queen, far beyond my deserts'. The part that seems most likely to have been written by Anne is a plea to the king that he might not 'cast so foul a blot on your most dutiful wife and the infant princess your daughter', and that 'myself may only bear the burden of your Grace's displeasure'.[26]

If the letter really was written by Anne, then it is unlikely ever to have reached her estranged husband. Instead, it was found among the possessions of her mortal enemy, Thomas Cromwell, at the time of his own arrest in June 1540. Regardless of its provenance, what is certain is that the letter later came into the ownership of Elizabeth. It may have been given to William Cecil, Lord Burghley, who passed it on to his royal mistress. They seem to have had several copies made for posterity, and the original was later passed on to an antiquarian, Robert Cotton. Evidently, Elizabeth wished this protestation of her mother's innocence to be preserved for future generations.

On the same day as Anne's arrest, her five alleged lovers had also been taken to the Tower. On 12 May, four of them – Henry Norris, an intimate of the king, Francis Weston and William Brereton, who served in Henry's privy chamber, and Mark Smeaton, a musician in Anne's household – were tried and found guilty. Five days later, Anne and her brother were tried separately in the great hall at the Tower. Seated on the same raised dais on which her husband's chair of state had been placed during their triumphant stay at the Tower three years earlier was her uncle, the Duke of Norfolk, who had been appointed to preside over her trial. The documents prepared for it mention Anne's father as a member of the jury, but it is not clear whether he actually attended.

Anne remained impassive as the evidence against her was read out to the crowded courtroom. Driven by her 'frail and carnal lust', she had kissed her brother by 'inserting her tongue in his mouth, and he in hers'. Much was made of the fact that she had written to tell him she was pregnant – the insinuation being that the child was his, not the king's. The courtroom heard how she had incited others in her entourage to yield to her 'vile provocations' and that she had taken Henry Norris to her bed just six weeks after giving birth to Elizabeth.[27]

When the time came for Anne to speak, she gave 'so wise and discreet answers to all things laid against her, excusing herself with her words so clearly as though she had never been faulty to the same'. George Wyatt later concurred that the 'spotless Queen in her defence had cleared herself with a most wise and noble speech'.[28] Although the mood in the courtroom shifted from one of vocal hostility to respectful silence, it was not enough to alter the outcome. That had already been decided, given that the king had sent for an expert executioner from Calais several days before the trial took place. The verdict was swiftly delivered: Anne was found guilty of treason and adultery and sentenced to death. When told of how she had conducted herself throughout the proceedings, the king remarked: 'She has a stout heart, but she shall pay for it.'[29]

The same verdict was brought at the trial of Anne's brother George. As well as committing incest with his sister, he was accused of having cast doubt on the paternity of his niece, remarking: 'With his [Henry's] problems, it's hard to see how the king ever produced Elizabeth.'[30] If he had ever spoken such dangerous words, it had probably been a poorly judged joke. But the fact that it was quoted in his trial proved damaging to his young niece. To make matters worse, Chapuys made the unlikely claim that Archbishop Cranmer had declared Elizabeth was Anne's bastard by Henry Norris.[31] Again, this was probably nothing more than tittle-tattle, put about by a man famously hostile to Anne. But it is partly thanks to such scurrilous remarks that Elizabeth would spend the rest of her life trying to shake off the stain of illegitimacy. She was the 'little bastard', the 'concubine's daughter'; a bad seed who was destined to ruin herself as her mother had done. Such comments resonated deeply with the young Elizabeth, who years later wrote in a private prayer that God 'seest whereof I came, of corrupt seed; what I am, a most frail substance'.[32] Added to this was the fact that her mother had been accused of witchcraft – that, too, was believed to be hereditary.

Among the surviving papers from Anne's trial in The National Archives, there are some important omissions – notably, the details of the evidence produced in court, witness depositions and the statements made by Norris and Smeaton. There is a theory that these were later destroyed by Elizabeth to suppress proof of her mother's guilt. But if she had wished to do so, she would surely have been more thorough and ensured that the indictment containing the charges against her mother, with all its lurid and scandalous details, was also consigned to the flames. More likely is that they were destroyed on the orders of her father or Cromwell in response to doubts about the strength of the evidence, or that they have simply been lost in the intervening centuries.[33]

After the trial, Anne was taken to the Lieutenant's Lodgings (now known as the King's House), where she was to spend her final days as the guest of Sir William Kingston. At the same time, one of the women who had been appointed to spy on the fallen queen was discharged, her duties now at an end. It has been claimed that at Anne's request, she was replaced by her sister Mary's daughter, Katherine. Although Mary's first husband William Carey recognised Katherine as his child, she may have been the result of her mother's affair with the king. Katherine was only about twelve or thirteen years old, but if she really was summoned to attend her aunt then perhaps Anne wished for the comfort of her sister's daughter, knowing that she was unlikely ever to see her own again.

As she waited for the day of her execution, Anne veered between calm acceptance and wild hysteria. 'I heard say the executioner was very good, and I have a little neck,' she told Sir William Kingston, putting her hands around it and 'laughing heartily'.[34] Meanwhile, at court rumours abounded that the king was planning to disinherit his daughter Elizabeth. A gleeful Chapuys reported: 'The Concubine's little bastard will be excluded from the succession.'[35] On 16 May, Anne received a visit from her former chaplain, Archbishop Thomas Cranmer. After her arrest, he alone had spoken out in her defence, telling the king that he could not believe her guilty of the charges against her and that: 'I had never better opinion of woman.'[36] The purpose of his visit now was to persuade Anne to agree to an annulment. This might seem odd, given that she had already been sentenced to death. But Henry's intention was to remove their daughter Elizabeth from the line of succession, leaving the way clear for the children of his forthcoming marriage to Jane Seymour. It was also rumoured that he was planning to legitimise his bastard son, Henry FitzRoy, so that he could make him his heir.

Cranmer could not have had an easy task. Anne had always fiercely defended her daughter's rights and lobbied tirelessly to have her recognised both in England and abroad as the king's only true heir. But, holed up in the Tower awaiting her execution, she no longer held any of the cards. It seems that Cranmer used as an incentive the prospect of commuting her sentence to exile in a nunnery – Anne cheerfully told her ladies afterwards that 'she was to be banished'.[37] Knowing that otherwise she had just days, if not hours, left to live, it must have been an irresistible prospect. Perhaps, too, she judged that her daughter would be better served by having her mother alive, even if it was in exchange for her legitimacy.

The following day, Cranmer declared the king's second marriage null and void 'in consequence of certain just and lawful impedi-ments which . . . were unknown at the time of the union, but had lately been confessed to the Archbishop by the lady herself'.[38] Quite what these impediments were remains a mystery: they were not published at the time and, if they were ever recorded on paper, it has not survived. Most likely is the theory expounded by Charles Wriothesley, who assumed that the queen had confessed to a pre-contract with Henry Percy, Earl of Northumberland. The earl himself had written to Cromwell a week earlier to say that he would stand by his denial of a betrothal 'to his damnation'.[39] By contrast, Chapuys opined that the annulment was 'on account of the King having had connection with her [Anne's] sister, and that, as both parties knew of this, the good faith of the parents cannot make the said bastard [Elizabeth] legitimate'.[40] Whatever the grounds, in agreeing to the annulment, Anne had unwittingly blighted her daughter's life for nothing. She had been tricked: all talk of a pardon ceased and there was now no reason to delay her execution.

Early in the morning of 17 May, the five men condemned for adultery with the queen were led up to Tower Hill for their execution. As the highest in rank, Anne's brother George was the first to die – a privilege, given that the axe would be sharper so the death swifter. From the scaffold, he made a defiant speech in defence of the evangelical beliefs that he and his sister had cherished. 'I have been a setter-forth of the word of God and one that hath favoured the Gospel of Christ,' he declared, then ruefully admitted: 'If I had followed God's word in deed as I did read it and set it forth to my power, I had not come to this.'[41] When it was the turn of Henry Norris, he declared before the assembled crowds: 'In his conscience, he thought the Queen innocent of these things laid to her charge, and he would die a thousand deaths rather than ruin an innocent person.'[42] He was the only one of Anne's alleged lovers to speak out in her defence and, later, her daughter would reward his family richly for it.

Chapuys claimed that Anne was made to witness the full horror of the five men's executions 'to aggravate her grief.'[43] But Kingston, who recorded every detail of Anne's final days, makes no mention of this and it is unlikely that his prisoner would have been able to see the scaffold site from where she was lodged. She would, though, have heard the cheers from the baying crowds as each of the men accused of being her lover had their head smitten off.

Two days later, it was Anne's turn. At nine o'clock in the morning, she was escorted from her lodgings to a scaffold that had been erected on the north side of the White Tower, outside the building that today houses the Crown Jewels. A warrant that Henry issued to Sir William Kingston the day before reveals how he planned every detail of his wife's execution with chilling precision.[44] The concessions he made also hint at a sense of guilt at sending an innocent woman to her death. Having commuted Anne's sentence from burning to beheading, he had granted her the privilege of a private execution, rather than staging it on Tower Hill, where thousands of spectators routinely gathered to watch the dispatching of his latest victim. Even so, there were as many as a thousand witnesses to her final moments.[45] The king had invited Henry FitzRoy, as if to make the point to Anne that their lack of male heirs was her fault, not his.

After mounting the steps to the scaffold, the fallen queen turned to address the crowd. Given her nature, it might have been expected that she would use the opportunity to rail against the injustice of her fate. Instead, while she made no admission of her guilt, she meekly accepted the judgement against her and had nothing but praise for her estranged husband. 'Good Christian people, I am come hither to die, for according to the law I am judged to die, and therefore I will speak nothing against it,' she began. 'I am come hither to accuse no man, nor to speak anything of that, whereof I am accused and condemned to die, but I pray God save the king and send him long to reign over you, for a gentler nor a more merciful prince was there never: and to me he was ever a good, a gentle and a sovereign lord.'[46]

This act of calm acquiescence was deliberate. Through it, Anne hoped to soften Henry's heart towards her – and, more importantly, their daughter. She knew that Elizabeth's prospects were bleak. Not yet three years old, the child was about to be rendered motherless as well as illegitimate, and there were few if any courtiers who would be willing to risk the king's displeasure by acting in her defence. She may also have had Elizabeth in mind when she added a final, plaintive plea: 'If any person will meddle of my cause, I require them to judge the best.' Perhaps more than anyone else she was leaving behind, it was her daughter whom she wished to think well of her – and, perhaps, to rehabilitate her reputation. She could not have predicted with what vigour and commitment Elizabeth would dedicate herself to the task.

Having delivered her speech, Anne turned to her ladies and told them not to be sorry for her death. She also begged them to forgive any harsh treatment that she had meted out in the past, and gave one of them her prayer book. After kneeling with her priest and saying some final prayers, with great composure she removed her French hood, unclasped her necklace and paid the swordsman. One of her ladies blindfolded her and the crowd sank to their knees out of respect. As Anne began to pray aloud, the Calais executioner quietly reached for the sword that he had hidden under the straw and beheaded her with a clean strike, a prayer still on her lips. The sombre crowd looked on aghast as Anne's eyes and mouth continued to move for several seconds when her head was held aloft. Despite the care that had been taken over her execution, nobody had thought to order a coffin. In haste, an arrow chest was brought from the nearby ordnance store and Anne's weeping ladies lifted her body into it. Three hours later, she was laid to rest a few feet away, in the Tower chapel of St Peter ad Vincula.

Reports of Anne's final moments quickly spread across England and abroad. Her courage as she met her death was widely praised, even by her enemies. In Calais, Lord Lisle heard that she had 'died boldly'.[47] Lancelot de Carles described how she 'rose above womanly courage'. Similar language would be used by her daughter Elizabeth when declaring that though she was a 'weak and feeble woman', she had 'the heart and stomach of a king'.[48]

Henry VIII's scandalous second wife has gone down in history as 'Anne of a thousand days', the queenship for which she had fought so hard ending in less than three years. But during her brief tenure she had changed England forever, sparking a religious and political revolution that would echo down the centuries, bringing turbulence and bloodshed in its wake, but also a new national identity. For the first time in the history of the English monarchy, the king, not the pope, was head of the Church in England. The statutes that had enacted both this and Anne's marriage to Henry had bolstered the power of Parliament, giving it an effective voice in the succession – which would later bring her bastardised daughter to the throne. Once unleashed, Parliament's authority could not be checked and would ultimately lead to the destruction of the monarchy.

Anne had brought religious reform out of the shadows of academia and established it firmly among the English élite. It was thanks to her patronage that a host of evangelicals were able to secure positions of influence in the English church, some of which endured well into the reign of her daughter. The reformist scholar and bishop John Aylmer later told Elizabeth that her mother was 'the chief, first, and only cause of banishing the beast of Rome, with all his beggarly baggage'.[49]

Anne's influence on her daughter had been no less profound. Even though she had only been in Elizabeth's life for two years and eight months, she had left an indelible mark – one that would shape her daughter's outlook, beliefs, character and, above all, her future reign. Anne had had the qualities that could have made her a great queen, but she had also had a number of fatal flaws. It was in learning from both that Elizabeth would be able to realise her mother's ambitions and become the most celebrated monarch not just of the Tudor age but of the entire history of the British crown.

CHAPTER 5

'Storms and tempests'

ALTHOUGH EDWARD HALL noted that 'the king wore white for mourning', his actions made a lie of any pretended grief at the passing of his second wife.[1] The day after Anne's execution, he was betrothed to her former lady-in-waiting, Jane Seymour. 'The king hath come out of hell into heaven for the gentleness in this [Jane] and the cursedness and the unhappiness in the other,' remarked Sir John Russell with satisfaction.[2] In a similar vein, Chapuys compared the king's relief at finding a more suitable queen to 'the joy and pleasure a man feels in getting rid of a thin, old and vicious hack in the hope of getting soon a fine horse to ride'.[3] All traces of Anne were removed from the royal palaces: her initials, emblems and portraits. The king even ordered that their daughter Elizabeth be kept out of sight. He never spoke Anne's name again and it was as if his scandalous queen, for whom he had overturned England's entire religious, political and social life, had never existed. Never again would he allow a wife such influence as Anne had enjoyed. When her successor tried to persuade Henry to reprieve certain monasteries, he warned her to 'attend to other things, reminding her that the last Queen had died in consequence of meddling too much in state affairs'.[4]

Elsewhere, the assassination of Anne's character rapidly grew both widespread and vicious. Writing almost fifty years after the event, Nicholas Sander asserted that she had lost her virginity to her father's butler at the age of fifteen and had subsequently bedded his chaplain and the King of France before enticing Henry into her bed. He concluded: 'Anne Boleyn was everywhere regarded as a woman of unclean life.' Inspired by hints of Anne's witchcraft, Sander claimed that she had a sixth finger on her right hand and a large 'wen' (a boil or mole) under her chin. Such blemishes were commonly thought to be the 'Devil's Mark' – a symbol of having made a pact with Satan.[5]

And yet, at the same time, doubts were expressed about the justice of Anne's fate. Alexander Ales later told Elizabeth how his landlord, who had witnessed the execution, invited some others who had been there to dinner a day or so later. Discussing the dramatic events of the past few weeks, they agreed that there had been little grounds for her condemnation.

> It is no new thing, said they, that the King's chamberlains should dance with the ladies in the bedchamber. Nor can any proof of adultery be collected from the fact that the Queen's brother took her by the hand and led her into the dance among the other ladies . . . It is a usual custom throughout the whole of Britain that ladies married and unmarried, even the most coy, kiss not only a brother, but any honourable person, even in public.

One of Cromwell's servants wryly remarked: 'For just as she [Anne], while the King was oppressed with the heavy cares of state, was enjoying herself with others, so he, while the Queen was being beheaded, was enjoying himself with another woman.' Even Chapuys admitted: 'There are some who murmur at the mode of procedure against her and the others, and people speak variously of the King, and it will not pacify the world when it is known what has passed, and is passing, between him and Mistress Jane Seymour.'[6]

Closeted away at Greenwich, Elizabeth was apparently oblivious to the earth-shattering event that had just taken place five miles away at the Tower. She had lost not only her mother, but her place in the royal succession, her importance to her father – and by extension to England. Robbed of her chief protector, henceforth Elizabeth would be buffeted by the 'storms and tempests' of life as a royal outcast.[7] The speed with which all of this had unravelled was encapsulated by an Italian diplomat who reflected on the event two decades later: 'Not long after the marriage of Anne Boleyn, the Lady Elizabeth was born, and immediately declared heir to the Crown, in which grade she remained a very short time, because her mother being beheaded on suspicion of adultery, she in like manner was deposed from the succession, and proclaimed a bastard.'[8]

There is an unsubstantiated account that immediately after Anne's execution, Lady Bryan took Elizabeth to Hampton Court so that she might be comforted by her father. The story goes that when she approached the king with her young charge in her arms – just as Anne Boleyn had done shortly before her death – and asked him if he wished to see his daughter, he thundered: 'My daughter? My daughter? You old devil, you witch, don't dare to speak to me!' Terrified by this outburst, Lady Bryan fled with Elizabeth and went in search of Cromwell, who counselled her to take the child to Hatfield until the king's anger had abated.[9] It is unlikely, though, that a seasoned courtier such as Lady Bryan would have misjudged the situation so badly – or defied the king's instructions to keep Elizabeth hidden away at Greenwich.

On 21 May, Henry ordered that his younger daughter and her household should leave Greenwich for Hunsdon, thirty miles north of London, and that Elizabeth should continue to be kept hidden away. Sir John Shelton, who had overall charge of her household but would soon be removed from his position, wrote to Cromwell: 'I perceive by your letter that my lady Elizabeth shall keep her chamber and not come abroad, and that I shall provide for her as I did for my Lady Mary when she kept her chamber.'[10] Henry may have wished to shield his youngest daughter from the scandal surrounding her mother's trial and execution, but the impression is more of punishment than of protection.

Not long afterwards, the king ordered that Elizabeth's household be reduced. It was still combined with that of his elder daughter but, in a direct reversal of when it was first established three years earlier, Mary's side of the establishment would now enjoy superiority and have the freedom to detach itself from Elizabeth's if required. The elder princess's privy chamber comprised twenty-five staff with the promise of more, while Elizabeth's numbered just seventeen. Evidently anxious to ensure that his younger daughter would not turn out like her mother, the king insisted that her household be filled with 'ancient and sad [serious] persons'. Later, when a young gentlewoman asked to be part of it, Henry complained that there were already too many young people in Elizabeth's household and the woman was rejected in favour of one 'of elder years'.[11]

In the newly reordered household, one of Elizabeth's most trusted attendants, her great-aunt, Lady Anne Shelton, was dismissed. The king's choice of replacement was either brutally insensitive or deliberately vindictive. Lady Mary Kingston, wife of the Constable of the Tower, had been appointed to attend – and spy upon – the fallen queen in her final days. Along with her husband, she had accompanied Anne to the scaffold and watched her final moments at close quarters. She had paid a visit to Hunsdon a week later, perhaps to tell Mary about it – although it seems she spared the younger princess the ghastly details. Lady

Kingston served Elizabeth and her sister Mary until April 1539. The latter showed her great favour and the two women became very close. By contrast, Elizabeth seems to have kept her mother's former gaoler at arm's length.

Young though she was, Elizabeth soon realised that something was badly wrong. 'Why Governor, how hap it yesterday Lady Princess and today but Lady Elizabeth?' she demanded of Sir John Shelton.[12] But if her attendants knew enough of recent events to change the way that they addressed her, they were given no other guidance as to how to proceed. Now married to his third wife, the king evidently wished to avoid any reminders of his second. He did visit Mary at Hunsdon in August 1536 and probably saw his younger daughter there too. But such contact was both rare and fleeting and Elizabeth's household was therefore obliged to act *in loco parentis*, filling the gaping void left by her mother's execution and her father's neglect.

In contrast to his treatment of Elizabeth, the king welcomed his elder daughter Mary, now aged twenty, to court and 'made much of her', giving her 'many jewels belonging to the unjust Queen'.[13] Chapuys gleefully reported that Mary was 'every day better treated, and was never at greater liberty or more honourably served than now . . . she has plenty of company, even of the followers of the little Bastard [Elizabeth], who will henceforth pay her Court'.[14]

The new queen also made much of Mary and showed no interest in her younger stepdaughter. As a former attendant of Mary's mother, whom she had greatly admired, it was natural that Jane should favour her over Elizabeth, the daughter of her arch-rival. But Jane may have also been aligned with Mary in her religious views. When a Catholic revolt broke out in the early months of her queenship, she tried to persuade her husband to pardon the rebels, receiving a sharp reprimand for her pains. Even before she married the king, Jane had expressed 'great love and reverence' towards Mary and had tried – unsuccessfully – to persuade Henry to restore her to the succession.[15] Undeterred, once she and Henry were married, she continued to champion her elder stepdaughter's cause. Chapuys reported that she had 'spoken to the King as warmly as possible in favour of the Princess, putting before him the greatness and goodness of all her kindred'.[16] Mary responded with effusive gratitude and affection, thanking Jane for her 'motherly joy' and 'most prudent counsel'. She soon began to address the new queen as her 'good mother' – a mark of respect that she had never accorded Anne Boleyn.[17] Just a few short weeks before, Mary had been the neglected daughter of another former wife whom her father had denounced. It was a salutary lesson for her half-sister of just how quickly fortune's wheel could turn at court.

In early June 1536, the king convened Parliament in order to have his marriage to Anne Boleyn formally 'adjudged unlawful'. It was vague about the reasons, citing only 'certain entirely just, true and lawful impediments hitherto not publicly known . . . confessed by the Lady Anne before the most reverend father in God, Thomas, Archbishop of Canterbury'.[18] In the first week of July, Parliament repealed the statute declaring Elizabeth the king's lawful heir and formally pronounced her illegitimate. A new Act of Succession left no room for doubt about the piecemeal destruction of her rights and status. Her parents' marriage having been annulled because of Anne's incestuous adultery, Elizabeth was to be 'taken, reputed and accepted to be illegitimate, and utterly excluded and barred to claim, challenge or demand any inheritance as lawful heir to your Highness by lineal descent'.[19] Instead, the crown would pass to the children Henry had by his new wife, Jane Seymour. Interestingly, it also provided that if he had no legitimate heirs, he could choose his successor – thus paving the way for Henry FitzRoy.

If the king had such plans, however, they soon lay in tatters. By the time that he witnessed Anne Boleyn's execution, FitzRoy was already gravely ill with what may have been tuberculosis. He died four days after the Succession Act took effect, aged just seventeen. Although he had lavished honours on his bastard son in life, Henry ordered that he be buried with as little fuss as possible. The Duke of Norfolk, whose son had been FitzRoy's closest companion, arranged for the young man to be quietly laid to rest in his family vault at Thetford Priory in Norfolk.[20] But no sooner had the modest ceremony been performed than the king furiously upbraided the duke for showing too little respect towards his late son. It seems that when it came to the succession, Henry was increasingly sensitive and unpredictable.

The death of her half-brother made no difference to Elizabeth's situation. Not only had she been rendered illegitimate; a general pardon had been issued to anyone who had been imprisoned for slandering Anne or calling her daughter a bastard. This opened the floodgates for the vicious rumours that had already begun to leak out before Anne's execution. Most of these centred around the slander that Elizabeth was not Henry's daughter. Even his council declared that they believed she was the offspring of an incestuous affair between Anne and her brother, George Boleyn. Others, such as the outspoken Imperial ambassador, Chapuys, thought that another of Anne's alleged lovers, Henry Norris, was the more likely father and even went so far as to say that Cranmer had declared this the basis of the annulment of Anne's marriage to Henry.[21] Elizabeth's half-sister Mary later claimed that Anne's musician, Mark Smeaton, was the father – a claim that was supported by Nicholas Sander. They perhaps drew inspiration from the fact that of the five men accused of adultery, Smeaton had been the only one to plead guilty – although he was also the only one to have been tortured. Mary asserted that her sister had his 'face and countenance'.[22] Such rumours quickly spread abroad and were embellished along the way. In the Low Countries, it was reported that Elizabeth was the result of a casual affair between Anne Boleyn and 'a poor man'. Meanwhile, Dr Ortiz, Charles V's ambassador in Rome, confidently predicted: 'It is intended to declare the child not to be the King's.'[23]

There was little basis for any of these rumours: indeed, Henry himself never expressed any doubt that Elizabeth was his. Alexander Ales later told her: 'Whereas she [Anne] left you, her only child, your father always acknowledged you as legitimate; nor could those letters which were written by your mother to her brother, which were produced as the concluding and conclusive proof that your mother deserved capital punishment, persuade the illustrious King that you were not his daughter.'[24] Nevertheless, the rumours provide a stark illustration of just how far her daughter's status had fallen. In the space of a few short months, she had gone from being heir presumptive to a 'cursed bastard', as her mother had once described the king's elder daughter. When, in 1538, a marriage between Elizabeth and one of Charles V's nephews was mooted, the emperor 'noted the life and death of her mother', which put a stop to the idea before it had taken root.[25] 'In what ill case the young Lady Elizabeth now was, any one may guess,' observed the seventeenth-century chronicler John Strype, 'she being degraded into a meaner condition upon the Queen her mother's divorce and death.' A later commentator concurred: 'The blood of her mother, soon put to death by the King, sprinkled even to her cradle with the blot of bastardy.'[26]

Parliament's judgement on Elizabeth's legitimacy seems to have caused great consternation among her household. Shortly before Elizabeth's third birthday, Lady Margaret Bryan wrote a furious letter to Thomas Cromwell, complaining that she had been given no guidance about Elizabeth's new status or how to manage her upbringing. The council had formerly directed everything from Elizabeth's weaning to her regular moves between palaces, and Anne had kept in regular contact with her daughter's Lady Mistress. But now Lady Margaret was left 'succourless . . . as a redeless creature'.[27]

'Now as my Lady Elizabeth is put from that degree she was in, and what degree she is at now, I know not but by hearsay,' she protested. 'I know not how to order her or myself, or her women or grooms.' As the most senior woman in the household, Lady Margaret would have been besieged by her subordinates, all anxious to know whether they should start looking for positions elsewhere. There were signs of dissension, too, as Lady Margaret's authority was challenged by Sir John Shelton, who insisted that Elizabeth should dine in state, rather than privately in her rooms. Perhaps he was trying to uphold the pretence that Elizabeth was still a princess and heir to the throne to protect her status, as well as his own. 'It is not meet for a child of her age to keep such rule,' Lady Margaret complained. 'If she do, I dare not take it upon me to keep her Grace in health; for she will see divers meats, fruits, and wine, that it will be hard for me to refrain her from.' Lady Margaret may have also wished to keep her young charge away from the whispers of attendants less discreet than herself.

The Lady Mistress went on to complain that Elizabeth was rapidly outgrowing her clothes. 'I beg you to be good to her and hers, and that she may have raiment,' she implored, 'for she has neither gown nor kirtle nor petticoat, nor linen for smocks, nor kerchiefs, sleeves, rails [night dresses], body stitchets [corsets], handkerchiefs, mufflers, nor begins [night caps].'[28] Now, more than ever, Elizabeth needed the regular supply of dresses, shoes and other accessories that her mother had assiduously provided. Perhaps, though, Lady Margaret was being disingenuous. Anne had continued to order new clothes for her daughter until shortly before her death. Lady Margaret's letter was written just six weeks later, so it is hard to believe that Elizabeth had outgrown all of them. More likely, perhaps, is that her Lady Mistress was trying to ensure that Elizabeth was not neglected by the king and his council. This was not entirely selfless: Lady Margaret was an ambitious woman and had no desire to become side-lined in a court where she was used to the exalted status that came with raising the king's children. Tellingly, she added an appeal to Cromwell that Elizabeth might be 'set abroad' (in other words, go to court) on special occasions, assuring him 'that she shall so do as shall be to the King's honour and hers'.

Lady Margaret ended the letter on a more tender note, betraying her fondness for the motherless child in her care: 'My Lady has great pain with her teeth, which come very slowly. This makes me give her her own way more than I would.' She went on to praise Elizabeth's character and precociousness, assuring Cromwell that she was 'as toward a child and as gentle of conditions as ever I knew in my life'. With an apology for her 'boldness in writing thus', Lady Margaret signed off the letter.[29] It worked the desired effect – at least in part. The records contain no further pleas for clothing, which suggests that Cromwell had put this to rights. He also supported Lady Margaret's request for Elizabeth to eat in her rooms and instructed Sir John Shelton accordingly.

If the king's younger daughter was better provided for, she still remained an outcast. No invitations to court were forthcoming – in contrast to Mary, who spent more and more time there – and neither her father nor his courtiers showed any inclination to visit her. While Mary enjoyed a succession of lavish gifts from the court, her sister received nothing. Service to Elizabeth had formerly been a great honour; now the members of her household had been left out in the cold, just as she was. Upon Cardinal

Wolsey's fall seven years earlier, all but a handful of his vast array of attendants had deserted him. But the household at Hunsdon, closely tied to the Boleyns through blood or other connections, had no such option.

There were few others upon whom Elizabeth could have relied for support. Among her maternal relations, those who were not at Hunsdon had either been put to death or disgraced. Elizabeth's grandfather, Thomas Boleyn, had been replaced as lord privy seal on 29 June by Cromwell, the architect of his daughter's fall. The following year, he was obliged to surrender his Garter collar to Cromwell, too, and was removed from the commission of the peace in his native Norfolk. With few resources at his disposal, Thomas was forced to provide annuities from estates given to him by the crown for the king's new favourites. A papal report of 1538, the same year as his wife Elizabeth's death, described the once influential courtier as being 'of little power'.[30] Only Anne's former ally, Archbishop Cranmer, stood by him and tried to untangle his beleaguered affairs.

The surviving sources provide little clue about the impact of this increasingly bleak situation upon Elizabeth herself. We do not know how or even when she was told of her mother's fate, although her question to Sir John Shelton suggests she had immediately appreciated that something important had changed. Given her tender age, it is possible that her attendants kept the full truth from her until later. But then, childhood was much shorter in Tudor times: the age of six was believed to mark the transition to adulthood. Moreover, Elizabeth was a precocious and strong-willed child who was unlikely to have been satisfied with vague or evasive answers to any questions that she asked about her mother. Even if Lady Margaret Bryan was discreet, she was just one member of a large household in which gossip would have been rife. Some of the attendants may even have resented being obliged to stay and serve the king's bastard daughter so would not have held back in telling her of Anne's fate.

Evidence from Elizabeth's later life suggests that while the rest of the country – and probably some members of the household at Hunsdon – were condemning Anne as an adulteress and traitor, there were enough benevolent influences to offer her daughter an alternative view. Among them was Elizabeth's closest blood relative on her mother's side: her cousin and possibly half-sister, Katherine Carey. Although her date of birth is not certain, Katherine was about nine years older than Elizabeth. The two young women quickly established a close bond and Katherine would later become one of Elizabeth's most trusted and cherished companions. If she had attended Anne in the Tower, then she was one of precious few people in Elizabeth's orbit who could provide reliable details of her mother's final days, rather than just second-hand reports and rumour.

With no contemporary evidence of the psychological impact of Anne's death upon her daughter, it is tempting to assess it from a modern perspective. Historians and psychologists alike have speculated that such a traumatic realisation must have had a deep and enduring impact upon Elizabeth's entire outlook and behaviour. 'The harm done to Elizabeth as a small child resulted in an irremediable condition of nervous shock,' asserted one author. 'In the fatally vulnerable years she had learned to connect the idea of sexual intercourse with terror and death.'[31] Another has argued that by depriving Elizabeth of a female role model in her formative years, Anne's death inhibited her daughter's feminine attributes, leading to 'a lively dread of pregnancy and childbirth'.[32] In short, Anne's execution caused Elizabeth to cling on to that most famous trait: her virginity.

Certainly, the fact that her mother had been condemned for treasonous adultery and put to death at the orders of her father must have been at least as shocking to Elizabeth as it was to Henry's subjects. Anne was the first anointed queen in the history of the English monarchy to have been executed. For ten years, she had dominated the court and the kingdom, her scandalous courtship with the king bringing revolution and destruction in its wake. Henry may have wished to erase her from history after her fall, but she would remain the subject of frenzied gossip and debate for many years to come – not least among her daughter's household.

Elizabeth's dismay at learning of all this was perhaps tempered by the fact that for most of her childhood, Anne had been a distant figure, making only occasional visits to her daughter. Having been established in her own household from the age of three months must have fostered a sense of independence from her parents at court. While she would have missed the steady supply of new clothes and other gifts from her mother, it is unlikely that she felt bereft at her now permanent absence. At her tender age, she would probably have felt a greater wrench if one of her nursemaids or governesses had been suddenly taken away from her.

And yet, as Elizabeth grew to maturity, she became distrustful, cautious and full of fear – even if the latter was often suppressed by the outward courage that she inherited from Anne. As an adolescent, she would become increasingly neurotic and emotionally unstable, sometimes overcome with inexplicable feelings of dread. Plagued with a deep-seated anxiety, she occasionally fell prey to debilitating panic attacks. The physical manifestations of the psychological trauma she had suffered included fainting fits, stomach upsets and amenorrhea. It was increasingly apparent that the sudden and brutal loss of her mother had left an indelible mark on the young Elizabeth.

CHAPTER 6

'A child toward'

As the upheaval of Anne Boleyn's execution began to subside and Elizabeth's household adjusted to the changed circumstances, her upbringing became more settled. It may have lacked the excitement and prestige of former times but, after having her mother so brutally snatched away, stability was something to be prized. Meanwhile, at court there were signs that, yet again, all was not well with her father's new marriage. Now aged forty-five, Henry was past his sexual prime and there were rumours of impotence. Anne Boleyn had reportedly remarked that her husband lacked 'vigour', and Chapuys speculated that if the king decided to get rid of Jane Seymour, he could do so easily, since she was likely still a virgin. As the months wore on and the new queen showed no signs of pregnancy, speculation began to mount. The king confided in Chapuys that he feared he would have no children by Jane. He had other reasons to regret their hasty marriage. Jane's plainness and modesty had formed an appealing contrast to her predecessor, but now that Anne was out of the way Henry could not help comparing his new wife to the other, more beautiful women of the court.

In December 1536, the king's younger daughter was invited to join the Christmas celebrations at Greenwich. It was the first time she had returned there since her mother's execution seven months earlier. Her invitation may have been prompted by her sister Mary, whose attitude towards Elizabeth had been transformed by Anne Boleyn's execution. To her credit, rather than pushing home her advantage as the favoured daughter, Mary took pity on Elizabeth and petitioned their father to look kindly on her. Even before her own restoration to court, she had written to him: 'My sister Elizabeth is well, and such a child toward, as I doubt not but your Highness shall have cause to rejoice of in time coming.'[1] But to Henry, his younger daughter was an uncomfortable reminder of his previous marriage, particularly as she bore a striking resemblance to Anne. During the Christmas festivities, he invited Mary to sit opposite himself and the new queen, while Elizabeth was positioned out of sight. The French diplomat Cardinal du Bellay did report, though, that the king was 'very affectionate' towards Elizabeth and 'loves her very much'.[2]

To Henry's elation, in early 1537, his new wife finally fell pregnant. Everything progressed well and in September Jane began her confinement at Hampton Court. She was given a richly appointed suite of rooms that probably contained some of the treasures prepared for her predecessor's lying-in four years earlier. At two o'clock in the morning of 12 October, after a long and gruelling labour, the queen was delivered of a healthy boy. The king and court were transported with joy at the birth of the 'noble imp Prince Edward', recorded Hall. 'Great fires [were] made through the whole realm and great joy made with thanksgiving to almighty God, which had sent so noble a prince to succeed in the crown of this realm.'[3]

The celebrations at Hunsdon were likely more muted. Although Elizabeth had already been declared illegitimate and removed from the succession, for as long as the king lacked a son, there had been hope that she might one day be restored. Now, her status had been dealt a blow from which it seemed unlikely ever to recover. At a little over four years old, Elizabeth looked set to be relegated to the side-lines of history. At the christening three days later, her sister Mary was accorded the honour of godmother, while Elizabeth bore the train of her new brother's christening robe. A concession was made to her 'tender age' and she was carried by one of the noblewomen present.[4] Now her father had his 'precious jewel', he was prepared to be magnanimous towards his younger daughter, who was referred to as 'the Lady Elizabeth the King's daughter'. Also present was Elizabeth's grandfather, Thomas Boleyn, who was tasked with bearing a taper in the procession. His feelings at seeing the granddaughter who, a short time before, had been the heir to England and now had little prospect of ever inheriting the throne were kept hidden.

The king's good humour was brought to an abrupt end when his 'noble and gracious' wife fell gravely ill.[5] Jane seems to have contracted an infection soon after the birth and her condition rapidly deteriorated. Her death on 24 October plunged the court into mourning. Elizabeth was unlikely to have shared their regret. Jane Seymour had done nothing to supply the place of her late mother: if anything, she had worked against her younger stepdaughter by so obviously favouring her elder. What struck a much crueller blow to Elizabeth was the loss of her Lady Mistress, Margaret Bryan, who was transferred to the new prince's household shortly afterwards. Of all her attendants, Lady Margaret was the one with whom Elizabeth had formed the closest attachment. She had been with her from the moment that she had first left court, providing a treasured link to her mother and helping to fill the maternal void during the long periods between Anne's visits. This role had become even more vital during the months after Anne's death. But now it had been withdrawn just as suddenly as her mother's presence.

The blow was softened by the fact that, for a time at least, Prince Edward was to join his sisters' household. So, while Lady Margaret would no longer be Elizabeth's constant companion, she continued to live under the same roof. Elizabeth's former Lady Mistress revelled in her new position. There was no prospect of Edward ever being supplanted in the king's affections, or of his status being diminished. Her letters were full of praise for the young prince, towards whom she showed greater indulgence than she ever had towards Elizabeth or Mary. 'His grace . . . was as full of pretty toys as ever I saw child in my life,' she wrote to Cromwell, before pestering him to send 'a good jewel to set on his cap'.[6] As the prince grew into a demanding toddler, she indulged his every wish. 'The minstrels played, and his grace danced and played so wantonly that he could not stand still,' she reported with evident delight.[7]

Loss had become a dominant theme in Elizabeth's young life. In the space of four years, she had been deprived of her mother, her Lady Mistress, her Shelton relatives and her stepmother – not to mention her status as the king's legitimate daughter and heir. An awareness of the precariousness of life made her inclined to cling tightly to those around her and throughout her life she would form intense relationships with her attendants. Upon Lady Margaret's transfer to Edward's household, Katherine ('Kat') Champernowne, who had entered Elizabeth's service a year earlier, was promoted to the position of governess. Still in her teens, she was much closer in age to Elizabeth than Lady Margaret had been and was of an altogether different character. Her enlightened education had given her a stronger sense of independence than most women of her age, and her keen intellect was appealing to the precocious child for whose education she was now responsible. Kat also had a lively sense of fun and supplied the affection that Elizabeth craved. Her influence on the young princess would be profound. Elizabeth later reflected: 'She hath been with me a long time, and many years, and hath taken great labour, and pain in bringing of me up in learning and honesty.'[8]

As queen, Elizabeth was notoriously hostile to the idea of her ladies marrying, not least because it would divert their attention from her service. But when her beloved Kat fell in love with John Astley, a member of Elizabeth's household, she seemed to heartily approve of the match. This was probably because he hailed from a Norfolk family with strong Boleyn connections: his mother's sister, Lady Elizabeth Boleyn, was Anne Boleyn's aunt. Elizabeth was evidently proud of their kinship. The inscription on John's tomb in All Saints Church, Maidstone, declares: 'He was justly acknowledged to be allied to the most illustrious Princess Queen Elizabeth (by her mother's kindred).'[9] Astley's sharp intellect also appealed to Elizabeth: the Cambridge scholar Roger Ascham, who would exert a profound influence over her education, commended his ability to speak Italian. John and Kat married in 1545 but remained dedicated to Elizabeth's service and would enjoy their royal mistress's favour throughout their lives.

Elizabeth's nursemaid, Blanche Parry, also rose to prominence after Margaret Bryan's defection. Blanche's steady, stabilising presence formed a marked contrast to Elizabeth's more exuberant governess, but they were qualities that she came to appreciate more as she grew to maturity. Showing no inclination to marry or, in contrast to Lady Margaret, to pursue her own ambitions, she devoted her life to Elizabeth's service and would become the benchmark by which she measured all her other ladies.

Another, more surprising, maternal figure for Elizabeth during this time was her half-sister Mary, who invested a great deal of effort into her upbringing and education. She also showered her with gifts, which was something that Elizabeth had not enjoyed since her mother's death. Although she had every reason to resent him, Elizabeth also grew close to her half-brother. With only four years separating them, they often shared lessons and both developed a passion for the reformist faith – the only point of discord with their elder half-sister Mary. This was encouraged by Anne Boleyn's former chaplain, Matthew Parker, who had stayed true to the promise he had made to her six days before her death. He had kept in contact with Elizabeth and sometimes visited her, such as in 1540 when he came to Hatfield to preach a sermon.[10]

In March 1539, Elizabeth's maternal grandfather, Thomas Boleyn, died at Hever Castle, aged about sixty-two. It is a testament to his skills as a courtier, as well as to the king's esteem, that he had continued in royal service to the end – albeit on the fringes. In January 1538 he and his wife Elizabeth had been reported to be 'again now at court and very well entertained'.[11] Thomas was buried at the nearby St Peter's Church and his funeral effigy still bears the falcon badge that his daughter made famous. The king paid his chaplain to say masses for his former father-in-law's soul. Thomas was survived by his daughter Mary, but she had not appeared at court since her banishment two years earlier and it is unlikely that she had any contact with her niece Elizabeth. She died in obscurity at Rochford Hall in Essex, a Boleyn property, in 1543.

The loss of her grandfather had no discernible impact on Elizabeth, who had had little to do with him either before or after her mother's execution. She had plenty of distractions from her household and its regular removes between palaces. Sometimes she shared a residence with Mary and sometimes with Edward. It was during the latter times that Elizabeth stood a greater chance of seeing her father, who lavished attention on his son and visited whenever matters of state allowed. At the beginning of 1540, Henry married for the fourth time. Anne of Cleves brought him a valuable alliance with a continental duchy that, like England, had rejected papal authority, but on a personal level the marriage was a disaster. Although beguiled by the portrait that he had commissioned from Hans Holbein, when Henry first met Anne in person, he was apparently so repelled that he was unable to consummate their union and immediately set about trying to dissolve it.

The king's younger daughter was unaware of this when she

wrote to welcome her new stepmother to England: 'Permit me
to show, by this billet, the zeal with which I devote my respect to
you as queen, and my entire obedience to you as my mother.' The
letter could have been composed by a seasoned courtier, rather
than a six-and-a-half-year-old girl – albeit an extraordinarily precocious one. Elizabeth had clearly learned a great deal since her
mother's death and was eager to cultivate the new queen, assuring
her: 'I hope your Majesty will have as much goodwill for me as I
have zeal for your service.'[12] It was perfectly judged. Anne was so
charmed by the letter that she asked the king if Elizabeth might
come to court. Her request was instantly rebuffed. Irritated by this
reminder of another marriage that he would rather forget, he
ordered Cromwell: 'Tell her [Elizabeth] that she had a mother so
different from this woman that she ought not to wish to see her.'[13]

A few months later, the king's new marriage was dissolved.
Thomas Cromwell, who had been instrumental in arranging it,
was beheaded for treason on the same day that his master married
for a fifth time. Although Henry had forgiven his chief minister
for matching him with Anne of Cleves, Cromwell's influence had
already been on the wane as his royal master had begun to lose
faith in his religious reforms. The king had welcomed the riches
that these had brought him – the dissolution of the monasteries
in particular – and revelled in his status as supreme head of the
new Church of England, but at heart he was conservative in
matters of religion and sought ways of returning to some of the
traditional Catholic practices. At the same time, Henry's physical
health had declined sharply following his serious accident while
jousting in 1536, which made him increasingly irascible and para-
noid. As a result, it had taken shockingly little effort on the Duke
of Norfolk's part to persuade the king that his faithful servant
Cromwell had been plotting against him.

Henry's new bride was Anne Boleyn's attractive young cousin,

Catherine Howard, who was probably more than thirty years his junior. The marriage had an immediate and positive impact on Elizabeth's status. To pave the way for it, a statute had been passed in 1540 authorising marriage between cousins. This also stipulated that no union could be dissolved because of any pre-contract, which reversed Elizabeth's bastard status – albeit unintentionally.[14] Her close kinship with the new queen also worked in her favour. On the day that Catherine was publicly acknowledged as queen at Hampton Court, she asked that Elizabeth be placed opposite her at the celebratory banquet because she was 'of her own blood and lineage'.[15] This honour was repeated on other occasions. By contrast, Elizabeth's half-sister Mary, who had made her distaste for her father's new wife all too obvious, was left out in the cold.

This was not set to last. In November 1541, the king was presented with evidence of his young wife's adultery with Thomas Culpepper, a trusted member of his own privy chamber. Equally damning was the revelation that she had not been a virgin at the time of their marriage. History seemed to be repeating itself as Catherine was taken to the Tower to await her fate. But, in contrast to her late cousin Anne, her guilt was beyond doubt. In December 1541, Thomas Culpepper and another of Catherine's former lovers, Francis Dereham, were put to death. Catherine herself was beheaded on 10 February 1542, along with her close attendant, Jane Boleyn, sister-in-law of Elizabeth's late mother, who had facilitated her adulterous liaisons.

Elizabeth had witnessed a succession of stepmothers come and go over the past few years, but none of them affected her so deeply as Catherine Howard. By now, she would have learned the full details of her mother's downfall and execution, and this was all too similar. Already keenly alive to the danger inherent in royal marriages, this confirmed her opinion. From that day, she was said to have vowed: 'I will never marry.'[16]

CHAPTER 7

'No words of Boleyn'

Although Elizabeth's father had been plunged into a deep depression by his fifth wife's betrayal, he was soon on the hunt for a replacement. It was rumoured that he might remarry Anne of Cleves, with whom he had enjoyed better relations since the annulment of their marriage than he had during it. Elizabeth had also grown close to Anne, who was entranced by her clever, witty and affectionate former stepdaughter. She once told the king: 'To have had [her] for a daughter would have been greater happiness to her than being queen.'¹ Elizabeth visited Anne at Richmond Palace and perhaps also at Hever Castle, which the king had gifted his fourth wife as part of a financial settlement.² If she had spent time at Anne Boleyn's former home, it must have been an emotional experience for Elizabeth, whose reverence towards her late mother seemed to grow with each passing year.

In 1543, Henry chose an entirely new bride: the twice-widowed Katherine Parr, a member of his daughter Mary's household. They were married on 12 July at Hampton Court Palace. Elizabeth and her sister were among the eighteen guests. Although Elizabeth was sent back to her own household soon afterwards, she seems to have quickly struck up a rapport with her new stepmother and referred to herself as Katherine's 'humble daughter'.³ It was one that would deepen over the next three years and Katherine, an intelligent woman who was fiercely committed to religious reform, exerted a profound influence over Elizabeth's education and upbringing.

During the summer of 1544, the new queen acted as regent while Henry embarked on a last-gasp attempt at military glory in France. From the beginning of his reign, he had dreamed of emulating the achievements of illustrious medieval predecessors such as Edward III and Henry V by conquering large swathes of territory across the Channel. But apart from a couple of short-lived victories in northern France in 1513, he had enjoyed little success. With her husband away, Katherine invited his younger daughter to keep her company at Hampton Court and, while there, encouraged her to read the works of Marguerite of Navarre. Elizabeth needed no persuasion: Marguerite had been a close acquaintance of her mother during her years at the French court, and the two women had renewed their association when Anne became queen. In 1535 Anne paid her friend the highest possible compliment by sending her a message that her 'greatest wish, next to having a son, was to see you again'.[4] Her affection was evidently reciprocated because Marguerite presented her with the original manuscript of her controversial poem, *Le miroir de l'âme pécheresse*, which was published in 1531. It is likely that Anne had bequeathed this to her daughter. Marguerite's writings therefore offered Elizabeth, who was now almost eleven years old, the tantalising prospect of absorbing some of the intellectual influences that had shaped her mother's outlook at a similar age.

Anne's former acquaintance also strengthened Elizabeth's commitment to what would become known as the Protestant faith. The theme of Marguerite's poem, *Le miroir*, was one that profoundly resonated with Elizabeth: the inadequacy of the human soul. Among the subjects it covered were bastardy, adultery and incest, all of which she had been plagued with since her mother's execution. It did, though, offer the hopeful message that one could be saved by faith alone – a cornerstone of Protestantism and one that both Elizabeth and her stepmother firmly believed in. Given its resonance to her own history, when Elizabeth undertook a painstaking and precocious translation of *Le miroir* in 1544, it may have been as much to compliment her mother's memory as a fitting New Year gift for her stepmother.[5]

One of the most revealing parts of Elizabeth's translation concerned the treatment of adulterous wives. In Marguerite's original, she stated that no husband would forgive such a wife and that many would have them judged and put to death. It is interesting that Elizabeth changed the gender in this section so that it read: 'There be enough of them, which for to avenge their wrong, did cause the judges to condemn *him*[6] to die.' Of course, this may have been a simple mistake. But the rest of Elizabeth's translation is painstakingly accurate, so it is tempting to conclude that the change of gender was deliberate and that, through this poem, she was venting her long-suppressed anger towards her father. With an apparent slip of her pen, she condemned Henry to the death that he had made Anne suffer.[7]

Elizabeth embroidered a beautiful cover for the book, which was bound in exquisite blue cloth (the colour of France), and carefully stitched little forget-me-nots onto the spine. It was customary to decorate gifts with this flower in the hope that the giver would always be remembered. But in choosing it, the princess was perhaps making a tacit reference to Anne Boleyn, whose memory she would cherish and honour for the rest of her life.[8]

In the same year that Elizabeth worked this gift for her stepmother, she and her half-sister Mary were restored to the line of succession, if not to their legitimate status. This was at least partly thanks to Katherine's benign influence, although even before she became Henry's sixth wife there had been signs that he was thawing towards his younger daughter. In September 1542, he had invited both Elizabeth and her elder sister to dine with him while he was on a visit to inspect coastal defences in Essex. She had evidently impressed him because he had subsequently begun making plans to marry her to the Earl of Arran, son of the Scottish regent, and praised her as being 'endowed with virtues and qualities agreeable to her estate'.⁹

Perhaps to mark the occasion of his daughters being made heirs to the throne once more, the king commissioned a spectacular dynastic portrait. At the centre of the composition is Henry, flanked by his late wife Jane Seymour and their son Edward. The princesses Mary and Elizabeth are at either side of them. On the surface, it is a depiction of family unity (albeit an idealised one, given that Jane had been dead for several years) and the two princesses stand in an aspect of meek compliance. But Elizabeth used this portrait to make a daring statement of loyalty to her late mother. Visitors who peer closely enough at the painting, which now hangs at Hampton Court Palace, will see that she is wearing Anne's famous 'A' pendant.¹⁰ Now aged about twelve or thirteen, Elizabeth had gained enough experience of her father's court to appreciate the colossal risk she was taking. She knew just how fragile her newly won favour was and that an act of such bold defiance could send her back to obscurity. She knew, too, that her father wanted no reminders of the woman whom he had condemned for adultery and treason; that Anne's name must not even be spoken in his presence. But when it came to her mother, Elizabeth's actions would always speak louder than her words.

Elizabeth apparently escaped any reprisals for this act of teenage rebellion. It is likely that she and the other sitters were painted separately, and the necklace was discreet enough to escape her father's notice. But she may have repeated the risk when she sat for another portrait in 1546. The artist on this occasion was William Scrots and the painting was probably for the king.¹¹ He must have been struck by the physical similarity between the princess and her mother. She had the same 'black and pleasant' eyes, slender face and pointed chin.[12] Impeccably dressed as she was in a gown of crimson silk and cloth of silver tissued with gold, it is obvious that she had inherited Anne's sense of style, too. What is most intriguing about the portrait, though, is that Elizabeth chose to wear a pearl choker and necklace that she may have inherited from her mother. In the portraits of Anne painted during Elizabeth's reign, she is shown wearing an almost identical set, the only difference being the gold jewel hanging from the choker, which in Anne's case is a 'B'. Sadly, none of Anne's jewels have survived (or at least, not in their original form) so it is not possible to say for certain whether her daughter inherited them. Even if the ones she wore in this portrait were not Anne's, though, the fact that they were so similar was a tribute to her late mother. Elizabeth also wears a French hood edged with pearls, just like Anne.

It is possible that Elizabeth's father did not live to see the painting completed. Dogged by ill health since the jousting accident in 1536, he was morbidly obese and in constant pain from his ulcerated legs. He briefly attended the Christmas celebrations at Greenwich in 1546, to which Elizabeth was also invited. It would be the last time she saw her father. Soon afterwards, he retreated to Whitehall Palace with just a few close attendants. From there, he ordered two of Elizabeth's closest relatives on her mother's side to the Tower. Henry Howard, the proud and arrogant young Earl of Surrey, had boasted of his royal blood by quartering the royal arms on his shield – an ill-advised move given the intense paranoia by which the king was gripped in his later years. Surrey's father, Thomas Howard, Duke of Norfolk (Anne Boleyn's uncle) was tainted by association and a warrant was drawn up for his execution.[13] Surrey was beheaded on 19 January, the last victim of an increasingly brutal and tyrannical king. It was a chilling reminder to the thirteen-year-old Elizabeth that when it came to the crown, blood was not thicker than water.

Elizabeth was with her brother Edward at Enfield, a royal manor house to the north of London, when they received the news that their father had died. Edward was now king of England at the tender age of nine, although on his deathbed Henry had appointed a council to rule for him until he reached maturity. This was led by Edward's maternal uncle, Edward Seymour, as Lord Protector. There is no contemporary evidence for how the young king and his sister reacted to their father's death, but later accounts have the siblings clinging to each other and weeping piteously. It is possible that, despite what he had done to her mother, Elizabeth loved and revered him – certainly she always spoke of him with pride. Perhaps she believed that he had been duped by the 'evil counsellors' to whom her mother's chaplain had referred shortly before Anne's downfall. But it was also politically expedient for a princess of questionable legitimacy to remind people of her connection to the late king. In private, it was a very different story.

Upon the king's death, a detailed inventory of his possessions was taken. The original still survives and includes a list of those items that his daughters were given for their own households. As the elder, more favoured princess, Mary was at liberty to select an array of rich furnishings from among her father's vast treasure. Elizabeth's choice was more frugal and mostly confined to religious items, reflecting her already intense piety. But it also included something that was closely connected with her mother: a set of tapestries depicting Christine de Pizan's *The City of Ladies*. Anne Boleyn had encountered the work during her time in the courts of the Netherlands and France, and an English translation had been published in 1521. The ideas it propounded about female education and leadership were a source of profound inspiration for Elizabeth. The author included stories of numerous female saints who refused to marry. Elizabeth would have identified with one of these in particular: the warrior queen Synoppe, who 'had such a great and lofty heart, that not for a day in her life did she deign to couple with a man, but remained a virgin her entire lifetime'. Significantly, Synoppe also 'avenged her mother's death in great style'.[14]

The inventory reveals that the six large tapestries were 'delivered to the Lady Elizabeth . . . towards the furniture of her house'.[15] Each measured an average of eight by five metres, so if hung together they would have required a room or hall with a perimeter of almost fifty metres. To have such a prominent visual reminder of Christine de Pizan's work hanging on the walls of her home was a clear demonstration of how much it had influenced Elizabeth – and of how greatly she revered her mother's memory.

By contrast, Elizabeth showed little loyalty towards her late father. Within three months of Henry's death, her stepmother Katherine married Thomas Seymour (brother of the late Queen Jane) in secret. She would probably have married him years earlier if she had not come to the king's notice. Conducted with such unseemly haste, the marriage caused a scandal at court. Princess Mary refused to have anything more to do with Katherine and urged Elizabeth to follow her example, considering the 'scarcely cold body of the King our father so shamefully dishonoured by the Queen our stepmother'.[16] Elizabeth's reply was philosophical. She told her half-sister that they must 'submit with patience to that which could not be cured'.[17] Honouring the memory of a father who had put her mother to death was, it seemed, of less importance to Elizabeth. Shortly afterwards, she went to live with Katherine and her new husband at their home in Chelsea.

Of course, this may not have been a deliberate act of disrespect towards a father who had destroyed her mother. Elizabeth was a good deal more pragmatic than her half-sister and saw in Chelsea the prospect of a settled and happy life with a stepmother she adored. She thrived in the intellectually stimulating atmosphere of Katherine's household, where she was tutored by the renowned scholar, Roger Ascham. Seymour's ward, Lady Jane Grey (a great-niece of Henry VIII), joined Elizabeth's studies for a time and shared her Protestant faith. As the princess developed beliefs and opinions of her own, her mother's influence became ever more pronounced. During Edward's reign, Bishop John Hooper, a staunch reformist, approvingly noted: 'His sister, the daughter of the late king by queen Anne, is inflamed with the same zeal for the religion of Christ. She not only knows what the true religion is, but has acquired such proficiency in Greek and Latin, that she is able to defend it by the most just arguments and the most happy talent; so that she encounters few adversaries whom she does not overcome.'[18]

Some time before Elizabeth moved to Chelsea, she had appointed Thomas Parry as her cofferer – effectively, her business manager. As with so many other members of her household, he had Boleyn connections. His wife Anne's first husband had been Adrian Fortescue, the son of Anne Boleyn's aunt, Alice. Parry was also related by marriage to William Cecil and may have introduced the latter to Elizabeth's service. Cecil would go on to become her longest-serving and by far her most trusted adviser.

Elizabeth was developing sexually as well as intellectually. A striking young woman with the fine features, pointed chin and dark eyes of her mother, she had an abundance of the trademark red hair of the Tudors. As the half-sister of the new king, she was an attractive prospect to any suitor – and a fatally irresistible one to her new stepfather. It seems Thomas Seymour thought the daughter of the 'Great Whore' would be easy prey. He started paying surprise visits to Elizabeth's bedchamber early in the morning, before she was up and dressed. What he passed off as innocent fun – tickling her in bed, slapping her 'on the buttocks familiarly' – spelt grave danger for Elizabeth. After years of veering from undoubted royal heir to the bastard daughter of a notorious concubine, her legitimacy was as precarious as her reputation. Now she was on the verge of becoming embroiled in a sexual scandal that was both adulterous and incestuous: Seymour was her step-uncle as well as her stepfather. In the eyes of the world she was simply playing out her destiny as the 'bad seed' of her notorious mother.

Seymour's behaviour towards his stepdaughter eventually aroused the suspicions of his wife, who was pregnant with his child. Matters reached a head when Katherine discovered her husband and Elizabeth in a clinch. In June 1548, barely a year after her arrival, Elizabeth was ordered to leave Chelsea. She never saw her beloved stepmother again: Katherine died in childbirth that September. Although there were rumours that Elizabeth herself was pregnant by the time she left Chelsea, there is no reliable evidence to support them. Even so, it had been a damaging episode for a young woman whom many believed would go the same way as her mother.

Following his wife's death, Seymour renewed his attentions towards Elizabeth. Ambitious for power, he seemed intent upon making her his wife. To do so, he would need the king's permission, but he knew he was unlikely to secure it because he was at loggerheads with his brother Edward, whom Henry VIII had appointed Lord Protector during his son's minority. Rumours soon began to circulate that Thomas planned to marry the king's half-sister in secret. His earlier brush with scandal had evidently been enough to make him wary of reviving any memories of Elizabeth's mother. Thomas Parry recalled a conversation in which Seymour had told him that he was going to Boulogne, which the English pronounced 'Boleyn'. To avoid any doubt, Seymour added:

'No words of Boleyn.'[19] To a more cautious man, his previous entanglement with his stepdaughter would have been more than sufficient deterrent. But Seymour was ruthlessly, fatally ambitious and Elizabeth was too tantalising a prize to resist.

In January 1549, Seymour was arrested on the charge of high treason and committed to the Tower, along with three of Elizabeth's closest attendants: Kat Astley, her husband John and Thomas Parry. Elizabeth herself was confined to Hatfield, where she was subjected to intense interrogation. Terrified for her servants, who were holed up in the fortress that she would forever associate with her mother's death, Elizabeth showed her mettle and refused to admit any guilt. She also demanded John Astley's release, 'for he is my kinsman'.[20] Parry was less stoical. While Kat Astley remained tight-lipped, he gave his interrogators all the lurid details of Seymour's scandalous behaviour towards Elizabeth at Chelsea. Elizabeth was painfully aware that her mother had been condemned on far less evidence. But, like Anne, she gave no hint of her inner turmoil and steadfastly protested her innocence.

Both of the princess's attendants were subsequently released, although Kat was temporarily removed from Elizabeth's service – much to the princess's grief. 'She took the matter so heavily, that she wept all that night, and lowered all the next day,' reported one of Mary's officials. 'The love that she beareth her is to be wondered at.'[21] Elizabeth herself escaped any reprisals, but Seymour was condemned for treason and executed on the orders of the king's council in March 1549.

For the fifteen-year-old Elizabeth, to have been at the heart of a sexual scandal that reached its bloody conclusion at the Tower was a deeply disturbing echo of her mother's fate. From that moment onwards, she presented herself as a woman of impeccable virtue, eschewing the brightly coloured, richly decorated gowns that she had loved since childhood in favour of the sober garb of a Protestant lady. Bishop John Aylmer opined: 'I am sure that her maidenly apparel, which she used in King Edward's time, made the noblemen's daughters and wives ashamed, to be dressed and painted like peacocks, being more moved with her most virtuous example.'[22] It was a talent for reinvention that Elizabeth had inherited from her mother, and she would employ it to ever greater effect in the years to come. For now, she became such a shining example of modesty that it inspired her cousin and former study partner, Lady Jane Grey. When Princess Mary presented Jane with a rich gown of gold and velvet, she refused to wear it, declaring: 'It were a shame to follow my Lady Mary against God's word and leave my Lady Elizabeth which followeth God's word.'[23]

As the scandal began to subside, Elizabeth welcomed a new chamberlain into her household. Sir Henry Parker was a long-established courtier and respected scholar, who had gained renown during Henry VIII's reign for his translations from Latin to Italian. The latter made him an acceptable addition to the princess's household, but what further recommended him was his strong Boleyn connections. His daughter Jane had been married to Anne Boleyn's brother, George. Although her testimony helped implicate her sister-in-law for adultery, there is little evidence for Jane being the scheming, embittered woman who single-handedly brought down a queen, and it is likely that she had had little choice but to fall in with Cromwell's plot. Her father had avoided being tainted by the scandal of her condemnation as an accomplice to Catherine Howard's infidelities and had continued in royal service. He held the position of chamberlain to Elizabeth from 1550 until 1552, but died before she came to the throne.

At around the same time, Elizabeth became acquainted with another Boleyn associate. Two years after the death of her aunt, Mary Boleyn, in 1543, her widower William Stafford married his distant cousin Dorothy. As a committed Protestant, William prospered during Edward VI's reign and it may have been at this point that his second wife became acquainted with the young Elizabeth. It was the beginning of a friendship that would last a lifetime.

The princess's household accounts during her residence at Hatfield from 1551 to 1552 provide an intriguing glance into her private world. Drawn up by her cofferer, Thomas Parry, the accounts were checked and signed by Elizabeth, who seemed to have inherited both the eye for detail and the parsimony of her grandfather, Henry VII. In the space of a year, she gave only a tiny proportion of her income in 'alms to diverse poor men and women' (£7. 15s. 8d.). Yet she gave ten times that amount to Edmund Boleyn, 'her grace's kinsman'. The identity of this man is not known, but he evidently knew that he could count on the princess's generosity, thanks to his Boleyn blood.[24] There are also entries for payments made at the christening of the children of 'Mr Norrice' and 'Mr Carie'. These men might have been members of her household, but it is possible that they were Henry Norris, son of the man who had been executed for adultery with Elizabeth's mother, and Henry Carey, son of Mary Boleyn and first cousin of the princess. Both men would become closely affiliated with Elizabeth in the years to come, but their connection may have begun earlier than has often been supposed.[25]

Elizabeth was soon back in her half-brother's favour after the Seymour controversy. Edward had always been closer to Elizabeth than to Mary, thanks to their shared passion for the reformed faith. During his reign, relations between the two sisters became increasingly strained and, because of her refusal to conform, Mary found herself out in the cold. But the young king was increasingly subject to the will of John Dudley, who had ousted Edward Seymour as the dominant force in government. The first indication that this spelt trouble for Elizabeth came in the spring of 1553 when Dudley took ownership of Durham Place, a sumptuous mansion on the Strand in London where Anne Boleyn and her father had lodged prior to her marriage to Henry, and which had subsequently been granted to her daughter. When Elizabeth heard that she was required to surrender it to Dudley, she expressed her annoyance that the decision had been taken 'without first knowing her mind'.[26]

Not long afterwards, Edward suddenly announced his intention to disinherit both of his half-sisters in favour of his first cousin once removed, Lady Jane Grey, because of her staunch Protestantism. Even though Elizabeth was of the same faith, the king feared that she, like Mary, might marry a foreign, Catholic prince. He was also heavily influenced by Dudley, who had married his son Guildford to Lady Jane Grey. Both of Edward's sisters were declared illegitimate by letters patent because their mothers' marriages to Henry VIII had already been 'clearly and lawfully undone'.[27] In answer to opposition voiced in his government, the young king pronounced: 'It was the fate of Elizabeth to have Anne Boleyn for a mother; this woman was indeed not only cast off by my father because she was more inclined to couple with a number of courtiers rather than reverencing her husband, so mighty a king, but also paid the penalty with her head – a greater proof of her guilt.'[28] It was a bitter blow for Elizabeth and a striking illustration of the different influences with whom they had been surrounded. As the son of the woman who had supplanted Anne Boleyn and whose memory would be forever revered because she was the only one of Henry's wives to give him a male heir, Edward had been raised to believe every word of the slander against his father's wicked 'concubine'.

By the time Edward drew up his 'Device for the Succession',

it was obvious to those closest to him that he was dying. A bout of measles the previous year had dangerously weakened his immune system and by early 1553 he was showing signs of tuberculosis. He died on 6 July, aged just fifteen. Four days later, Lady Jane Grey was proclaimed queen.

But the late king's sister Mary, whom most people viewed as the rightful heir, was quick to rally support. Upon hearing that Edward was dying, she had fled to East Anglia before Dudley and his followers could act against her. Setting up camp at Framlingham Castle, the ancient fortress of the dukes of Norfolk, she attracted ever greater numbers to her cause. Although most were religious conservatives opposed to the radical policies of Edward's reign, many reformists also viewed her as his rightful successor.

Bolstered by this support, Mary wrote to the council, demanding that she be recognised as queen. Having heard that people were gathering in ever greater numbers to support Edward's elder sister, on 19 July the council capitulated and abandoned Jane. Dudley, who had ridden over to Norfolk to take possession of Mary, was captured, sent to the Tower and executed the following month. His daughter-in-law Jane now resided there, not as queen, but as a prisoner.

CHAPTER 8

'The school of affliction'

H AVING KEPT A low profile during the turbulent events that
followed Edward VI's death, Elizabeth wrote at once to
congratulate her half-sister. In a triumphant mood, Mary was
apparently prepared to forget the tensions of the past and invited
Elizabeth to join her ceremonial entry into London. But soon
those same tensions resurfaced. As the sisters rode through the
city, Elizabeth, not Mary, won the greatest acclaim. She might
have been illegitimate, but she had grown into an attractive,
charismatic young woman. The new queen lacked her popular
touch and responded awkwardly to the cheers from the crowds,
whereas her younger sister showed them a 'merry countenance'
and spoke to many of them with 'most tender and gentle
language'.[1] 'Her figure and face are very handsome, and such an
air of dignified majesty pervades all her actions that no one can
fail to suppose she is a queen,' remarked Giacomo Soranzo, the
Venetian ambassador in France.[2]

There were soon other, graver causes for discord between the
two sisters. Even though, as Soranzo observed, in matters of
religion Elizabeth 'adapted herself to the will of her Majesty',
Mary's Catholic-dominated government viewed her half-sister as
a threat that could not be ignored.[3] The Spanish ambassador,
Simon Renard, never missed an opportunity to drip poisonous
words in the new queen's ear. He warned that Elizabeth was

'clever and sly' and might 'conceive some dangerous design' against the new queen.[4] Such comments may have been slanderous, but they succeeded in reopening old wounds. 'She still resents the injuries inflicted on Queen Catherine, her lady mother, by the machinations of Anne Boleyn, mother of Elizabeth,' noted Renard with evident satisfaction.[5] Mary confided to him that she thought Elizabeth would grow to be like her mother, 'who had caused great trouble in the Kingdom'.[6] Every time Mary looked at her sister, she was likely reminded of Anne Boleyn and the pain and misery that she and Catherine of Aragon had suffered at her hands.

Memories of their respective mothers were also stirred during the first Parliament of the reign, which passed an Act declaring Catherine's annulment void and confirming Mary's legitimacy. Elizabeth's bastardy, on the other hand, was upheld. But the new queen was determined to go further still because, according to the statute passed in 1544, her half-sister was still heir to the throne. She therefore made clear her intention to repeal this and appoint her cousin, Lady Margaret Douglas, daughter of Henry VIII's elder sister, as her heir. Mary subsequently accorded her cousin a place of honour at court and gave her precedence over Elizabeth at its formal gatherings. Much as they wished to get Elizabeth out of the way, however, the shrewdest among the new queen's advisers persuaded her that disrupting the succession in this way would cause more trouble than it solved. Mary reluctantly agreed to abandon the scheme.

But for Elizabeth, the damage had been done. Renard dismissed her as having 'too doubtful lineage on her mother's side', and the Venetian ambassador, Giovanni Michiel, went further still, describing her as 'the illegitimate child of a criminal who was punished as a public strumpet'.[7] Rather than being bowed by such treatment, Elizabeth displayed the same resilience that her mother had shown when surrounded by a hostile court. Soon after her coronation, Anne had told a disdainful Venetian envoy that 'God had inspired his Majesty to marry her'.[8] Showing a similarly 'proud and haughty' face to her enemies, Elizabeth insisted upon her legitimacy. 'Although she knows she was born of such a mother, she nevertheless does not consider herself of inferior degree to the Queen [Mary], whom she equals in self-esteem; neither does she believe herself less legitimate than her Majesty, alleging in her own favour that her mother would never cohabit with the King unless by way of marriage, with the authority of the Church, and the intervention of the Primate of England; so that even if deceived, having as a subject acted with good faith, the fact cannot have invalidated her mother's marriage, nor her own birth, she having been born under that same faith'.[9] The exchange is an exceptionally rare example of Elizabeth referring to Anne directly. It is telling that it was prompted by the question of her own legitimacy – a subject that had always touched her closely.

For all Elizabeth's public defiance, she harboured the same fears that had plagued Anne when her influence at court had been on the wane. In late November 1553, as she accompanied her sister to chapel, there was a cry of 'Treason!' Instantly, Elizabeth was gripped with terror, assuming that the cry was against her. One of Mary's ladies was obliged to comfort her and rub her stomach until she calmed down.[10] Shortly afterwards, Elizabeth begged the queen to let her leave court and take up residence at her country estate of Ashridge. Renard urged that this was too dangerous a course, given the support that Elizabeth had among the 'heretics', and advised Mary either to keep her sister at court or 'shut her up in the Tower'. Much to Elizabeth's relief, the queen decided to grant her request. But she soon learned that distance did not guarantee safety. Almost from the moment it began, Mary's reign had 'set her [Elizabeth] apprentice in the school of affliction', as one contemporary shrewdly observed.[11]

By the time of her accession, Mary was thirty-seven years old. If she was to secure the succession, it was vital that she marry as soon as possible. She had already made her choice: Philip of Spain, son of her cousin, the Holy Roman Emperor, Charles V. As a Catholic prince from her mother's homeland, he was the perfect candidate and Mary was deaf to the urgings of her council that England would become a mere satellite of the mighty Spanish empire – a fear shared by many of her subjects.

When the marriage settlement was agreed in January 1554, it sparked rebellion. The leader was Sir Thomas Wyatt, son of Anne Boleyn's former suitor, who had been briefly imprisoned in the Tower in 1536 on suspicion of adultery with her. Thomas Wyatt the younger amassed a considerable body of supporters – perhaps as many as fifteen thousand – among commoners and noblemen alike, including Lady Jane Grey's father. Although there was a strong Protestant undertone to the uprising, the participants claimed that their primary motive was 'to prevent us from over-running by strangers'.

In January 1554, Wyatt and his supporters marched towards London. On 1 February, Mary dispatched the Duke of Norfolk to crush the rebels before they reached the capital. But his troops deserted, leaving the queen and her council virtually undefended. This was the first serious test of Mary's queenship and she rose to the challenge. Rallying the loyal troops that had gathered at the Guildhall in the heart of London, she gave a rousing speech that proved a decisive factor in defeating the rebels, although many had already deserted their leader and little blood was shed. The rebellion might have been quickly suppressed, but it had seriously destabilised a regime in its infancy, and those closest to the new queen urged that she rid herself of any rival claimants.

Henry Grey's involvement had sealed the fate of his daughter. Even though Jane had had nothing to do with Wyatt or his supporters, she and her husband Guildford were beheaded on 12 February 1554.

Another woman who had been implicated in the plot was of even closer kinship with the queen: her half-sister Elizabeth. Like Lady Jane, she was almost certainly innocent, but Wyatt and his followers had openly plotted to put her on the throne in Mary's stead and to marry her to Edward Courtenay, Earl of Devon, the last of the Yorkist line. Furthermore, they had written to tell her of their plans – although Elizabeth stoutly denied that she had ever received their letter. Many suspected traitors had been condemned for less – her own mother included. The fact that Wyatt's family was so closely associated with Anne Boleyn did not help matters. When Elizabeth heard that she was to be taken from Ashridge to London for interrogation on the very same day that Lady Jane Grey and her husband were executed, she suffered a complete mental and physical collapse. Too weak to stand, she had to be carried in a litter all the way to Whitehall Palace – a journey of some thirty-five miles that took an agonising eleven days.

Elizabeth arrived in the capital on 23 February, the day that Henry Grey was beheaded, and was installed at Whitehall Palace. Although she was in a state of nervous exhaustion, she showed the same presence of mind as her mother had after her own arrest in May 1536. Having been told that she was about to be taken to the Tower, she insisted on writing to the queen, assuring her of her innocence and loyalty. Aware that the low tide that enabled boats to pass safely under the narrow arches of London Bridge would soon be at an end, she wrote the letter deliberately slowly. By the time she had finished, her captors had – literally – missed the boat. Given the pressure she was under, the letter is extraordinarily impressive: eloquent, persuasive and in the same beautiful script that Elizabeth had spent her childhood perfecting. She even thought to score lines across the unused section above her signature, to prevent her enemies from adding any defamatory text. As well as defending her actions, Elizabeth begged to be allowed to see her half-sister, since: 'I have heard in my time of many cast away for want of coming to the presence of their prince.'[12] She knew that her mother had been denied this right and had paid a heavy price.

Elizabeth's plea went unanswered. The letter had delayed, but not avoided, her journey to the Tower and she was taken there the very next day – 18 March, Palm Sunday – 'by water privily', as Wriothesley noted, so as not to attract attention.[13] It was cold and pouring with rain, and, as the sight of the fortress came into view, with the famous onion domes that her father had added to the central keep in honour of her mother's coronation, Elizabeth was overcome with foreboding. To be taken prisoner in the same place that Anne had been put to death was the stuff of nightmares. Upon arriving at the landing stage, she refused to get out of the boat. Eventually, one of her ladies persuaded her to disembark and she mounted the riverside steps, just as Anne had done eighteen years earlier. Looking up to the heavens, she exclaimed: 'Oh Lord! I never thought to have come in here as a prisoner; and I pray you all, good friends and fellows, bear me witness, that I come in no traitor, but as true woman to the queen's majesty as any is now living.'[14]

Henry Radcliffe, Earl of Sussex, one of Elizabeth's Howard cousins, had accompanied her to the Tower. Although he was a staunch supporter of Mary, he broke down in tears when he saw one of the officials 'lock the doors very straightly'. 'What will you do, my lords?' he demanded. 'She was a king's daughter, and is the queen's sister; and you have no sufficient commission so to do.'[15] His words fell on deaf ears.

Contrary to later, Protestant, tracts, Elizabeth was not taken to a dungeon or to the Bell Tower, where Thomas More and Bishop Fisher had spent their final days. But she might have preferred either of those to the place of her incarceration: the very same suite of apartments that her mother had been lodged in before her coronation and, less than three years later, her execution. Although it was a natural place to house a royal prisoner, it was probably intended to increase Elizabeth's terror. The apartments comprised three principal rooms – a presence chamber, dining chamber and bedchamber – and had their own private garden. But they had been little used since Anne's day, and the general air of neglect must have rendered their mournful associations even more pronounced.

John Bridges, Lieutenant of the Tower, showed every respect towards his prisoner and invited her to take her meals in his lodging. Elizabeth perhaps derived less comfort from this than he anticipated, given that it had been here that Anne Boleyn had spent her last two days on Earth. She was also allowed to walk along the walls as far as the Beauchamp Tower, from where she could clearly see the site of her mother's execution – and the scaffold built for her cousin Lady Jane Grey the previous month. She probably knew that the Beauchamp Tower had housed some of the men condemned for adultery with her mother. One of them had left their mark on a wall of the tower that can still be seen today. Compared to some of the elaborate graffiti by prisoners desperate to leave a lasting legacy before they met their end, this one was simple and crude, carved in a hurry. It shows a falcon perching on a tree stump – the most famous of Anne Boleyn's royal badges. But this falcon has no crown or sceptre. Just days – perhaps even hours – later, the man who carved it was led up to Tower Hill and beheaded.

As well as permitting the princess daily walks around the Tower, Bridges allowed Elizabeth's servants to buy food for her (at her own expense), rather than suffer the usual fare offered to prisoners. More importantly, this protected the princess from any attempts to poison her. But these privileges came to an abrupt end when Bridges' superior, Sir John Gage, Constable of the Tower, heard of them. Thereafter, Elizabeth was confined to her rooms and forbidden pen or paper in case she thought to communicate with any of her supporters. Her health soon began to suffer. A week after she had been lodged in the Tower, a group of interrogators arrived and told her that 'her fate should depend on her answers'. They included Stephen Gardiner, Bishop of Winchester, who had been one of her mother's most bitter enemies. 'My lords, you do sift me very narrowly,' Elizabeth complained.[16] But she proceeded to defend herself as stoically as her mother had, even though she must have been painfully aware that it had served Anne little purpose. Years later, she recalled that she had been so convinced that she would meet the same fate that she had asked if she might be executed with a sword rather than an axe, because she had heard that it was a swifter death.

A few days later, it seemed that Elizabeth's worst fears were about to be realised when the Constable of the Tower received a warrant for her execution. Thankfully, he had the presence of mind to check its validity with the queen. It was a fake – the work of Stephen Gardiner and his faction, who had long been hostile to Elizabeth. Mary was shocked upon hearing of it and railed against the perpetrators 'for their inhuman usage of her sister'.[17] Although she took no further action against them and did not order Elizabeth's release, she started to refer to her as 'my sister' again and had her portrait reinstated in the royal gallery.

Elizabeth was unaware of any of this, so the psychological torture of her imprisonment dragged on. On 5 May, Sir Henry

Bedingfield, 'a man unknown to Her Grace and therefore the more feared', replaced Sir John Gage as Constable. He came with an escort of one hundred soldiers, which struck terror into his young prisoner. Convinced that her execution was imminent, Elizabeth asked in alarm if the scaffold used for Lady Jane Grey's beheading was still in place. Her gaolers assured her that it had been removed and that 'her Grace needed not to doubt of any such tyranny; for God would not suffer any such treason against her person'. Shortly afterwards, she learned that Bedingfield was to escort her from the Tower to a different place of imprisonment.[18] This was cold comfort: Bedingfield had been the custodian of Catherine of Aragon after her banishment from court and Elizabeth suspected that he had been given secret instructions to have her quietly murdered.

On 19 May 1554, the princess was filled with foreboding as she was escorted out of the royal apartments, just as her mother had been. But as she passed under the huge edifice of the Coldharbour Gate, instead of turning right to the site of Anne's execution, she was taken left, underneath the Bloody Tower and out to the riverside steps. Her imprisonment in the fortress had ended on the same day that her mother's had – albeit with a very different outcome.

Even when she had left the Tower and was being cheered by the crowds who had gathered to show their support, Elizabeth was still paralysed by fear and convinced that she was 'like a sheep to the slaughter'.[19] When she was lodged at Richmond Palace that night, she summoned one of her servants in terror and cried: 'This night . . . I think to die.' The trauma of the experience would stay with her. Years later, she recalled: 'I stood in danger of my life, my sister was so incensed against me.'[20]

Mary ordered that Elizabeth be taken to the gloomy palace of Woodstock in Oxfordshire, where she remained for a year under

intense scrutiny and suspicion. Bedingfield was under strict instructions not to 'suffer my lady Elizabeth's grace to have conference
with any suspect person out of my hearing, that she do by any
means either receive or send any message, letter or token to or
from any manner of person'.[21] As had happened after her mother's
arrest, most of her closest attendants – Kat Astley included – were
replaced with those appointed by the council. The queen also
assigned an additional guardian to ensure her sister did not escape.
But Sir John Williams would prove an ally – one who would open
up an unexpected connection to her mother's past. He had been a
trusted court official throughout the reigns of Henry VIII and
Edward VI, and had been one of the first to declare his support for
Mary when Lady Jane Grey claimed the throne. As a reward, she
had appointed him sheriff in Oxfordshire and Buckinghamshire,
and he played a key role in defending the Home Counties during
the uncertain early days of her reign. Williams was subsequently
entrusted with a number of other important commissions, including
taking the high-profile prisoners of conscience, Hugh Latimer,
Nicholas Ridley and Anne Boleyn's former chaplain and Archbishop
of Canterbury, Thomas Cranmer, to Oxford in March 1554.

Williams escorted Elizabeth from the Tower to Woodstock and
they broke the sixty-five-mile journey with an overnight stay at
his Oxfordshire home, Rycote House. There, he provided hospitality fit for a princess, not a prisoner. Even though he was her
guard, Williams was a genial and pleasant man and the pair soon
struck up an accord. This would be the first of many occasions
when Williams would entertain Elizabeth at his home. Possibly
without the queen's knowledge or sanction, he arranged a number
of short visits for her during the year after her arrival at Woodstock
to help relieve the tedium and isolation of her existence there.

On one of these occasions the princess became acquainted with
Williams's daughter Margery and her husband, Henry Norris.

Henry was the son of the courtier of the same name who had been one of five men executed for adultery with Elizabeth's mother in 1536 – and the only one to protest her innocence from the scaffold. Before Anne's fall, the younger Henry and her nephew, Henry Carey, had been tutored in her household by the Frenchman Nicholas Bourbon, whom she had rescued from persecution in France. His father's execution rendered him an orphan because his mother had died some years before. Henry VIII evidently took pity on him (and perhaps felt a measure of remorse for his father's death) because he allowed him to remain at court as his ward. The king subsequently gave him various court offices and restored most of his father's lands to him, which made Henry Norris a rich young man. He enjoyed even greater favour during the reign of Edward VI, who made him a Knight of the Shire upon his accession and then a gentleman of his privy chamber. He also entrusted him as a witness to the 'Device' that altered the succession in favour of Lady Jane Grey. This should have meant that he was left out in the cold when Mary took the throne, but the fact that he was the son-in-law of one of her staunchest supporters meant that he continued to enjoy royal favour.

Their connection to her late mother ensured that Elizabeth quickly established a close bond with the Norrises – one that would endure for the rest of their lives. Rycote would also claim a special place in her heart. She stayed there in July 1555 after being summoned to attend her sister in London. By then, Sir John Williams had been dismissed from his post amid rumours that he was sympathetic towards Protestants. Given his closeness to Elizabeth, as well as to William Cecil, Robert Dudley and other known reformists, these were probably true.

Another man connected with her mother's past joined Elizabeth during her house arrest at Woodstock. Sir John Fortescue was the stepson of her cofferer, Thomas Parry. He was the eldest of three sons born to Sir Adrian Fortescue, who had been summarily executed in 1539, possibly because of his Catholic leanings. It may have been Adrian's Boleyn blood that had helped seal his fate: his mother Alice had been Anne Boleyn's great-aunt. Sir John would serve Elizabeth for the rest of her life and be rewarded with numerous grants and promotions, becoming master of the wardrobe, a member of her privy council and chancellor of the exchequer.

Although Elizabeth drew comfort from such allies during her time at Woodstock, the emotional strain of her imprisonment soon began to show. Upon receiving reports that her sister was 'sickly', Mary sent physicians to attend her. After performing their ministrations, which including letting her blood, they remained with her for four or five days, until they were assured of her recovery. But still the source of Elizabeth's anxiety remained. She was 'oppressed by continual sorrow . . . fraught full of terror' at the thought that she might at any moment be quietly put to death. According to Foxe, she was right to be suspicious. He claimed that some 'ruffians' were 'appointed violently to murder the innocent lady'.[22] Living under a cloud of suspicion that she could do little to shake off was unbearable. During her confinement at Woodstock, she etched the following words on her window with a diamond:

Much suspected by me
Nothing proved can be

The same words had applied to Anne Boleyn, who had been condemned by rumour and hearsay alone. The lack of proof had made no difference. Her daughter knew that if the queen was so minded, she could have her put to death on the same fragile basis.

From the beginning of her reign, Mary had made it clear that she intended to reverse her father and half-brother's reformation and return England to the Roman Catholic fold. Although this was welcomed by many of her subjects, it sparked widespread unease among those who had embraced the new faith. Even some Catholics were opposed to the idea because they had profited from the dissolution of the monasteries and had no desire to surrender their newly won lands and riches. But the queen was deaf to their protests and in February 1555 she ordered that anyone who persisted in practising the Protestant faith should be put to the flames. Over the next three years, 290 'heretics' were burned at the stake, including Cranmer, Latimer and Ridley (the 'Oxford Martyrs'), earning her the sobriquet 'Bloody Mary'.

As a Protestant, Elizabeth was a natural figurehead for all those opposed to her sister's regime. She had been as discreet as possible in the practice of her faith, attending mass when at court during the early days of Mary's reign. But the beliefs espoused by her mother and reinforced by Elizabeth's reformist education were too deeply embedded for her to relinquish. Her name continued to be linked to plots against the crown, even though her experience in the Tower had taught her to keep at a safe distance from them. Members of her household were also under surveillance, and in May 1556 Kat Astley (who had been restored to Elizabeth's service the year before) was arrested and taken to the Tower, along with Elizabeth's Italian master, Battista Castiglione.[23]

As the Marian persecutions gathered pace, many of England's prominent reformists fled to exile on the continent. They included Dorothy and William Stafford, whose staunch Protestantism had served them well during Edward's reign but now plunged them into jeopardy. Together with their young family, they escaped to Geneva in March 1555. They took with them their cousin, Elizabeth

Sandys, who had been a long-serving member of Elizabeth's household until 1554, when Queen Mary had dismissed her because of her Protestant beliefs. During their time in Geneva, the Staffords became closely acquainted with John Calvin, one of the most influential figures in the Reformation, and in January 1556 he stood as godfather to their youngest son, who was named in his honour.

Elizabeth's first cousin, Katherine Carey, also sought refuge abroad. Katherine had married Sir Francis Knollys, a prominent courtier, in 1540. It proved a successful union and produced no fewer than sixteen children – two of whom had been named for Elizabeth and her mother Anne. The Knollyses had thrived during the reigns of Elizabeth's father and brother, but like the Staffords their known Protestantism spelt danger when Mary came to the throne. Elizabeth remained close to Katherine throughout this time and was bereft – though no doubt relieved – when in around 1556 she learned that her cousin and her family were going to escape to Germany for their safety.

Even though she was still under the close scrutiny of her sister the queen, Elizabeth took a significant risk by writing a letter of farewell, assuring Katherine of her continued friendship and vowing that she would do everything possible to protect her interests. 'The length of time and distance of place, separates not the love of friends, nor deprives not the show of good will . . . when your need shall be most you shall find my friendship greatest,' she averred.

> Let others promise, and I will do, in words not more in deeds as much. My power but small, my love as great as them whose gifts may tell their friendship's tale, let will supply all other want, and oft sending take the lieu of often sights. Your messenger shall not return empty, nor yet your desires unaccomplished . . . And to conclude, a word that hardly I

can say, I am driven by need to write, farewell, it is which in one way I wish, the other way I grieve.

Elizabeth signed the letter: 'Your loving cousin and ready friend, Cor Rotto [Broken Heart].'[24] It is possible that Katherine's daughter Lettice went to join Elizabeth's household at Hatfield while her parents fled to exile. If so, it marked the beginning of an explosive relationship.

During these turbulent years of her sister's reign, Elizabeth could draw comfort from the knowledge that she was still Mary's immediate heir. The idea of supplanting her with Lady Margaret Douglas had come to nothing: for all her stubbornness, Mary knew from the experience of Lady Jane Grey's brief ascendancy that the people of England would not support a disruption to the succession. Neither was there any real prospect of Mary having a child. Although she had displayed signs of early pregnancy soon after marrying Philip of Spain in July 1554 and had been so convinced of her condition that she had entered her confinement eight months later, she had eventually admitted that she had been mistaken. Now approaching her fortieth year, and having suffered from menstrual problems throughout her life, the chances of her conceiving were slim – particularly as her husband had spent most of their marriage overseas.

Although Mary continued to cling to the hope that she would have a child, she was just enough of a realist to make alternative plans. Knowing that her sister would not convert to her own faith, she therefore resolved to find her a Catholic husband. The chosen candidate was Emmanuel Philibert, Duke of Savoy, who had been suggested by her own husband, Philip. But when Mary summoned Elizabeth to court in late 1556 so that she could tell her of the scheme, she was shocked by her sister's reaction. Elizabeth became almost hysterical and pleaded with Mary not to make her enter such a match, protesting: 'The afflictions suffered by her were such that they had not only ridded her of any wish for a husband, but that they had induced her to desire nothing but death.' She then burst into 'a flood of tears'.[25] This was more than mere play-acting: her mother's fate and that of her stepmothers – Catherine Howard in particular – had left Elizabeth with a profound fear of marriage. Whenever the issue was raised in the years to come, her reaction would be just as extreme.

In 1557, the Venetian ambassador Giovanni Michiel described the queen-in-waiting as: 'A young woman believed to be no less beautiful in her soul than in her body, though her face is pretty rather than beautiful, her figure, is however, tall and well-shaped, with good colour, though olive skinned, and beautiful eyes and hands, as she is well aware.'[26] This echoes the description of Anne when she first made her appearance at court thirty-five years earlier – the complexion and eyes in particular. In later years, Elizabeth enhanced her image as the Virgin Queen by having her ladies apply thick white lead makeup to her face, neck and hands. Like her mother, the princess was striking, rather than conventionally attractive – her 'beauty was of no common order', as one contemporary put it.[27]

As had been the case with Anne, her daughter's appeal derived more from her self-confidence than her looks. This confidence grew as the prospect of her sister giving birth to an heir faded. In the summer of 1557, Mary again believed herself to be pregnant and went through the same elaborate ritual as before, but this time few of her courtiers shared her conviction. 'They had small hope of issue by the Queen, being now 40 years old, dry, and sickly,' was the shrewd, if brutal, observation of seventeenth-century historian, William Camden.[28] It is possible that the swelling in Mary's stomach was caused by cancer. Even during her first confinement, it had been rumoured that 'she was deceived by a

Tympanie [tumour] or some other like disease, to think herself with child'.[29] By the time Mary emerged from her 'confinement' in early 1558, it was obvious to everyone who saw her that she was gravely ill.

Anxious to secure the succession, in April 1558 Mary sent Sir Thomas Pope to gauge her sister's reaction to another proposal of marriage from a foreign prince. Elizabeth was unequivocal. She reminded Pope that when her brother Edward was king, she had asked permission 'to remain in that estate I was, which of all others best liked me or pleased me', adding: 'I am even at this present of the same mind . . . I so well like this estate, as I persuade myself there is not any kind of life comparable to it.' When Pope urged that she would surely accept a suitor whom her sister approved of, Elizabeth insisted: 'I am not at this time otherwise minded, than I have declared unto you; no, though I were offered the greatest Prince in all Europe.'[30]

On 28 October, the queen added a codicil to her will, finally acknowledging that there would be no 'fruit of her body' and confirming that the crown would go to the next heir by law. But she could not bring herself to name Elizabeth specifically. As well as her fear that Elizabeth would swiftly undo all of Mary's efforts to reinstate Roman Catholicism, she was plagued by the old resentments against this daughter of the 'Great Whore'. She cried that Elizabeth 'was neither her sister nor the daughter of the Queen's father, King Henry, nor would she hear of favouring her, as she was born of an infamous woman, who had so greatly outraged the Queen her mother, and herself'.[31] But Mary was painfully aware that there were no other viable candidates to succeed her, as were the ambitious place-seekers who had been flocking to Elizabeth's household for months now.

In early November, Philip II's envoy, the Count of Feria, paid a visit to Elizabeth and reported that she 'already sees herself as the next Queen'.[32] She did not have long to wait. On 17 November, between four and five o'clock in the morning, Mary slipped from a life that had been marked by pain and sorrow. Her half-sister was now Queen of England.

CHAPTER 9

'The sore which was with age over-skinned'

THRONGS OF ELIZABETH'S subjects greeted her accession with wild celebrations. Across London, church bells were rung and at night bonfires were lit, around which thousands of people gathered to drink and make merry. As well as heralding a bright new beginning with a young and popular queen, there was a palpable sense of relief among many that the dark days of Mary's reign were at an end. By contrast, Elizabeth at twenty-five was a shining symbol of youth, hope and prosperity.

The new queen graciously acknowledged the people's acclamations but was shrewd enough to recognise that they were only skin-deep. Tudor society viewed women as the weaker sex and the accession of a queen regnant as little short of a disaster. 'To promote a woman to bear rule, superiority, dominion or empire above any realm, nation or city, is repugnant to nature,' railed the Protestant preacher John Knox, shortly after Elizabeth came to the throne.[1] Worse still, most of England's Catholics viewed her as an illegitimate usurper, 'the child of his [Henry VIII's] concubine Anne Boleyn'. Even favourable commentators such as the writer and politician Sir Robert Naunton remarked: 'By her mother she was of no sovereign descent,' although he conceded that the Boleyn family was 'noble and very ancient'.[2] If Elizabeth was to hold on to the throne, she knew that she would need to focus her efforts on bolstering her legitimacy – something that Anne had not survived long enough to do.

A remarkable document that still survives in the collections of the British Library provides a powerful assertion of the new queen's right to the throne. It is an exquisitely illuminated genealogical tree spanning numerous pages and showing Elizabeth's descent from Rollo, the first ruler of Normandy, and was presented to the queen early in her reign. Although most of the manuscript focuses upon her paternal ancestors, it is interesting that in a reference to a Norman count, Eustace, Boulogne is spelt 'Bullen'. The Boleyns were thought by some to have descended from the Counts of Boulogne, their name becoming anglicised over the years. A portrait of Eustace is included on the page, perhaps to draw attention to the connection.

However, the most significant part of the document is on the last page, which cites Elizabeth's parents as: 'The most excellent and victorious prince Henry VIII' and 'The most gracious princess Lady Anne, Marquess of Pembroke, the first wife to King Henry ye Eight was crowned Queen of England and France in Anno 1533.' Elizabeth is described as 'the sole daughter and heir to the high and mighty prince king Henry the eight'. The document therefore entirely disregards Catherine of Aragon and her daughter Mary, just as Anne Boleyn had tried to in life so that she might silence those who viewed her marriage to Henry as invalid.[3] Now her daughter was taking up the same theme to prove her legitimacy. 'I am the most English woman in the kingdom,' she proudly boasted. 'Was I not born in this realm? Were my parents born in any foreign country?'[4] As well as being a deliberate side-swipe at her half-Spanish predecessor, this was a tribute to her mother's ancestry.

On 23 November, the new queen left Hatfield for London. But rather than heading straight for the Tower, as tradition dictated (and as her immediate predecessors had done), she and her entourage stayed at Sir Edward North's residence in the Charterhouse, two miles away. Only after five days there did she finally set out for the Tower, splendidly arrayed in a gown of royal purple. As she approached the fortress where she had been held prisoner four years earlier and where her mother had been executed, 'there was great shooting of guns, the like was never heard before. In certain places stood children, who made speeches to her as she passed; and in other places was singing and playing with regals.'[5] Elizabeth betrayed no sense of unease but showed a smiling face to the crowds as they cheered her entry.

The new queen was lodged in the same apartments that had been refurbished for her mother and in which she herself had been held prisoner. She left there on 5 December, the 'trumpets playing and melody and joy and comfort', no doubt reflecting the relief she felt at being free of the fortress.[6] Two and a half weeks later, Elizabeth moved to what would become her principal residence: Whitehall Palace, a vast maze of buildings that sprawled over twenty-three acres and lay close to the Parliament in Westminster. Of all the London palaces, it was the one with the most positive association with her mother. Anne Boleyn had been installed there as Henry's queen-in-waiting, along with her mother, father and brother, after Cardinal Wolsey (its original owner) had been obliged to vacate it following his dismissal from court. The king had immediately begun refurbishing and extending the palace to Anne's taste, and they had married there in secret in January 1533, when Anne was pregnant with Elizabeth. Taking up residence there as queen was a fitting tribute to the ambitions that Anne had cherished for her unborn child.

Upon Anne's execution, Henry VIII had removed, repurposed or simply painted over all visual reminders of his second wife. A huge bill for painting at Hampton Court in August and September

1536 suggests a wholesale redecoration of the palace interiors, including the Great Hall and queen's lodgings, the latter being extensively remodelled. Meanwhile, the King's Beasts carved by Henry Corant and Richard Rydge in 1535–6 were swiftly adapted: Anne's leopard (her secondary badge) was re-carved into Jane Seymour's panther 'by new making of the heads and the tails', as the building accounts record.[7] At least one of Anne's leopards survived intact, however, and has recently been discovered by a specialist in early oak antiques. The remnants of tenons on the underside suggest that it was once displayed on top of an onion dome or roof so that it could be seen for miles around.

Some of Anne's initials and emblems also survived in the palaces that her daughter now occupied. They tended to be in places so hard to reach that Henry's workmen had judged it not worth the effort of taking them down. Dozens of Boleyn falcons still decorated the Great Hall ceiling at Hampton Court, although they had been painted black to make them less visible, and Anne's arms and initials were also in abundance. The same initials decorated the doorways of the gatehouse turrets at St James's Palace, where Elizabeth often stayed. When she visited King's College Chapel, Cambridge, in 1564 to hear evensong and watch a pageant, she sat close to the choir screens adorned with her mother's falcon badge and her parents' initials, 'HA'.

One of the best examples of Anne's falcon has recently come to light, after being purchased at auction. Painstaking restoration has brought it back to something approaching its dazzling former glory. Gilded throughout, the carved oak falcon is crowned and holds a sceptre while sitting atop a tree stump of red and white roses. Given its similarity to those that still survive in Hampton Court's Great Hall ceiling, this example probably once decorated the royal apartments there. The quality of the workmanship and gilding suggests that it was made for a more visible part of the palace – perhaps the queen's 'new lodgings', which were decorated throughout with Anne's arms and badges.[8] How this single falcon survived when all others within reach were destroyed is a mystery. It is tempting to speculate that it was spirited away by a supporter of Anne and deliberately saved for posterity, but, unless new evidence is uncovered, this is impossible to prove. Anne's falcon became increasingly prominent in Elizabeth's palaces and pageantry as her reign progressed. The fact that it was closely associated with chastity, as well as with Anne herself, heightened its appeal to a young queen who made a virtue of her unmarried state.

In January 1559, Elizabeth opened the first Parliament of her reign. Much has been made of the fact that, in contrast to Mary, Elizabeth did not attempt to overturn the annulment of her parents' marriage or to contest her mother's conviction. Neither did she repeal the 1536 Succession Act, which had declared her illegitimate and removed her from the line of succession, or the 1544 version, which had named her as one of Henry VIII's heirs but upheld that his marriage to Anne Boleyn had been unlawful. This meant that the new queen was technically still illegitimate. Elizabeth had sought the advice of Sir Nicholas Bacon, Lord Keeper of the Great Seal, as to whether the legislation of her father and sister's reigns could be repealed. After trawling numerous legal documents, Bacon had warned against unpicking this complex web of legislation and urged that the queen 'would not new gall the sore which was with age over-skinned'. Instead, he advised that she use her forthcoming coronation to proclaim her right to the throne. As he put it: 'The English laws have long since pronounced, that the Crown once worn quite taketh away all defects whatsoever.'[9]

This was sound advice and Elizabeth followed it. Neither did she make any move to have her mother's remains taken from the Tower chapel to a more fitting place of burial.[10] By contrast, her successor James I would honour his own executed mother by having her reinterred in Westminster Abbey. 'No word was ever uttered for the purpose of making her legitimate, or clearing away the taint of her birth,' Sander scornfully remarked; 'on that point the silence was complete.' He concluded that 'bastards [have] no title to the crown of England'.[11]

Elizabeth's actions should not be taken as a tacit admission of Anne Boleyn's guilt, or that her parents' marriage had been invalid. Rather, the new queen was too great a pragmatist to draw attention to such controversies, painfully aware that at least half of her subjects viewed her as the heretical daughter of the 'Great Whore'. Besides, she could not redeem her mother's reputation without condemning her father's. Political expediency therefore decided her against digging up the past – literally and metaphorically.

The new queen did, though, assert her right to the throne through two new Acts that were passed in her first Parliament. 'The Act of Recognition of the Queen's Title' simply willed all her subjects to acknowledge her right to the throne, without grounding this right upon anything other than the power of Parliament. It referred only to the new queen's 'most noble father', from whom her right to the throne descended, and upheld the terms of the 1544 Act of Succession. The second Act is often overlooked but is just as significant, if not more so. 'An Act whereby the Queen's Highness is restored in blood to the late Queen Anne her Highness' Mother' made Elizabeth the legal heir of her mother and all her Boleyn relatives. As a convicted traitor, Anne Boleyn had forfeited her titles and property to the crown, which meant that in terms of inheritance law her daughter was motherless. Passed on 10 February 1559, this second Act restored the legal bond between mother and daughter and meant that Elizabeth was 'enabled in blood' to inherit the property of Anne and all her

Monumental brass effigy of Thomas Boleyn, St Peter's Church, Hever. The only known likeness, it shows a resemblance to his daughter, Anne, whose portraits show the same pointed chin.

Hever Castle, Kent. Originally purchased by Anne's great-grandfather Geoffrey Boleyn in the 1450s, it became the family's principal seat thanks to its being within easy reach both of the court and Dover.

Portrait of a woman, thought to be Mary Boleyn. The dates of birth of Thomas Boleyn's three surviving children are not certain, but Mary is commonly cited as the eldest.

Christine de Pizan lecturing to a group of men. Christine's literary works have earned her the reputation as one of the earliest feminists. Her influence on Anne Boleyn was profound.

Marguerite of Navarre, sister of Francis I, King of France. One of the greatest intellectuals of the French court, Marguerite forged a close acquaintance with Anne during her time there.

This recently-discovered chair, which is carved with 'Ab', is thought to have been made for Anne during her years at the French court. The decorative carvings symbolise a union between England and France.

This gold ring, unearthed by a metal detectorist close to Boleyn land in Kent in 2019 and bearing their heraldic bull's head, may have belonged to Thomas Boleyn or his son George. It has recently been acquired by Historic Royal Palaces.

The oldest of Anne's three surviving Books of Hours, this was made in Bruges in c.1450 and bears the inscription: 'Le temps viendra [The time will come] je anne boleyn', with her armillary sphere emblem inserted before her name.

Henry VIII by Joos van Cleve, c.1530-5. Painted at the height of Henry and Anne's relationship, this shows the king in his prime – before a jousting accident of 1536 sparked a dramatic physical decline.

Anne Boleyn. With her dark eyes and long, slender face, Anne bears a striking resemblance to her daughter – perhaps deliberately so, since most of the surviving portraits of her were painted during Elizabeth's reign.

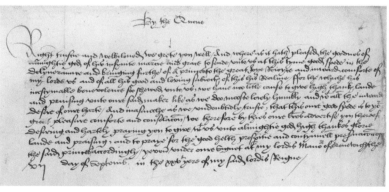

Letter 'By the Quene' announcing Elizabeth's birth, September 1533. Drafted before the event, when Anne was confident she carried the male heir Henry craved, an 's' had to be hastily added to the word 'prince'.

This christening robe from Sudeley Castle in Gloucestershire (former home of Katherine Parr), is believed to have been worn by the future Elizabeth I at her christening in Greenwich in September 1533.

Holbein's design for the silver-gilt table fountain that Anne gave to Henry at New Year 1534, four months after giving birth to Elizabeth.

'Certain detts due to the late Quene Anne'. This account in The National Archives was drawn up shortly after Anne's execution in 1536. Among the last items she purchased were 'pyrwykes', a device to straighten the fingers, and a cap of taffeta – both for her daughter.

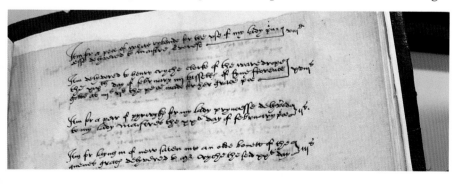

Anne Boleyn says a final goodbye to her daughter Princess Elizabeth, by Gustave Wappers, 1838.

A carving of Anne's falcon badge in the Beauchamp Tower, Tower of London. Made in haste by one of her alleged lovers, it is devoid of the crown and sceptre that it carried during Anne's brief tenure as queen.

This portrait of the twenty-eight year old Princess Mary was painted in 1544, the year that she and her younger sister Elizabeth were restored to the line of succession.

An engraving showing Princess Elizabeth as a prisoner in the Tower during the reign of her sister Mary in 1554. Elizabeth was suspected of conspiring with the rebel, Thomas Wyatt.

The L. Elizabeth Prisoner in the Tower

Katherine Carey, Lady Knollys. The daughter of Mary Boleyn, Katherine was extremely close to her cousin Elizabeth. It was rumoured they shared the same father because Henry VIII had had an affair with Mary Boleyn before paying court to Anne.

Detail from The Family of Henry VIII, showing Elizabeth (then aged about thirteen) wearing her late mother's 'A' pendant.

Detail from Princess Elizabeth by William Scrots, c.1546. Although it was probably painted for her father, Elizabeth's French hood and drop pearl necklace echo those worn by her mother.

Elizabeth presented this book to her last stepmother, Katherine Parr, as a New Year's gift in 1544. It is her own translation of *Le miroir de l'âme pécheresse* [Mirror of the Sinful Soul] by her mother's former companion, Marguerite of Navarre.

Plea roll of the Court of Queen's Bench, 1572, showing Elizabeth enthroned beneath her mother's motto, *Semper Eadem*.

Detail from an illuminated genealogical tree showing Elizabeth I's descent from Rollo, the first ruler of Normandy. This section refers to her parents and cites Anne as Henry's 'first wife', deliberately overlooking Catherine of Aragon.

Anne's falcon badge in *The Ecclesiaste*. The book advocated religious reform and may have been translated by her brother George as a gift upon her marriage to Henry.

Illustration for the 1578 edition of George Cavendish's *The Life and Death of Cardinal Wolsey*, in which Anne Boleyn is shown in very Elizabethan style. Her kirtle is embroidered with the honeysuckle emblem that she and her daughter favoured.

Bed valance made for Anne and Henry and embroidered with their intertwined initials, along with the honeysuckle and acorn emblems they used during their marriage.

In this portrait, which was probably painted in the 1580s, the sleeves of Elizabeth's dress are embroidered with honeysuckle and acorn emblems.

Anne Boleyn's leopard. Recently discovered by Paul Fitzsimmons, a specialist in Tudor oak antiques, it may have been on prominent display in one of the royal palaces and swiftly removed after her fall.

Tympanum at St Margaret's, Tivetshall, Norfolk, showing Anne's white falcon surmounted by her daughter Elizabeth I's arms and surrounded by emblems of other Tudor monarchs.

Henry and Anne's intertwined initials in the Great Hall, Hampton Court. Their survival is an oversight: the king ordered the removal or overpainting of his second wife's emblems after her fall.

Silver-gilt cup made for Anne in 1535 and later passed to her daughter. Elizabeth I subsequently gifted it to her physician, who gave it to St John the Baptist Parish Church in Cirencester, where it is still on display.

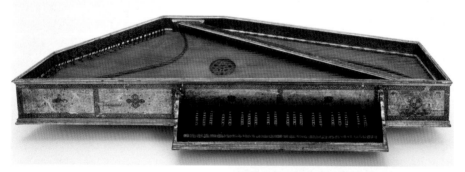

Elizabeth I's virginals, decorated with her mother's crowned falcon (below) and the royal arms.

Locket ring containing portraits of Anne and her daughter. Made in the 1570s, Elizabeth I kept the ring until her death in 1603. It is now in the collection at Chequers House, the Prime Minister's country residence.

This carved oak falcon was one of many commissioned by Henry VIII to decorate Hampton Court in honour of his new queen, Anne Boleyn, in 1533. A remarkable survivor, it was recently acquired at auction and beautifully restored.

Linen tablecloth showing Elizabeth I beneath her mother's crowned falcon with sceptre. Commissioned by Sir Thomas Gresham in 1571 for a banquet attended by the queen, it still survives at Gresham College, London.

Shortly before her death, Anne Boleyn committed her daughter's spiritual care to her chaplain, Matthew Parker. Upon becoming queen, Elizabeth made him her first Archbishop of Canterbury.

Henry Carey, Baron Hunsdon, son of Mary Boleyn and first cousin of Elizabeth I, who showed him great favour throughout his life.

Thomas Howard, fourth duke of Norfolk. A paternal cousin of Elizabeth, he was found guilty of involvement in the Ridolfi Plot of 1572. But it took her four attempts before she finally issued the warrant for his execution.

Detail from The Ditchley Portrait, 1592. Close to Elizabeth's left ear, she wears a jewel in the form of an armillary sphere – the earliest known symbol used by her mother.

Elizabeth I visiting her mother's childhood home, Hever Castle. There is no record that she ever made such a visit, but the scene is imagined by Walter Henry Sweet in this watercolour.

Katherine Howard (née Carey), Countess of Nottingham. The eldest daughter of Elizabeth's first cousin, Henry Carey, Katherine attended the queen for more than forty years and became one of her closest companions.

Katherine's husband Charles, first earl of Nottingham, was a cousin of Anne Boleyn and became one of Elizabeth's most trusted advisers.

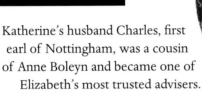

The Rainbow Portrait, c.1602. One of the last portraits of Elizabeth to be painted, she wears a gown decorated with her mother's honeysuckle and armillary sphere motifs.

'ancestors and cousins'. Although it was only two lines long, the Act provides a touching glimpse of the affection that Elizabeth bore towards her mother. It refers to 'Her Highness' . . . *Mother'. The comment at the asterisk is *Deest in originali* ('Lacking in the original'), which draws attention to the fact that the queen inserted the word 'dearest' before 'Mother' in the final version of the Act. She might not have been able to assert Anne's innocence or revoke the annulment of her marriage to Henry, but through this simple Act she could restore the maternal bond that had been so cruelly severed almost twenty-three years earlier.[12]

On the very day of her accession, Elizabeth had issued a memorandum for the appointment of 'Commissioners for the Coronation'. Setting aside her natural caution, she lavished £16,000 (equivalent to around £3.7 million) on the event. Like Anne, her aim was to create such a dazzling spectacle that it would blind her subjects to the shaky foundations upon which her queenship was based. And she borrowed heavily from the symbolism created for the 1533 coronation.

It was now a long-established tradition that a new monarch would spend a night or two at the Tower before progressing through the streets of London to their crowning at Westminster Abbey. On 12 January, Elizabeth was duly conveyed to the Tower from Whitehall in a flotilla of barges that had been decked out 'as sumptuously as possible'. An Italian resident of London was so overawed that he claimed it 'reminded one of Ascension Day in Venice'.[13]

Disembarking, Elizabeth stooped to pat the earth and declared: 'Some have fallen from being princes of this land to prisoners in this place. I am raised from being prisoner in this place to be the prince of the land. That dejection was a work of God's justice. This advancement is a work of his mercy.'[14] The allusion to her mother was clear. More memories would have been stirred as she was once more escorted to the apartments in which she and her mother had been held prisoner, and in which she had stayed again after becoming queen. She endured the ordeal for the sake of royal tradition – something that she knew she must strictly uphold to emphasise the continuity of the succession. But it is telling that throughout the rest of her long reign she rarely stepped foot inside the Tower.

On 14 January, the new queen left the fortress for her procession through the city. The spectacular pageantry that was staged along the route bore a striking similarity to that designed for her mother's coronation: indeed, Elizabeth had ordered John Leland and Nicholas Udall, who had masterminded Anne's coronation, to instruct Richard Mulcaster, who designed her own. The only difference was the weather: in contrast to the hot June day of Anne's, snow fell as her daughter made her stately progress to Westminster. The same Latin verses sounded in Elizabeth's ears and much of the elaborate decoration lining the route was in the same classical style that Anne had arranged.

The idea of the new queen bringing peace, not war, had been invoked in Anne's procession and would be reinforced by her daughter, both at her coronation and throughout her reign – notably in Hans Eworth's celebrated painting, *Elizabeth I and the Three Goddesses*. Elizabeth also borrowed her mother's theme of transformation and renewal, with depictions of London as a 'New Jerusalem'. She wore the crown of St Edward's during the coronation itself, just as her mother had, and, like her, wore a smaller, more comfortable crown for the procession. In fact, she may have even worn the crown that had been made for her mother. Certainly it was among the royal jewels listed in an inventory of 1574, along with the same gold sceptre surmounted with a dove that Anne had used for her crowning.[15]

Elizabeth chose to wear her hair loose, as Anne had done. As a further tribute to her mother, she too dressed in white, with a heavily brocaded silk surcoat and a mantle of ermine. Her litter was also draped in white cloth of gold, like Anne's. The preponderance of white was intended to emphasise the new queen's virtue and purity, her transformation from a mere mortal into a divine one. It had been harder for Anne to pull this off, given that she had been very visibly pregnant at the time. But the daughter she carried then could now flaunt and celebrate her own virginity. This would become the dominant theme of all the carefully stage-managed and increasingly elaborate set-pieces of her reign: the entertainments and ceremonies, the pageantry and progresses. She would take it further still, not just evoking an image of the Virgin Mary, but becoming her: untouched and untouchable, a divine presence for her subjects to worship on Earth.

A series of lavishly directed vignettes had been constructed along the processional route. The first, on Gracechurch Street, was by far the most significant. Three storeys high, it was labelled 'The uniting of the two houses of Lancaster and York' and was set upon a huge model of a rose bush. On each level were large statues of Elizabeth's ancestors: Henry VII and Elizabeth of York on the lowest tier, Henry VIII and Anne Boleyn on the middle, and Elizabeth seated in majesty at the top. In front of Anne was 'a white [falcon] and a gold crown on its head and gilt sceptre in its right talon, the other resting on a little hill, and surrounded by small branches with little roses in front, the coat of arms and device of the said Queen'.[16]

This was the first time in more than twenty years that Anne had been publicly – and positively – represented. The fact that Elizabeth gave her mother equal status with her father demonstrates not only her loyalty towards Anne but her determination to prove that she was the child of a legitimate marriage and, therefore, the rightful successor to her half-sister Mary. To hammer home the point, a small boy stood atop the central arch and, as the queen drew level, gave a speech explaining the details of the symbolism, to which Elizabeth listened 'most attentively, evincing much satisfaction'.[17] A fortnight later, a detailed account of the pageant was printed, in which Anne Boleyn was described as 'mother to our most sovereign lady queen, Elizabeth that now is'.[18]

Another significant pageant was staged on Cheapside, close to St Paul's Cathedral. Two enormous artificial hills had been built, one barren and wasted and the other green and fertile. An old man representing 'Time' emerged from a cave that had been constructed between them, followed by his daughter 'Truth' – an unsubtle reference to Queen Mary's motto, 'Truth the Daughter of Time'. In Truth's hands was an English translation of the Bible that had been banned during Mary's reign. When Truth presented this to the new queen, Elizabeth kissed it reverently and thanked the city for its gift. The symbolism could not have been more obvious: the reformed faith, championed by Anne and adopted by her daughter, had triumphed.

Through her coronation, Elizabeth sought to restore her mother's reputation – and, therefore, her own. It was a resounding success, inspiring her with the confidence to stage similarly lavish set-pieces in the years to come. But a short while later, she received a brutal reminder of the full horror of Anne's death. Alexander Ales, the Scottish Protestant refugee who had described Anne's final plea to her husband, wrote an extraordinary letter to the new queen, in which he shared a premonition he had had of her mother's death twenty-three years earlier. 'On the day upon which the Queen was beheaded, at sunrise, between 2 and 3 o'clock, there was revealed to me (whether I was asleep or awake I know not), the Queen's neck after her head had been cut off, and this so plainly that I could count the nerves, the veins and the arteries.'[19] Viewed through modern eyes, this appears shockingly insensitive. But in an age when people at all levels of society – Elizabeth included – enjoyed blood sports such as hunting, bear-baiting and cock fighting, or gathered in their thousands to witness the latest beheading, such sensibilities did not necessarily apply. Even so, Ales's letter must have tarnished the glister of the new queen's coronation.

But the letter had an even more profound impact upon Elizabeth. Running into several pages, it presented Anne as the victim of a Catholic conspiracy. According to Ales, shortly before her downfall, Anne had persuaded the king to send an embassy to the Schmalkaldic League, an alliance of Lutheran princes in Germany against the Holy Roman Emperor, Charles V. This had provoked Charles to draw together his Catholic allies – the pope included – and prepare for hostilities against all those of the reformed faith. Hearing of this, England's Catholic bishops (including Stephen Gardiner, Elizabeth's interrogator during her imprisonment in the Tower in 1554) had conspired in Anne's downfall. According to Ales, they had enlisted the help of Thomas Cromwell, 'the King's ear and mind, to whom he had entrusted the entire government of the kingdom'. Although a reformer himself, Cromwell 'hated the Queen' because she had threatened to tell the king that he and his allies were profiting from the Reformation. He therefore set his spies to watch Anne's private apartments 'day and night', bribe her attendants and incite them to betray her by affirming 'that the King hates the Queen, because she has not presented him with an heir to the realm, nor was there any prospect of her doing so'. Having fabricated evidence of Anne's adultery, Cromwell presented it to his royal master, who did not hesitate to have her condemned. If Elizabeth already believed that her father's advisers had tricked him into having her mother put to death, Ales's account would have strengthened that conviction.

'It was easy to perceive that in the event of the Queen's death, a change of religion was inevitable,' Ales went on, and he recalled 'the tears and lamentations of the faithful who were lamenting over the snare laid for the Queen'. His account of Anne's trial made it clear to Elizabeth, in case she did not already know it, how weak the case against her had been. 'The Queen was accused of having danced in the bedroom with the gentlemen of the King's chamber and of having kissed her brother, Lord Rochfort.' Ales rightly judged that, given the evidence was hardly enough to condemn Anne, 'there must have been some other reason which moved the King', and concluded: 'Possibly it might be the same as that which induced him to seek for a cause of divorce from his former Queen, namely, the desire of having an heir.' Determined to present Anne's downfall in religious terms, Ales believed that Elizabeth's father had also been embittered against her mother because of the failure of the embassy to conclude an alliance with the Schmalkaldic League. He admitted, though, that Henry's abandonment of Anne may have had something to do with his growing interest in Jane Seymour: 'For so ardent was he when he had begun to form an attachment, that he could give himself no rest.' Ales went on to describe Henry's callous disregard for Anne's death while he immersed himself in all the pleasures that the court – and his new love, Jane Seymour – could offer. 'Now was he openly insulting her,' he scornfully reflected. This was the closest that anyone came to criticising Henry VIII during Elizabeth's lifetime. The fact that Ales escaped any reprisals suggests that she privately shared his views about her father's culpability in her mother's fate.

Not content with offering this long and detailed defence of the new queen's mother, Ales avowed:

It has often occurred to me that it was a duty which I owed the Church, to write the history, or tragedy, of the death of your most holy mother, in order to illustrate the glory of

God and to afford consolation to the godly. No one, as far as I know, has as yet published such a work; I have been admonished from heaven by a vision or dream which I shall presently narrate, to make it known to the world.

If this was an open invitation for Elizabeth to patronise such a work, she did not take him up on it. Neither is there any evidence that she acted on Ales's hint that he might be rewarded for his letter – he even included an address for any financial gifts to be sent. But his words had left a profound impression on the new queen, stoking her already fierce loyalty towards her late mother. It also strengthened her determination to avenge Anne's death by firmly establishing the religion of which her mother had been such a passionate advocate.

Elizabeth's accession had sparked a flurry of celebratory prose among Protestant writers, all rejoicing that at last God's will would be done. They were also quick to praise Anne Boleyn as the inspiration for the new queen's reformist beliefs. John Foxe, whose *Acts and Monuments* first appeared in 1559, proclaimed: 'What a zealous defender she was of Christ's gospel all the world doth know, and her acts do and will declare to the world's end.' He also hailed Elizabeth's accession as 'the evident demonstration of God's favour' towards Anne Boleyn 'in maintaining, preserving, and advancing the offspring of her body, the lady Elizabeth, now queen'.[20] Other Protestant writers eagerly drew comparisons between the religious stance of the new queen and that of 'Queen Anne the mother of this blessed woman'. John Aylmer, who had fled to Switzerland during Mary's reign and returned to England as soon as he received news of Elizabeth's accession, praised Anne as 'the crop and root' of the English Reformation.[21] It was a theme that continued throughout Elizabeth's reign. Writing in the 1570s, John Bridges described Anne as 'a sweet sacrifice to God and a most holy martyr' whom Henry VIII had unjustly put to death, while Ralph Holinshed referred to her 'zeal of religion'.[22]

William Latymer, formerly chaplain to Anne Boleyn, presented Elizabeth with an essay praising her mother's virtues in general and her religious activities in particular.[23] Latymer had suffered for his association with the fallen queen and had been arrested for importing heretical books from Flanders on her behalf. Anne had been unable to intercede for him because by then she was in the Tower, awaiting death. Upon Mary's accession, he had lost all his preferments because of his Protestant faith, but Elizabeth restored these to him when she became queen. In his 'Cronickille of Anne Bulleyne', he began by drawing a direct comparison between mother and daughter: 'When I considered with myself . . . the manifold gifts of nature and virtuous qualities which set forth and magnify your royal name, I could not but remember the excellent virtues, and princely qualities wherewith your majesty's dearest mother, the most gracious lady, queen Anne, was adorned and beautified in the time of his majesty's noble reign.' As one of only a few people known to Elizabeth who could remember her mother, Latymer declared his determination 'that the same might not be utterly forgotten, but be commended to immortal memory'. He also hoped that the new queen would seek to emulate her mother: 'Your majesty as in a mirror or glass might behold the most godly and princely ornaments of your most gracious and natural mother; not a little to your highness' comfort, and to the alluring of others by like example to embrace virtue, charity, equity and godliness.' More specifically, he urged the new queen to fulfil her mother's wishes for reforming the English church.

After spending almost her whole life having to conceal her loyalty to Anne, who was widely condemned as the 'Concubine' and 'Great Whore', reading a work dedicated to celebrating her virtues and achievements must have been highly gratifying. Latymer provided numerous examples of Anne's genuine piety and of her reforming zeal. He also praised her as: 'So rare a patroness of learning, who omitted no time that might be employed either to the furtherance of the purity of scriptures or to the extirpating and abolishing of the blind ignorance and abuses grown in this land.' Latymer ended by lamenting 'the sudden departing of so good a princess, the fame of whose just deserts . . . shall yet remain as fresh in store as she were daily in sight'. More positively, he reiterated his hope that her daughter would carry on the godly work that Anne had begun. Elizabeth took this to heart. She made much of Latymer thereafter, raising him to Dean of Peterborough and Canon of Westminster. She also made him her personal chaplain, just as he had been to her mother, and his influence can be felt in the religious debates of her reign.

An even clearer demonstration of Anne's influence on her daughter's religious beliefs came with Elizabeth's appointment of Matthew Parker, her mother's former chaplain, as her first Archbishop of Canterbury. Parker accepted with some reluctance because he did not consider himself worthy of the position and was also suffering from a 'painful infirmity' after a horse-riding accident. But, as he confided to Sir Nicholas Bacon: 'My heart would right fain serve my sovereign lady the Queen's majesty, in more respects than of my allegiance, not forgetting what words her grace's mother said to me of her, not six days before her apprehension.' A short while later, he wrote to the queen herself, pleading his 'great unworthiness' of 'so high a function'. He admitted, though: 'I am . . . for the great benefits which sometime I received at your grace's honourable mother's benevolence (whose soul I doubt not but is in blessed felicity with God), most singularly obliged, above many other, to be your faithful bedesman.' Elizabeth ignored his pleas and he went on to serve her in that post for the rest of his days. His reluctance never wavered – but neither did his promise to Elizabeth's mother. In May 1572, he told William Cecil, Lord Burghley: 'If I had not been so much bound to the mother, I would not so soon have granted to serve the daughter in this place.'[24] The fact that Elizabeth promoted him to the highest ecclesiastical office in the land and refused to let him relinquish it was a testament to the faith she placed in her mother's judgement, as well as her determination to honour her memory.

A former protégé of Parker, William Bill, whose fellowship at Cambridge Anne Boleyn had funded, also enjoyed favour in her daughter's reign. He was elected Lord High Almoner in the year of Elizabeth's accession and assisted Parker in drawing up the new religious settlement. He was installed as Dean of Westminster in June 1560 but died the following year. Another influential reformer who owed his career to Anne and was favoured by her daughter was William Barlow. He had been appointed in 1534 as prior of Haverfordwest Priory in Wales, which had been in Anne's gift as Marchioness of Pembroke. After fleeing to exile during Mary's reign, Barlow had returned upon the accession of Elizabeth, who made him Bishop of Chichester. Along with Parker and Bill, he helped shape the religious settlement.

Committed Protestant though she was, Elizabeth had learned enough from her sister's example not to force her new subjects to conform. The contemporary philosopher and statesman, Francis Bacon (son of Sir Nicholas), shrewdly observed that she 'would not open windows into men's souls.' In April 1559, Parliament agreed a new Act of Supremacy, whereby the queen's title was changed from 'supreme head' to the less contentious 'supreme governor' of the Church of England. At the same time, an Act of Uniformity was introduced, which imposed a new Book of Common Prayer. This was based upon Edward VI's second book of 1552, but again the more controversial elements were watered down. It was passed by Parliament with the narrowest of margins, and all of Elizabeth's bishops voted against it. Clearly, the religious divisions still ran deep.

Religion was not the only subject from which contemporaries drew favourable comparisons between the new queen and her mother. In 1559, a scholar named William Barker published a book entitled *Nobility of Women*. In the dedication, he praised Anne Boleyn for having 'employed her bountiful benevolence upon sundry students, that were placed at Cambridge, among the which it pleased her highness to appoint me'.[25] Elizabeth would go on to become just as active a patron of learning as her mother had been. As a prolific scholar herself, her court attracted such towering literary and artistic figures as Edmund Spenser, Sir Philip Sidney, William Shakespeare, Francis Bacon and Nicholas Hilliard. In time, it would become the envy of the world.

CHAPTER 10

'Of her own blood and lineage'

FROM THE BEGINNING of her reign, Elizabeth made a great show of honouring some of her Tudor forebears. She visited the tomb of her 'dear Uncle, late Prince Arthur', in Worcester Cathedral and ordered the reburial of the dukes of York at Fotheringhay. But as queen, she would show no mercy towards her paternal cousins. Lady Margaret Douglas, Countess of Lennox, was twice consigned to the Tower during Elizabeth's reign for scheming to align her family more closely with the throne, while the sisters of Lady Jane Grey were imprisoned for marrying without the queen's permission and died miserable and alone. Tempting though it is to interpret this as Elizabeth's vengeance against her father, it was more likely statecraft: her Tudor kin had royal blood running through their veins so were more of a threat to her throne than her Boleyn relatives ever could be.

In establishing her new court, Elizabeth showed the greatest favour towards her maternal kin and supporters. After learning that she was queen, she had been escorted from Hatfield to London by an entourage of loyal attendants, among them Sir John Williams, her former guardian at Woodstock and father-in-law of Henry Norris. Even though he was by now approaching sixty and in poor health, the new queen expressed her gratitude for the 'good turns' he had done her by appointing him lord president of the Council of the Marches in 1559. He died in post later that year and was buried with great pomp in Thame church, close to Rycote.[1]

Sir John's son-in-law enjoyed even greater favour. Elizabeth's friendship with Henry Norris and his wife Margery had been forged in adversity, when she had been her sister's prisoner. Now that she was queen, she felt at liberty to express the reason why she held him in such high esteem: that his father had 'died in a noble cause and in justification of her mother's innocence'.[2] This was one of the clearest indications Elizabeth ever gave of just how much Anne Boleyn meant to her. It was also one of the rarest because it was expressed in words, as well as actions.

The new queen wasted no time in restoring Norris's full landed inheritance to him, and upon his father-in-law's death he and his wife took possession of Rycote. They played host to Elizabeth there on several occasions and she sometimes took advantage of the privacy it offered by inviting her favourite, Robert Dudley, to accompany her. The Norrises spent a great deal of time at court during the 1560s. Although Margery was not given a formal appointment, she became an intimate of the queen, who gave her the nickname 'Crow' because of her dark complexion. When Robert Dudley's wife Amy died in mysterious circumstances in 1560, Elizabeth, who was anxious to avoid being tainted by the scandal, appointed Margery chief mourner at the funeral. In 1562, Henry Norris was assigned his first diplomatic mission as special envoy to Paris. Four years later, shortly after receiving a knighthood from the queen during a stay at Rycote, he was elevated to the prestigious role of English ambassador in France, and in 1572 he was created Baron Norris of Rycote. Henry, his wife and their six sons devoted the rest of their lives to royal service and were rewarded richly for it.

Elizabeth's favour did not extend to the families of the other men who had been executed for adultery with her mother. As with her Boleyn relatives, her support was won by merit, not just kinship or connection. William Brereton's family had had a distinguished record of court service, which had enabled him to rise rapidly in Henry VIII's favour, becoming a member of the privy chamber and possibly witnessing the king's secret marriage to Anne Boleyn. But in his native Cheshire, where he was steward of the Marcher Lordships, his behaviour was so ruthless that it sparked widespread resentment. He dominated local monasteries to his advantage and even ordered the judicial murder of his former deputy. His unscrupulous activities soon came to the attention of Thomas Cromwell, who subsequently involved him in Anne's downfall. Of all the men accused of adultery with her, Brereton was the least likely to have been guilty. Not only was he considerably older than the queen, but he was not part of her inner circle – Wyatt described him as 'one that least I knew' – and he was not even in the same location as Anne on the occasions cited for their alleged adultery.[3] His execution had simply been a convenient means of ridding Cromwell and his royal master of a troublesome character. Brereton left two sons, neither of whom received anything at Elizabeth's hands.

Francis Weston had been a more likeable character than Brereton, but his open flirtation with Anne Boleyn had helped seal her doom. Elizabeth had no direct contact with his family, although she did show favour to his widow's son by her second marriage. Henry Knyvet was appointed a gentleman pensioner in 1560, attained various distinguished positions in local administration, fought for the queen in Scotland and possibly also the Netherlands, and was knighted in 1574. But he seems to have earned Elizabeth's good graces through his distinguished service, rather than his tenuous connection to her mother.

The other man implicated in Anne's downfall was Mark Smeaton, who left behind no heirs and was of such humble origins that his family had no court connections. He was also the only man to have confessed to sleeping with the queen and it was his testimony that had helped condemn the others, so Elizabeth had little reason to favour any of his family or associates.

Immediately after becoming queen, Elizabeth created her cousin and 'nearest kindred', Henry Carey, son of Anne Boleyn's sister Mary, Baron Hunsdon and gifted him the royal palace of that name.[4] One of her childhood homes, it was a splendid red-brick mansion nestled in the tranquil Hertfordshire countryside, a day's ride from the court in London. In 1559, Carey's royal cousin made him a substantial grant of lands in Hertfordshire, Kent and Essex worth £4,000 per annum (equivalent to more than £900,000 today). He was also given a generous pension and a host of court offices, including master of the queen's hawks and captain of the gentlemen pensioners – the latter effectively making him her personal bodyguard. His wife Anne was honoured with the position of lady of the bedchamber at the beginning of the reign. In 1561, her husband was elevated to the highest military order in the land when he was made a Knight of the Garter. Later, in the perilous time of Mary, Queen of Scots' flight to England, Elizabeth entrusted Carey with the task of helping restore order in the north as governor of Berwick. He proved so effective in this office that he was subsequently made warden of the east marches. The new queen demonstrated a real affection for her cousin throughout his life, calling him 'my Harry', and signing her letters 'Your loving kinswoman'.[5] She also promoted all four of his sons to high office.

As the new queen's cousin, Carey was her closest kin. But there was a rumour that he was even closer than that. In 1535, John Hale, vicar of Isleworth in Middlesex, claimed that a nun from nearby Syon Abbey had told him that the boy was Henry VIII's natural son by Mary Boleyn and that her sister Anne would 'not suffer [him] to be in the Court'.[6] But Hale was vehemently opposed to the king's second marriage and had also spread the slander that Henry had slept with Anne's mother. If Henry Carey had been his son, the king would surely have boasted of it to the world, as he did with Henry FitzRoy. At a time when the pressure to father a male heir was at its height, Henry would have welcomed further proof that the problem lay with his wives, not with him. Besides, the evidence suggests that by the time of Carey's birth in 1526, the king had long since abandoned Mary Boleyn; certainly he was already fixated with her sister.

Another family connected with Anne Boleyn emerged into the spotlight after 1558. Naunton recorded: 'The Howards were of the Queen's alliance and consanguinity by her mother, which swayed her affection and bent it towards this great house.'[7] Elizabeth's maternal great-uncle was William Howard, first Baron Howard of Effingham. His record of distinguished military and diplomatic service had not been enough to protect him from the wrath of Henry VIII when the adulterous liaisons of his niece, Catherine Howard, had been uncovered in 1541. Along with his wife and several of their servants, he was convicted of misprision of treason and sentenced to life imprisonment and the forfeiture of his goods. He had been pardoned after Catherine's execution early the following year and had resumed his military service. As a sign of her esteem, Elizabeth bestowed upon him the most senior office in the royal household: that of Lord Chamberlain, which required frequent attendance on the queen both at court and on her elaborate progresses. He was made a privy councillor in 1559 and attended meetings regularly throughout the following decade.

In what was by then a familiar pattern, when Howard's health began to falter and he was no longer able to discharge his duties as Lord Chamberlain, the queen kept the post in his family by appointing his nephew, Thomas Radcliffe, Earl of Sussex. Radcliffe was the brother of Henry, who had accompanied Elizabeth to the

Tower in 1554 and tried to defend her against Mary's officials, so she might already have been inclined to look favourably on him. Thomas had also served the Tudors as a diplomat and military man and was appointed lord lieutenant of Ireland early in Elizabeth's reign. It is a sign of how greatly she valued him that even though he made no secret of his antipathy towards her closest male favourite, Robert Dudley, he continued to enjoy her 'special favour and support'.[8]

Radcliffe's cousin, Charles Howard, who succeeded his father William as Baron Effingham in 1573, also enjoyed the benefits of kinship with the new queen. He was her first ambassador to France and was given a number of domestic offices. A regular participant in jousts and tournaments, Howard was prominent in every major court occasion. Elizabeth appreciated his straight-talking manner and was increasingly influenced by his advice as her reign progressed.

Another of Elizabeth's maternal relations who sought to benefit from her queenship was George Boleyn. He is often cited as the son of Anne Boleyn's brother, but there is no record of the elder George and his wife Jane having children, so it is more likely that the younger George was a more distant relative, especially as the evidence suggests he came from an impoverished background. Having graduated from Cambridge in 1552, he pursued a career in the Church and it may have been thanks to Elizabeth's influence that he gained his first clerical appointment at York Minster in 1559.

Of a 'choleric' nature, Boleyn made trouble wherever he went. He had a tendency to swear when provoked – an unfortunate habit for a churchman – and his temper often turned violent. In 1573 he was charged with threatening to nail the Dean of Canterbury Cathedral (where he served as prebendary) to the wall, thrashing a lawyer and attempting to strike a fellow canon.

Later, when he attacked one of the preachers with a dagger and was suspended for four months, he appealed against his sentence to the queen. This embarrassing Boleyn relative occasionally appeared at court, seeking further advancement at the queen's hands. But when she secured him the bishopric of Worcester, he turned it down. It must have been with some relief that Elizabeth heard that he had been installed as Dean of Lichfield Cathedral in 1576, a post that he managed to hold on to for the rest of his life.

An intriguing reference to Elizabeth's great-uncle, Sir James Boleyn, in the first New Year gift roll of her reign suggests that either they had become acquainted before she came to the throne or he was attempting to capitalise on their kinship now that she was queen. He gave 'sundry coins' in gold, to the value of £20 (around £4,700), which was more than any of the other knights listed in the same category. In return, his great-niece gave him a gold cup of similar value to those she gave her other knights.[9] There are no further references to Sir James in the gift rolls and he died in 1561. Although the lack of evidence does not necessarily mean that he and Elizabeth were not close, the fact that his wife had been hostile to Anne Boleyn and had helped gather evidence to condemn her was unlikely to have endeared him to the new queen.

Elizabeth appointed as her under treasurer Sir Richard Sackville, whose mother Margaret was her maternal great-aunt (the sister of Thomas Boleyn). He had risen to prominence during Edward VI's reign, when he was appointed chancellor of the court of augmentations and was knighted for his services. His known commitment to religious reform condemned him to a life of relative obscurity during Mary's reign, but he reaped the benefits of his Boleyn heritage when Elizabeth came to the throne. As well as conferring on Sir Richard his treasury post, the new queen appointed him to her council and gave him responsibility for many of the arrangements for her coronation. When her cousin Margaret Douglas was arrested in 1566 for conspiring to marry her son Henry, Lord Darnley to Mary, Queen of Scots, she entrusted her custody to Sackville. He also deputised for his royal mistress at funeral services held for foreign monarchs at St Paul's Cathedral. After Sir Richard's death, the queen transferred her favour to his eldest son Thomas, whom she created Lord Buckhurst, admitted to her privy council and appointed Lord Treasurer.

The new queen retained her sister's Lord Treasurer, William Paulet, Marquess of Winchester. Paulet had also served Elizabeth's father and brother. Originally a Catholic, he soon learned to adapt his beliefs to the changing times. When once asked how he had not only survived but thrived during the turbulent decades of his court service, he replied: 'I was made of the pliable willow, not of the stubborn oak.'[10] Paulet had been one of the judges in the trials of Anne Boleyn's alleged accomplices but, while Anne accused Henry's other councillors of twisting her words, she praised Paulet as 'a very gentleman'. It may have been this that recommended him to Elizabeth when she became queen. She admired his pragmatism, too, and once quipped: 'By my troth, if my lord treasurer were but a young man, I could find it in my heart to have him for a husband before any man in England.'[11]

In appointing the women who would serve her in private, Elizabeth showed the same bias towards her maternal relations. She also drastically reduced the size of her household. The number of ladies and gentlewomen of the privy chamber and bedchamber was decreased from twenty to eleven, and there were now just six maids of honour. This was the lowest number of female attendants that any queen had had for almost forty years and made the competition for places even more fierce than normal. The fact that nearly all of them went to the new queen's Boleyn relatives and associates, and that the posts became almost entirely hereditary, made her privy chamber virtually a closed shop.

Some of Elizabeth's ladies had served her since childhood and were collectively referred to as the 'old flock of Hatfield'.[12] Principal among them were Blanche Parry and Kat Astley, who had been part of her household for more than twenty years. One of Elizabeth's first acts after becoming queen was to bring Kat back from her enforced exile and appoint her chief gentlewoman of the privy chamber. This was the most prestigious post in the royal household and gave Kat unrivalled access to her royal mistress. Her husband John was awarded the honour of being made master of the jewel house. Blanche Parry, another of the 'old flock', became second gentlewoman of the privy chamber, with a generous allowance for clothes, servants, stabling and the like.[13]

On 3 January 1559, a privy seal warrant was issued appointing the queen's cousin Katherine Knollys a lady of the bedchamber. She and her husband Francis had remained on the continent until Queen Mary's death and had become prominent among the English exiles there. As soon as they received news of Elizabeth's accession, they made arrangements to return. Katherine immediately resumed her former closeness with Elizabeth and was described as being 'in favour with our noble queen, above the common sort', which may hint at the fact that the two women were probably half-sisters.[14] One contemporary noted that Elizabeth 'loved Lady Knollys above all other women in the world', which is corroborated by the lavish gifts that she bestowed on her each New Year.[15] Katherine and her family reaped the rewards of their connection. Her husband was admitted to the privy council and appointed vice-chamberlain of the household, as well as captain of the halberdiers. Her daughter Lettice, who may have been among Elizabeth's household at Hatfield for a time, also secured a salaried place as gentlewoman of the privy chamber. But Katherine, like the queen's other ladies, found that her privileged position came at a price. Elizabeth was every bit as demanding a mistress as her mother had been and Katherine would 'often weep for unkindness'.[16]

Another Boleyn cousin to join Elizabeth's service early in the reign was Henry Carey's daughter Katherine, who was appointed a gentlewoman of the privy chamber in January 1560. Given that she was then no more than fifteen years old – much younger than was usual for a woman in this post – it is likely that she was already well acquainted with the queen. The closeness between the cousins is also suggested by the fact that Katherine facilitated Elizabeth's relationship with her closest male favourite, Robert Dudley. In November 1561, the queen disguised herself as Katherine's maid in order to enjoy the secret pleasure of watching Dudley shoot at Windsor. Along with other senior ladies of the privy chamber, Katherine was entrusted with the safekeeping of the queen's jewels.[17]

In July 1563, Katherine married Charles Howard, son of the Lord Chamberlain. Although Elizabeth did not generally approve of her ladies marrying, this was one match that had her wholehearted support, thanks to Howard's blood ties to her mother. The newlyweds became the ultimate power couple of the Elizabethan court and their influence grew ever greater as the reign progressed. As with other favourites, their family reaped the rewards during the years that followed.[18]

Abigail Shelton, one of the daughters of Anne Boleyn's cousin Mary, who had been rumoured to have had an affair with Henry VIII, also joined the new queen's household – although the date of her appointment is uncertain. Another Shelton cousin, Mary, granddaughter of Elizabeth's former governor Sir John and his wife Lady Anne Shelton, was given the role of chamberer (the female equivalent of a groom) in 1571 but she soon became one of the queen's intimates and was occasionally her sleeping companion. Mary had strong Boleyn connections from both of her parents because her father was John and Anne's eldest son and her mother was Margaret Parker, elder sister of Jane Boleyn. With her red hair, dark eyes and prominent nose, she bore a striking resemblance to her royal cousin. It seems Elizabeth could not manage without her because when Mary took a brief leave of absence in October 1576, she received an urgent summons from Thomas Radcliffe, Earl of Sussex: 'I fear until you come her majesty shall not in the night have for the most part so good rest as she will take after your coming.'[19] Her influence with the queen was widely acknowledged and she remained in service for the rest of the reign. One courtier referred to 'that honourable place you are in and therein have continued you to the great good of the house from whence you are descended'.[20] Mary's dedicated service was not entirely disinterested, however, and she used her position to secure lucrative gifts in return for dropping a few favourable words in her royal cousin's ear.[21]

Inspired by her desire to honour her late mother, Elizabeth had created a tightly knit court in which almost all principal members were related by ties of blood, marriage or friendship. In this way, too, she expressed her pride in her Boleyn heritage – and helped atone for the sins of her Tudor father. This was typical of the way in which she used deeds rather than words to convey her true feelings. The bitter experiences of her childhood, as well as the example set by her sister, had taught her to set pragmatism above principle. Mary had spent her life trying to bring back the past – restoring her mother's legitimacy, reinstating Roman Catholicism, allying England with Spain – and in doing so had ridden roughshod over the wishes of her people. Much as she revered her own mother's memory, Elizabeth was shrewd enough to realise that the majority of her subjects would never share her opinion. She therefore focused her energies on realising Anne's ambitions by becoming the most successful of Henry's heirs.

CHAPTER 11

A French partisan

JUST OCCASIONALLY, ELIZABETH was sufficiently provoked to abandon her accustomed discretion about her mother. Her hackles had already been raised during negotiations for a new treaty with France in 1559. Her agents at Cateau-Cambrésis reported that their French counterparts had expressed unease about treating with a monarch whose claim to the throne was so questionable. The English queen furiously upbraided her representatives for not stamping down such objections immediately and told them: 'We may nor ever will permit any over whom we have rule or may have to make doubt, question, or treaty of this matter.'[1] In questioning her legitimacy, the French had touched a raw nerve. It was a subject about which Elizabeth had been sensitive since her mother's execution and, now that she was queen, she was quick to lash out at any who dared to debate the matter.

Then, in the summer of 1561, news reached Elizabeth of a defamatory tract that had been published in Paris. Her ambassador, Nicholas Throckmorton, reported to William Cecil that a man named Gabriel de Sacconay had 'devised' and printed the work, 'wherein he has spoken most irreverently of the Queen's mother'. The book denounced Anne as a 'Jezebel' and compared her to the 'heathen wives of Solomon' for persuading Henry VIII to turn his back on the 'true' Church of Rome. Their 'foul matrimony' was a result of lust and Anne had met with just punishment for her wickedness. Upon receiving Throckmorton's report, Cecil was greatly alarmed. He was close enough to the queen to know how she felt about her mother and that, for all her accustomed pragmatism, she was unlikely to turn a blind eye to such a vicious attack on Anne's reputation. This in turn could disrupt England's already fragile alliance with France. Perhaps hoping that the controversy would soon recede, he chose to keep it from his royal mistress. But while he waited to see how things would develop, hundreds of copies of the book were printed and news of it spread like wildfire across Paris and beyond. This forced Cecil's hand and in the middle of September, more than a month after he had heard of it, he reluctantly told his royal mistress the truth.

Elizabeth's reaction was one of furious indignation. She wrote at once to Throckmorton, ordering him to request an urgent meeting with Catherine de Medici, who was acting as regent during the minority of her son, Charles IX, and demand that the 'lewd and slanderous' book be immediately suppressed. He duly did so, but, while Catherine made a diplomatic show of dismay at the insult to the English queen's mother, she stopped short of having the book withdrawn from circulation. Instead, she asked for a copy to be brought to her so that she 'might cause it to be considered, and thereupon give order for the matter'. She then consulted her son, as if an eleven-year-old boy would be able to offer a considered opinion on the matter, which delayed things further. All the while, more and more people were reading the book, which suited Catherine's purpose perfectly. Her widowed daughter-in-law, Mary Stuart, whose marriage to Catherine's son, the Dauphin Francis, had been cut short by his premature death at the age of just sixteen in 1560, had recently left France for her native Scotland, where she was queen. Scotland and France were old allies and Catherine's interests would be well served if Mary succeeded in taking the English crown, too. As the great-niece of

Henry VIII, Mary had Tudor blood flowing through her veins and her Catholic faith made her an appealing prospect to at least half of Elizabeth's subjects.[2] A book that condemned Elizabeth's mother as a usurping whore, thereby casting grave doubt on her own legitimacy as queen, would bolster Mary's claim.

Eventually, an order was issued under Charles IX's name for de Sacconay to 'alter the offensive passages' and to sell no further copies in the meantime. Still, Elizabeth was not satisfied. She demanded that all copies of the book be completely destroyed and that the author be severely punished for his slanders. Catherine continued to offer fine words and promises, but she had not reckoned with Elizabeth's tenacity, nor her strength of feeling where Anne was concerned. For more than twenty years, Elizabeth had been obliged to ignore the insults levied at her late mother by courtiers, attendants, ambassadors and even members of her own family. Now that she was queen, although still mindful of the need to tread carefully where her own subjects were concerned, she could give full vent to her rage against Anne's enemies overseas.

Finally, in the second week of October, Throckmorton was able to report that the French king had issued a command for all the offending books to be confiscated. But Elizabeth was not prepared to forgive and forget. When her ambassador suggested that she thank Catherine and her son for their pains, she ignored him. Alarmed, he urged the danger of making an enemy of France and pointed out that Catherine was highly offended by Elizabeth's lack of courtesy. Only in late November did the English queen reluctantly send a note of thanks – not via Throckmorton, as etiquette demanded, but via her ambassador in Spain. This was a studied discourtesy that made it clear Elizabeth had not forgiven the French for slandering her mother.[3]

But the more positive associations between Anne Boleyn and

the country where she had spent much of her youth were revived the same year, thanks to the late Queen Claude's younger sister, Renée. Born in 1510, Renée had been a child of three when Anne had first entered her sister's service, but she had warmed to her immediately and the two girls had spent a great deal of time together. When Throckmorton was introduced to her during his embassy in 1561, Renée, by now the dowager duchess of Ferrara, confessed that she admired his royal mistress because she had been very fond of Elizabeth's mother.

The English queen felt a natural affinity for France – if not always the French monarchy – throughout her life. Fluent in the language, she had numerous French books in her library, some of which she had inherited from her mother. Anne's love of French literature had been well known. The author of the treatise presented to her at New Year 1530 had reflected: 'When I consider your great affection and perfect desire for the French tongue, I am not surprised that you are not to be found . . . without some French book in your hand which is useful and necessary for teaching and discovering the true and straight path of all virtue.' During Mary's reign, Charles V's ambassador, Simon Renard, had warned that Elizabeth would prove as troublesome as Anne because 'she would imitate her mother in being a French partisan'.[4]

The French author who influenced Elizabeth most was her mother's former companion, Marguerite of Navarre. One of the most powerful lessons that Elizabeth drew from Marguerite's works was that women were essentially weak, inferior beings and that only by emulating the characteristics of men could they hope to succeed. As queen, she regularly referred to herself in the masculine gender and would express her regret that she had been born 'a weak and feeble woman'. The fact that she would choose not to fulfil that most basic of womanly functions by marrying and producing an heir strengthened the impression that she was a woman in appearance, but a man in every other respect. Towards the end of her life, Sir Robert Cecil reflected that she had been 'more than a man, and, in truth, sometimes less than a woman'.[5] Elizabeth would take Marguerite's teachings a step further, though: as well as drawing attention to her 'male' characteristics, she would flaunt her femininity when she judged the occasion demanded it. At turns delighting, frustrating, enticing and enslaving the male courtiers who flocked to pay her homage, she would become as bewitching and sexually provocative as her mother. But while Anne had ultimately been condemned for it, Elizabeth would use her feminine power to triumph over a world of men.

Anne's example was a powerful influence on her daughter throughout her reign. But it proved a double-edged sword. As well as being an inspiring role model for Elizabeth, Anne was also a painful reminder of the cloud of illegitimacy that continued to hang over the new queen. Elizabeth's sensitivity about this found expression again two years after the de Sacconay controversy. John Hales, Clerk of the Hanaper, circulated a treatise in which he argued against Mary, Queen of Scots' title to the English throne. Even though this was to Elizabeth's advantage, she was so anxious to curb any discussion touching her own legitimacy as queen that she sent Hales to the Tower.

On 18 July 1565, Elizabeth lost the woman to whom she had been closest since Anne Boleyn's death and who had supplied the place of mother ever since. Kat Astley had served her faithfully – if not always wisely – for almost thirty years and the queen was reported to be 'greatly grieved' at her death.[6] She kept to her chamber for days, suspending all official business. She had once complained to Kat that she had 'so much sorrow and tribulation and so little joy' in the world.[7] The loss of her beloved governess brought the truth of this home to her now.

Three years later, the queen lost another cherished attendant. In December 1568, she and her court moved to Hampton Court Palace for the festive season. While there, her maternal cousin and confidante, Katherine Knollys, fell gravely ill. She had spent the previous ten years in tireless service to Elizabeth, despite the competing demands of mothering her numerous children. In contrast to other courtiers, she had not exploited her position for personal gain and was 'devoid of guile'.[8] Her husband had been no less assiduous in his duties and was at that time in Bolton Castle, supervising the imprisonment of Mary, Queen of Scots, who had fled to England after her reign north of the border collapsed. Hearing of his wife's condition, Sir Francis repeatedly begged to be allowed to visit her and complained bitterly at Elizabeth's 'ungrateful denial of my coming to the court'.[9] But no matter how much she valued her Boleyn relatives, Elizabeth rarely made an exception to her rule that royal service must come before everything else. William Cecil wrote to assure Sir Francis that his wife was 'well amended', which prompted the latter to write to Katherine, expressing an intense desire for them to retire from service and live 'a country poor life'.[10]

This wish, albeit whimsical, would never be fulfilled. Katherine's health deteriorated so rapidly that her royal mistress realised the seriousness of her condition too late. Cecil's protégé Nicholas White, who was at the palace for the Christmas celebrations, reported that the ailing Lady Knollys 'was very often visited by her Majesty's own comfortable presence'.[11] But Katherine slipped further into decline and died on 15 January 1569, aged just forty-six. Elizabeth was thrown into such 'passions of grief . . . for the death of her kinswoman and good servant' that she 'fell for a while from a prince wanting nothing in this world to private mourning, in which solitary estate being forgetful of her own health, she took cold, wherewith she was much troubled'.[12] When he visited the queen soon afterwards, White, who was rather a blunt man, noted that she was still beset by grief:

> She returned back again to talk of my Lady Knollys. And after many speeches past to and fro of that gentlewoman, I, perceiving her to harp much upon her departure, said, that the long absence of her husband . . . together with the fervency of her fever, did greatly further her end, wanting nothing else that either art of man's help could devise for her recovery, lying in a prince's court near her person.

It was an accurate, if rather tactless remark and he followed it up with another: 'Although her Grace were not culpable of this accident [i.e. Katherine's death], yet she was the cause without which their being asunder had not happened.' The queen replied disconsolately that she was 'very sorry for her death'.[13]

Elizabeth tried to assuage her guilt by laying out £640 (around £150,000 today) on a lavish funeral in Westminster. This was considerably more than the queen spent on the interment of two of her paternal cousins: the Duchess of Suffolk (who died in 1559) and the Countess of Lennox (1578). Katherine's epitaph, which can still be seen in the abbey, draws attention to her and Elizabeth's shared Boleyn heritage:

> This Lady Knollys, and the Lord Hunsdon her Brother, were the Children of William Carey, Esq; and of the Lady Mary his Wife, one of the Daughters and Heirs to Thomas Boleyn, Earl of Wiltshire and Ormond; which Lady Mary was Sister to Anne Queen of England, Wife to King Henry the Eighth, Father and Mother to Elizabeth Queen of England.

Elizabeth never missed an opportunity to remind her subjects that her mother was a true queen and, therefore, so was she. She continued to show favour to Katherine's family, notably her eldest son Henry, whom she honoured 'in respect of his kindred to us by his late mother'.[14]

CHAPTER 12

'Angry with any love'

$\mathbf{A}$s ELIZABETH'S REIGN progressed, she became ever more her mother's daughter. When her sister Mary was on the throne, the Spanish ambassador had remarked that Elizabeth had 'many characteristics in which she resembled her mother'.[1] Sir Robert Naunton, who wrote an account of notables at Elizabeth's court, believed that she had inherited all her best traits from Anne.

> Her mother was . . . as the French word hath it, more debonaire, and affable, virtues which might well suit with majesty and which descending as hereditary to the daughter did render her of a more sweet temper, and endear her more to the love and liking of the people, who gave her the name and fame of a most gracious and popular prince, the atrocity of her father's nature being allayed in hers by her mother's sweet inclination.[2]

His account was published after Elizabeth's death: he would not have risked such open criticism of her father during her lifetime, even if she privately agreed with it. Drawing favourable comparisons between mother and daughter, though, was always sure to win the queen's goodwill.

Like Anne, Elizabeth did not conform to the social conventions that made women subordinate to men in almost every aspect of their lives. Instead, she was determined to be mistress of her own destiny. This was evident from the moment she took the throne. When he met the queen-in-waiting three days before her accession, the Count of Feria shrewdly observed: 'She is determined to be governed by no one.'[3] The queen was also imbued with the same talent for crafting her public image as her mother had been. Keenly aware that most of Henry's subjects viewed her as a usurper, Anne had channelled her considerable energies into presenting herself as a divine ruler, notably by invoking images of the Virgin Mary at her coronation. Elizabeth had followed her example but, as with so many of the ideas borrowed from her mother, she would take it to another level. The cult of monarchy reached its height during her long reign, as she cultivated an image of herself as 'Gloriana', the Virgin Queen, whom God had appointed to bring peace and prosperity to her people. At the same time, she breathed new life into a court that had lost its glamour and vitality after her mother's demise, making it 'at once gay, decent, and superb', as one of her Boleyn relatives later reflected.[4] That word 'decent' is significant: ever watchful of her reputation not only as an unmarried queen but as the daughter of a notorious adulteress, Elizabeth was determined to ensure that revelry would never descend into licentiousness, or flirtatiousness into sexual transgression.

Not all the character traits that Elizabeth inherited from Anne were so positive. Like her mother, she was described as 'very vain' and thrived on the adoring attentions of her courtiers.[5] Her behaviour could be immoderate and, occasionally, hysterical, just as her mother's had been. Like Anne, she also had a vicious, sometimes violent temper and often vented her fury on her ladies, dealing them slaps or blows. On one occasion, when an attendant was clumsy in serving her meal, Elizabeth stabbed her in the hand. Even her Boleyn relatives were not immune from her temper. Robert Carey, son of her cousin Henry, Baron Hunsdon, recalled a 'stormy and terrible' encounter with the queen, during which he had been obliged to hold his tongue while she raged.[6]

Elizabeth's mood swings were just as sudden and dramatic as her mother's had been. 'When she smiled, it was a pure sunshine, that everyone did choose to bask in, if they could,' observed Elizabeth's godson, Sir John Harington, a regular at her court. 'But anon came a storm from a sudden gathering of clouds, and the thunder fell in wondrous manner on all alike.'[7] Like her mother, Elizabeth used her mercurial nature to devastating effect. Whereas Anne's regular and abrupt withdrawal of her affection had brought an ardent king to heel, Elizabeth achieved the same end with her entire court. Her ministers and attendants learned to their cost that her favour was not to be relied upon for long, which made them ever more eager to please her. 'All those to whom she distributed her favours were never more than tenants-at-will, and stood on no better terms than her princely pleasure, and their good behaviour,' observed Naunton.[8] Their fickle, changeable nature enabled both mother and daughter to wield greater power than sixteenth-century society would otherwise have allowed them. They did not just break the mould: they shattered it.

There was another deeply unconventional strategy that Elizabeth employed to both safeguard and assert her authority. Ironically, it concerned the same issue that from the beginning of her reign looked set to lose her the love and loyalty of her people. 'And, in the end, this shall be for me sufficient, that a marble stone shall declare that a queen, having reigned such a time, lived and died a virgin,' Elizabeth declared during the first Parliament of her reign in February 1559.[9] Few of its members believed her. 'There is a strong idea in the world that a woman cannot live unless she is married, or at all events that if she refrains from marriage she does so for some bad reason,' Elizabeth herself reflected.[10]

As queen, Elizabeth was not exempt from these conventions:

if anything, they applied to her even more. Many felt it was imperative that she find a husband as soon as possible so that he could advise and guide her – and, when required, assume the mantle of power so that she could fulfil her more natural function of childbearing. Shortly after her accession, Philip II had told her that she should marry him in order to 'relieve her of those labours which are only fit for men'.[11] All her subjects – from privy councillors to peasant farmers – shared the firm belief that the only way for Elizabeth to rule effectively and secure her throne was if she married and produced an heir. It seemed that the only person in England who held a different view was the queen herself.

There were sound political reasons why Elizabeth was reluctant to take a husband. In the world of Tudor marriage, men held all the power. If a husband proved violent, abusive or adulterous, his wife was expected to endure it. Upon marriage, a woman would relinquish any land or property she held and would have few legal rights over her husband. As queen, Elizabeth stood to lose a great deal more than most women. Even though her half-sister's marriage treaty had strictly defined the powers of her husband, the reality had been rather different and Mary herself had encouraged Philip to take the reins of government – with disastrous results. When Elizabeth told the Scottish ambassador Sir James Melville that she was resolved never to marry, he shrewdly replied: 'Your Majesty thinks, if you were married, you would be but Queen of England; and now you are both King and Queen. I know your spirit cannot endure a commander.' In a similar vein, Hieronimo Lippomano, the Venetian ambassador in France, referred to 'the ambition which the Queen has by her nature to govern absolutely without any partner'. Elizabeth herself, when provoked by her overbearing councillors, angrily pronounced: 'I will have but one mistress here, and no master!'[12]

But there were more profound, personal reasons behind Elizabeth's resolve to remain single – and they were bound up with her mother's fate. Anne Boleyn had been executed on her father's orders after being condemned as an adulterous whore. For Elizabeth, the trauma of this had been intensified by Catherine Howard suffering the same fate a few years later. Two more of her stepmothers had died in childbed and her sister Mary had endured the pain and humiliation of two phantom pregnancies before being all but abandoned by her scornful husband. Little wonder that by the time she reached adulthood, Elizabeth harboured a deep, visceral fear of marriage.

Although she would present a smiling face to potential suitors, alive to the political expediency of keeping them in play, the queen occasionally showed flashes of profound unease when the subject of marriage was raised. She told the French ambassador that she would leave herself entirely vulnerable if she took a husband, as he could 'carry out some evil wish, if he had one'. A German envoy was taken aback when she snapped that 'she would rather go into a nunnery, or for that matter suffer death' than marry.[13] She went even further a few years later, fiercely declaring that she 'hated the idea of marriage every day more, for reasons which she could not divulge to a twin soul, if she had one, much less to a living creature'.[14] On one of a number of occasions when Parliament petitioned her to marry, she retorted: 'I must confess my own mislike so much to strive against the matter . . . I would not forsake the single state to march with the greatest monarch in the world.'[15]

For the most part, the queen gave only the vaguest reasons for her reluctance to commit to any of the marriage alliances that were proposed during her long reign. But in 1561 she admitted to a Scottish envoy that her family history had played its part: 'Some say that this marriage was unlawful, some that one was a bastard . . . So many doubts of marriage was in all hands that I stand [in] awe myself to enter into marriage, fearing the controversy.' She went on to confide that certain events in her youth had made her afraid of marriage.[16] For the most part, though, she asserted that it was her position as queen, rather than her private feelings as a woman, that prevented her from taking a husband: 'As I think it [marriage] best for a private woman so do I strive with myself to think it not mete for a prince.'[17]

There was bitterness, as well as fear, in Elizabeth's response to the idea of marriage. By the time she became queen, she had learned the full truth of her mother's downfall, with all the shocking injustice it entailed. Driven by his all-consuming obsession with Anne, her father had overturned his kingdom to make her his queen. But as soon as he had her, his passion withered on the vine. He destroyed her for failing to give him a son and was betrothed to someone else the very next day. 'Affection,' Elizabeth once declared, 'is false'.[18]

Elizabeth did not just spurn the state of matrimony herself; she expected her ladies to follow suit. Those who did not share her prejudice found themselves in an invidious position. They could seek the queen's permission to marry, knowing that it would likely be refused; they could marry in secret and risk the inevitable storm if it was discovered; or they could forfeit their personal happiness by dedicating themselves entirely to serving their royal mistress, as she expected them to.

One naïve young recruit to Elizabeth's household soon learned this to her cost. A daughter of Sir Robert Arundell, she had only recently arrived at court when the queen asked if she intended to marry. Before anyone could warn her, the young woman eagerly replied: 'She had thought much about marriage, if her father did consent to the man she loved.' To her delight, the queen offered to speak to her father and arrange the whole matter. Not long afterwards, she relayed the joyful news that he had given his written consent to her marriage. 'I shall be happy and please your Grace,' the grateful girl exclaimed. 'So thou shalt,' replied the queen, 'but not to be a fool and marry.' She proceeded to confiscate Sir Robert's letter and sent his daughter on her way.[19]

Elizabeth's severity towards her ladies was at least partly justified. As an unmarried queen – particularly one with her family background – it was imperative that she safeguard her reputation as strictly as possible. Any sexual scandals in her household would reflect badly upon her, given that she set the moral standards of her court. Her mother had been no less stringent with her ladies. William Latymer, chaplain to both mother and daughter, observed that Anne 'would many times move them to modesty and chastity, but especially to the maidens of honour, whom she would call before her in the privy chamber, and before the mother of the maidens would give them a long charge of their behaviours'.[20]

Although she may have had good reason to punish her ladies for marrying, it is difficult to absolve Elizabeth completely from the charge of being 'angry with any love', as one of her courtiers put it.[21] Even Boleyn blood was no protection from the queen's wrath – if anything, it made it worse because she tended to regard her Boleyn relatives as part of an extended royal family and therefore expected them to seek her prior approval before marrying. In 1574, her cousin Mary Shelton secretly married Sir John Scudamore, a gentleman usher. Upon hearing of Mary's transgression, Elizabeth was 'liberal both with blows and evil words' and lashed out at her young cousin with a candlestick, breaking her finger. As one onlooker observed: 'Never woman bought her husband more dear than she hath done.'[22]

Anne Boleyn had shown similar cruelty towards members of her kin who fell in love. Her cousin Margaret or 'Madge' Shelton had been betrothed to Henry Norris, with whom Anne enjoyed a flirtatious relationship. She poked fun at Madge for the fact that Norris had not yet proposed, which prompted Francis Weston, another of Anne's male companions, to remark that Norris 'came more to her [Anne's] chamber for her than for Madge'.[23] This playful banter was later twisted into something altogether more sinister and both Norris and Weston lost their lives for it – as did Anne herself. Little wonder that Elizabeth guarded her reputation even more fiercely than her mother had.

Bound up in Elizabeth's attitude to marriage might have been a fear that she had inherited the fertility problems that had lain at the root of her mother's downfall. Her godson, Sir John Harington, observed: 'In mind, she hath ever had an aversion and (as many think) in body some indisposition to the act of marriage.'[24] On two, possibly three occasions during her short marriage to Henry, Anne Boleyn had miscarried or given birth to a stillborn child. There is a theory that she was rhesus negative, meaning that her body would reject all rhesus positive babies after the first pregnancy. Elizabeth's paternal relations did not instil her with much confidence either. Her sister Mary had suffered from menstrual problems throughout her life and the fact that her father struggled to sire a healthy male heir in almost forty years of trying suggests that the problem may have been with him, not his wives.

Elizabeth herself had displayed symptoms that suggest she might have had difficulty conceiving or carrying a baby to term. It was reported that her periods were irregular at best and sometimes entirely absent. The papal nuncio in France claimed: 'She has hardly ever the purgation proper to all women.'[25] Elizabeth Shrewsbury (better known as Bess of Hardwick) had confided to Mary, Queen of Scots that Elizabeth was 'not like other women' and that even if she had married, it could never have been consummated. As evidence, she cited the fact that an ulcer on the queen's leg had dried up at the same time as her monthly periods had ceased. The rumours became ever more outlandish as the years passed: there was even a suggestion that Elizabeth was really a man disguised as a woman.[26]

And yet, for every account of Elizabeth's infertility, there are several more claiming that she regularly slept with her male courtiers and had numerous bastards by them. The earliest such rumour had appeared in the aftermath of the Thomas Seymour scandal, but this was overshadowed by the gossip after she became queen. A widow named Dionisia Deryck claimed that Elizabeth 'hath already had as many children as I', but that only two of them had survived into adulthood. The playwright Ben Jonson, who claimed that Elizabeth 'had a membrana on her, which made her incapable of man', added that she had 'tried many'.[27] Most of the rumours centred on her relationship with Robert Dudley, whom she made Earl of Leicester in 1564. In 1587, a young man going by the name of Arthur Dudley persuaded the King of Spain that he was their illegitimate offspring. Interestingly, Arthur was said to have had a sixth finger on one hand – just like Anne Boleyn.[28] Even though she had by then ruled successfully for almost forty years, Elizabeth was still presented as the bad apple who had not fallen far from the tree.

The medical examinations that Elizabeth underwent as part of the various marriage negotiations suggest that she was perfectly healthy and able to bear many children. Even when she was a baby, her mother had arranged for her to be shown 'quite naked' to the French envoys who had been sent to treat for her marriage to Francis I's son. In 1566, the French ambassador, de la Forêt, quizzed one of the royal physicians as to whether she would be a suitable wife for the young French king, Charles IX. The physician's reply was unequivocal: 'Your king is seventeen, and the Queen is only thirty-two . . . If the King marries her, I will answer for her having ten children, and no one knows her temperament better than I do.' Another expert concurred that Elizabeth was 'likely to conceive & bear children without peril'. Her laundresses were regularly bribed by foreign agents to report on the state of the queen's sheets and underclothes, and all confirmed that, contrary to rumour, her periods were regular. Elizabeth herself once insisted: 'I am unimpaired in body'.[29] But the spectre of a blighted obstetric history continued to lurk in her mind. For all her intellectual brilliance and political guile, Anne Boleyn had been judged – and condemned – for the failure of her body. Her daughter was determined not to repeat that.

Elizabeth's resolve to remain the Virgin Queen might have been unshakeable, but that did not prevent her from indulging the provocative, flirtatious nature that she inherited from her mother. 'The Queen did fish for men's souls, and had so sweet a bait, that no one could escape her network,' observed Sir Christopher Hatton, one of her favourites.[30] Like Anne, she delighted in being at the centre of a game of courtly love that she herself had created – one that shaped her relationships with adoring favourites and sober advisers alike. She tickled Robert Dudley on the neck when conferring his knighthood and gave her councillors pet names: Cecil was 'Sir Spirit', Dudley 'Eyes' and Hatton 'Lids'. But having learned from Anne's example, Elizabeth made the boundaries much sharper. As a friend of Hatton cautioned: 'First of all you must consider with whom you have to deal, and what we be towards her, who though she does descend very much in her sex as a woman, yet we may not forget her place and nature of it as our sovereign.'[31] Anne had played the same game when she had been a single woman but had failed to adapt it when married to the king and had lost spectacularly. By both flaunting her femininity and fiercely guarding her virginity, Elizabeth proved that she could win it.

As her reign progressed and she grew more confident in her

queenship, Elizabeth increasingly made a virtue of her unmarried state, creating a cult-like image of herself as the Virgin Queen. She also cleverly cultivated the idea that she was married to England and was a mother to its people. From the beginning of the reign, her speeches were littered with references to this metaphorical state. In 1559, she replied to the House of Commons' petition to marry by telling them: 'Reproach me so no more . . . that I have no children: for every one of you, and as many as are English, are my children.' In another, she declared: 'I assure you all that though after my death you may have many stepdames, yet shall you never have any, a more natural mother, than I mean to be unto you all.'[32]

At the beginning of her reign, Elizabeth's unmarried state had been viewed as a problem to be fixed; by its end, it had become a virtue to be celebrated. Her decision to remain the Virgin Queen had been inspired by her mother and it condemned her father's dynasty to extinction. It is perhaps carrying the argument too far to say that this was a deliberate act of vengeance on Elizabeth's part, but it certainly handed her mother a posthumous victory.

CHAPTER 13

'Nearness of blood'

BY THE TIME Elizabeth had been queen for ten years, her maternal kin were so firmly embedded at court that she had come to trust and rely upon them utterly. But in 1569, a plot was uncovered that shook her belief in her Boleyn relations to the core. It centred around the captive Queen of Scots, who had been Elizabeth's prisoner since fleeing to England the previous year. Mary Stuart was the English queen's most deadly rival. Her claim to the throne of England was strengthened by the fact that she had – briefly – been Queen of France, before the untimely death of her young husband, Francis II, in 1560. In contrast to Elizabeth, Mary had no intention of remaining single and in 1565 she had married her half-cousin Henry Stuart, Lord Darnley, son of Lady Margaret Douglas. The marriage had quickly produced a son, James, but in all other respects it had been a disaster. An arrogant and violent man, Darnley had quickly alienated the powerful Scottish lords who controlled government. Matters had reached a crisis point when, three months before their son's birth in June 1566, Darnley had ordered Mary's beloved secretary, David Rizzio, to be dragged from her presence and stabbed to death in an adjoining room. He then kept his wife a virtual prisoner.

Soon, Mary had begun openly conspiring with a group of Scottish lords to rid herself and Scotland of her troublesome husband. They included the Lord High Admiral of Scotland, James

Hepburn, fourth Earl of Bothwell. In February 1567, Darnley was murdered while staying at the house of Kirk o'Field in Edinburgh. Events then rapidly spiralled out of control. Three months later, Mary scandalised the world by taking Bothwell – the chief suspect in Darnley's murder – as her new husband, possibly under duress. This fatally undermined her credibility as queen. On 15 June, the Scottish lords confronted Mary, Bothwell and their supporters at Carberry Hill. There was no battle because by then the Queen of Scots' forces had dwindled away. Bothwell fled into exile and Mary was taken to Edinburgh, where she was publicly denounced as an adulteress and murderer. She was subsequently imprisoned in Loch Leven Castle and on 24 July, a few days after miscarrying Bothwell's twins, she was forced to abdicate in favour of her infant son, who became James VI. The Earl of Moray, James V's illegitimate son, was appointed regent.

Keeping a close eye on events from England, Elizabeth had been swift to abandon her former pretence of 'sisterly' affection towards her royal cousin and had written to upbraid Mary for her reckless actions. 'How could a worse choice be made for your honour than in such haste to marry such a subject, who besides other and notorious lacks, public fame hath charged with the murder of your late husband,' she demanded.[1]

For almost a year, matters appeared more settled. Then in May 1568, the Queen of Scots escaped from Loch Leven and raised an army of six thousand men. They were routed by Moray's forces at the Battle of Langside on 13 May and Mary fled south with a greatly diminished band of men. Realising that to turn back would almost certainly mean death, the beleaguered queen made the fateful decision to throw herself on the mercy of her cousin.

The Queen of Scots had confidently expected she would soon be on her way northwards again, an English army in tow. But Elizabeth could hardly have risked such a move, given that the same army might one day be used to push Mary's claim to the English throne. She therefore decided to keep her cousin prisoner. Although in theory this gave Elizabeth the upper hand over her most dangerous rival, keeping the ousted Queen of Scots on English soil meant that she was within tantalising reach of the many English Catholics who wished to see her on the throne in Elizabeth's place. It was with good reason that William Cecil warned: 'The Queen of Scots is, and always shall be, a dangerous person to your estate.'²

The truth of this was soon proved. In January 1569, Mary was moved to Tutbury Castle in Staffordshire and placed in the custody of the Earl of Shrewsbury and his wife, Elizabeth (better known as Bess of Hardwick). A few months later, a group of powerful Catholic lords in the north of England conspired to overthrow Elizabeth and put the Queen of Scots on the throne. At the heart of the plot was Elizabeth's own cousin, Thomas Howard, fourth Duke of Norfolk. Frustrated at being given less authority than he thought he deserved, he had conspired to marry the Scottish queen so that he might share her power when she supplanted his cousin, and their descendants would then rule England. His involvement in the Northern Rebellion earned him a nine-month stay in the Tower. He could have faced a far worse punishment if Elizabeth, mindful of their kinship, had not been inclined to clemency.

Less than two years later, Norfolk was implicated in another plot. It took its name from the papal agent Roberto Ridolfi, who garnered support from the Catholic powers of Europe – Philip II in particular – for an invasion of England that would overthrow Elizabeth and set Norfolk and Mary in her place. When the plot was discovered, the duke was arrested and sent back to the Tower. In January 1572, he was tried and found guilty of thirteen counts of high treason and condemned to be hanged, drawn and quartered.

His execution was scheduled for 21 January, but Elizabeth flinched from signing his death warrant because of their 'nearness of blood'. Only in early February did she put her signature to it, but the night before the execution was due to take place she suddenly withdrew it. The queen was greatly distressed at the thought of sending the son of her mother's cousin to death where Anne herself had been beheaded and she suffered a severe bout of the stomach problems that often plagued her at times of stress.

When the queen was well enough to resume her duties, she came under intense pressure from the government to put Mary, Queen of Scots to death for her involvement in the plot. Elizabeth's refusal made it impossible for her to spare Norfolk, too, and on 9 April she signed another execution warrant. But, yet again, her conscience plagued her and two days later, she sent an urgent letter to Lord Burghley ordering him to withdraw it. Her long-suffering adviser noted that he had received it at two o'clock in the morning. Although Elizabeth had always prided herself on her political pragmatism, the execution of her mother's close kin touched her closely. In her letter to Burghley, she ruefully admitted: 'I am more beholden to the hinder part of my head' – the part of the brain that was thought to govern the affections.[3]

In all, it took five separate warrants before Elizabeth could go through with it. After signing the last of these on 31 May, she visited the Tower to make sure that the arrangements had been made in a proper and respectful manner. Norfolk's rank should have permitted him a private execution inside the walls of the Tower, like Anne, but it took place on the public scaffold on Tower Hill. Perhaps Elizabeth could not countenance sending him to his death on the same spot as her mother. The duke was, though, buried before the altar of the Chapel of St Peter ad Vincula, next to Anne. On the day of his death, Elizabeth's courtiers noted that she was in a deep melancholy.

Another man with Boleyn associations had been involved in the plot. William Barker was the author of *Nobility of Women*, which had praised Anne Boleyn as an active patron of learning. Alongside his academic career, he worked as a secretary to the Duke of Norfolk and became embroiled in his plotting. In desperation, he reminded Elizabeth of his connection to her late mother as a means of securing her pardon. 'As by her majesty's noble mother I first began at Cambridge tasting of her munificence, so by her majesty's clemency I may end the rest of my sorrowful days there,' he pleaded.[4] The connection likely saved him. He remained a prisoner in the Tower for two years but was then released and spent the rest of his life in quiet obscurity.

By the early 1570s, having seen off various challenges to her rule, Elizabeth's confidence as queen was evidently secure enough for her to abandon her former discretion about her mother and celebrate the fact that she was a Boleyn, not just a Tudor. She adopted one of Anne's mottos, *Semper Eadem* ('Always the Same'), which became increasingly prominent in her portraits and documents. A particularly fine example is a plea roll of the Court of Queen's Bench from Easter 1572. Elizabeth is shown in full magisterial splendour, a crown imperial above her head and the motto emblazoned on her throne's canopy.[5] She also had it engraved on several of her jewels.

The queen's subjects soon realised that complimenting her mother was a sure path to favour. On 23 January 1571, Sir Thomas Gresham, Founder of the Royal Exchange, hosted a banquet for Elizabeth at the Guildhall to commemorate the opening of the Exchange. For this, he commissioned some very fine damask table linen, some of which still survives at London's Gresham College. The design includes a half-length portrait of the queen wearing a French hood. Above her is her mother's crowned falcon carrying a sceptre, surmounted by the royal Tudor arms impaled with those of Anne Boleyn, including her leopard and griffin supporters. The style of Elizabeth's dress suggests that the pattern was based on that from the beginning of her reign – possibly for her coronation in 1559. The table linen is thought to have been woven in the Netherlands and may have been inspired by a set commissioned for Anne Boleyn, who had spent time there as a child.[6] An almost identical set of table linen was owned by the queen herself.[7]

Although at the beginning of her reign, Elizabeth had seemed content not to overturn the annulment of her parents' marriage, now that she felt more established on her throne she made moves to prove the union had been lawful. She was also prompted by Pope Pius V's bull of excommunication against her, issued in February 1570. The bull had revived the question of Elizabeth's legitimacy by calling her 'the pretended Queen of England' and encouraging her Catholic subjects to rise up against her. The timing was significant: Pius was trying to capitalise on the discontent caused by the arrival of Mary, Queen of Scots in England, as well as the rebellion led by Catholic lords in 1569. In December 1572, Archbishop Parker confided to Lord Burghley: 'One time her Majesty secretly told me of a pope's bull, wherein king Henry's marriage with queen Anne was confirmed. She willed me to seek it out.' The document in question was an order issued by Clement VII in 1528 to his legate, Cardinal Campeggio, authorising him to investigate the 'validity or invalidity' of Henry's first marriage. Parker did so 'as secretly and as prudently as I could', but he was unable to find any mention of it. A little under three months later, he was able to report: 'I have now found matter of that bull of the King's marriage.'[8] Anxious to avoid inflaming the religious tensions that threatened to tear her kingdom apart, Elizabeth chose not to publish it but kept it at hand in case of need.

Elizabeth's turbulent past had sharpened her judgement of character. Although she favoured her maternal kin throughout her life, she only promoted those who had earned her trust. Thomas Howard's betrayal had proved that Boleyn blood was no proof of loyalty. The same was true of Lettice Knollys, the daughter of Elizabeth's beloved former favourite, Katherine. The Spanish ambassador, de Silva, described Lettice as the best-looking woman in the court. With her dark eyes, auburn hair and pale skin, she bore a striking resemblance to the queen but was ten years younger, which put her at an advantage. Like Elizabeth, Lettice was vain, demanding and possessive and had inherited the Boleyn arrogance. She treated Elizabeth more as a cousin than a queen and refused to show her the required deference. Although de Silva referred to Lettice as a royal favourite, he was wide of the mark. The two women would probably have clashed earlier had it not been for Lettice's marriage to Walter Devereux, first Earl of Essex, which had taken her away from court in 1560.

Over the next few years, Lettice gave birth to five children in quick succession. She still occasionally attended court and was certainly there in 1565, when heavily pregnant with her son, Robert, because the Spanish ambassador noticed that the queen's great favourite, Robert Dudley, Earl of Leicester, was paying court to her. Elizabeth noticed it too and furiously upbraided Leicester for his disloyalty. It had almost certainly been his intention to make his royal mistress jealous so that she would at last agree to marry him. But what began as a ploy turned into a genuine attraction.

Although Lettice's marriage to the Earl of Essex had produced numerous children, the couple were ill-matched and when he was posted to Ireland in 1573, it presented his wife with an ideal opportunity to pursue her royal cousin's favourite. The fact that her husband's Staffordshire estate lay close to Leicester's home in Warwickshire ensured that they could conduct their affair away from the prying eyes of the court. By 1575, Lettice had become such a regular fixture at Kenilworth that she was invited to the lavish entertainments Leicester staged there for the queen that summer. Elizabeth remained tantalisingly out of reach, but her Boleyn cousin was only too happy to take her place. The following year, Lettice's husband died while in service in Ireland. Deeply embittered against his wife after hearing rumours of her infidelity, he left her virtually penniless. She petitioned Elizabeth for help, but when it became clear this would not be forthcoming, she set her sights on marrying her favourite.

In the summer of 1578, Elizabeth and her court went on a summer progress to East Anglia. The choice of location was partly motivated by politics: Norfolk had been the heartland of support for her half-sister Mary and there was still strong loyalty towards the Catholic Howards. Moreover, Norwich was the second city of the kingdom, with a population of just over 16,000 (admittedly far behind London's 200,000), so it was deserving of a royal visit. But, for the queen, there may have been another, more personal motive. The Boleyns came from Norfolk and her mother had probably been born there. This would be the first time that the forty-four-year-old queen had ever visited the land of her maternal ancestors.

The high point of the progress was a five-day visit to the county town of Norwich. On Saturday 16 August, Elizabeth entered the city through a gate emblazoned with her mother's falcon next to her own royal arms. She then passed through another gate decorated with Anne's 'falcon, with crown and sceptre, which is her own badge', before heading to the magnificent Norman cathedral for a service of thanksgiving.[9] The Erpingham Gate, which led into the cathedral precinct, was freshly painted with the arms of Anne's grandfather, Sir William Boleyn, and her great-grandmother, Lady Anne Boleyn. Inside the cathedral, a luxurious new throne had been made, upon which the queen could enjoy the service. This was placed on the north side of the high altar, opposite the Boleyn chantry chapel and the elaborate tomb of Sir William Boleyn. That evening, as Elizabeth sat enthroned listening to the *Te Deum*, her eyes were surely drawn to panels carved with the proud bulls' heads and gold and azure shields of the Boleyns.

On the last day of her visit to Norwich, the queen knighted five Norfolk gentlemen in the Great Hall of the Bishop's Palace. Two of them were her Boleyn relatives. Edward Clere of Blickling Hall hailed from an old Norfolk family and was related to the queen through their common great-grandfather, Sir William Boleyn. Clere was a great landowner and very wealthy – so much so that he was able to host Elizabeth and her sizeable entourage at his house in Thetford during the progress. Her other kinsman was Raphe Shelton, whose grandmother, a Boleyn of Blickling, was the aunt (and possibly namesake) of Queen Anne. Despite their blood ties, Shelton was a religious conservative and he and his family had enjoyed less favour during Elizabeth's reign than in that of her half-sister Mary. Before leaving the city, the queen received a gift of 'some falcons' from James VI of Scotland – an apt choice (no doubt inspired by his advisers as he was only twelve years old), given she was in her mother's heartland.[10]

The queen encountered another reminder of her Boleyn heritage at Kimberley Tower, a fifteenth-century moated manor house, where her mother and father had stayed in the year of Elizabeth's birth. The owner, Roger Wodehouse, was another grandson of Queen Anne Boleyn's aunt. His mother was Margaret Shelton, the daughter of Sir John Shelton, head of the young Elizabeth's household. It may have been from her that he inherited a richly embroidered silk valance, decorated with the intertwined initials of Henry VIII and Anne Boleyn, together with their personal motifs of acorns and honeysuckles. Given the quality and status of the valance, it might well have been used for the bed that the queen slept in at Kimberley.[11]

As Elizabeth and her court made its stately progress back towards London in September 1578, the Earl of Leicester rode ahead to his house in Wanstead, Essex, the last stopping-off place. In theory, this was to prepare it for the queen's arrival, but Leicester had an altogether different purpose in mind. His affair with Elizabeth's cousin had suddenly changed from a pleasurable diversion to something altogether more serious because Lettice was pregnant. Desperate for an heir, Leicester resolved to make her his wife. They married in secret at Wanstead on 21 September, two days before the queen and her entourage arrived.

Although the marriage quickly became one of the worst-kept secrets at court, the queen only learned of it a year later. According to one account, it was Jean de Simier, a French agent at court, who revealed the truth to her.[12] The result was explosive. Incandescent with rage, the queen vowed to send Leicester to 'rot in the Tower'. Soon afterwards, the earl sent his royal mistress a peace offering. His choice of gift was well judged: a 'fair cup of crystal fashioned like a slipper, garnished with gold, and a cover of gold, enamelled with a white falcon on top'.[13]

Elizabeth might have been prepared to forgive her favourite, but her greatest and most violent fury was directed towards her Boleyn cousin. When Lettice next appeared at court, the queen lashed out at her, boxing her ears and screaming that 'as but one sun lightened the earth, she would have but one Queen in England'.[14] She then banished Lettice from her presence, vowing never to set eyes on her again. Lettice was not the sort of woman to go quietly, though. Proud of her royal blood, she used her enforced distance from court to plan a series of secret marriage alliances for her children that would bring them closer to the throne. The first and most ambitious was a match between her daughter Dorothy and James VI. When this reached the queen's ears, she immediately put a stop to it, declaring that she 'would rather allow the King to take her crown away than see him married to the daughter of such a she-wolf.'[15] She later thwarted Lettice's plans to marry her and Leicester's new son Denbigh to Arbella Stuart, a great-great-granddaughter of Henry VII, who was described as being 'the nearest heir to the throne' after James VI and his mother, Mary, Queen of Scots.[16]

Undeterred, Lettice continued to provoke her royal cousin with some very public displays of magnificence. 'She now demeaned herself like a princess [and] vied in dress with the Queen,' one courtier observed. 'Still she is as proud as ever, rides through Cheapside drawn by 4 milk-white steeds, with four footmen in black velvet jackets, and silver bears on their backs and breasts, two knights and thirty gentlemen before her, and coaches of gentlewomen, pages, and servants behind, so that it might be supposed to be the Queen, or some foreign Prince or other.'[17] The queen's vehement dislike of her Boleyn cousin was so well known that Leicester's enemies used it to their advantage. In February 1586, after sending Leicester to command her troops in the Netherlands, Elizabeth heard that Lettice was preparing to join him 'with such a train of ladies and gentlewomen, and such rich coaches, litters, and side-saddles, as her majesty had none such, and that there should be such a court of ladies, as should far pass her majesty's court here'. This proved a malicious rumour, but it worked the desired effect. 'This information . . . did not a little stir her majesty to extreme colour and dislike,' reported Leicester's agent at court. Elizabeth declared 'with great oaths, that she would have no more courts under her obeisance but her own, and would revoke you from thence with all speed'. Leicester's brother also wrote to warn him that 'her malice is great and unquenchable'.[18]

CHAPTER 14

'*The time will come*'

A LTHOUGH THE QUEEN was plagued by tales of Leicester's new wife, she was busy conducting a courtship of her own. In 1579, negotiations opened for a marriage between Elizabeth and Francis, Duke of Anjou and Alençon. Even though he was more than twenty years her junior, she made much of the duke, nicknaming him her 'frog' and enjoying a close, flirtatious relationship with him during his visits to her court. The last of these was in October 1582, by which time it was obvious to all that the match would come to nothing. Nevertheless, the queen continued to show him every courtesy and arranged luxurious accommodation for him at a house close to Richmond Palace. It was noted that she personally supervised the furnishings of his rooms and quipped that he might recognise the bed.[1] This mischievous remark was a reference to the fact that the bed was the same one that had once formed part of an earlier Duke of Alençon's ransom – and that Elizabeth's mother had given birth to her in almost fifty years earlier.

Anne Boleyn's bed was by no means the only memento that her daughter kept in her palaces. The best source for these is a detailed inventory of Elizabeth's jewels and plate that had been completed in 1574 after four years of painstaking work by her officials. Although Henry VIII had done his best to wipe his scandalous second wife from the face of history, a number of Anne's effects had passed to her daughter. They included a silver-gilt basin and table fountain presented by Anne as a gift to her husband at New Year 1534. Designed by Hans Holbein, it was an extraordinarily beautiful piece, set with diamonds, rubies and pearls. It featured three women with swollen bellies and 'water running out at their breasts' and was emblazoned with Anne's falcon emblem.[2] The gift was perhaps intended by Anne both as a celebration of her proven fertility (it was given at the first New Year after Elizabeth's birth) and a promise of more children to follow. Another survivor from Anne's time was a gilt-bronze clock presented to her by Henry VIII, reputedly on the morning of their secret betrothal ceremony in late 1532. The weights are engraved with 'H' and 'A', true lovers' knots and the couple's mottos: *Dieu et mon droit* and 'The Most Happy'.[3]

Other items associated with her mother that had been recorded in the inventory taken after her father's death in 1547 do not appear in the 1574 inventory. They include a beautiful silver-gilt cup with the Boleyn falcon sitting proudly on top. It was made for Anne in 1535 and must have passed to her daughter at some point because Elizabeth later gifted it to her physician, Richard Master, who had served her from the beginning of her reign. In 1563, he gave it to St John the Baptist Parish Church in Cirencester, where it is still on display. The cup is similar to something that Henry VIII ordered for Anne from the Flemish goldsmith Thomas Trappes, who was paid £90 (equivalent to around £40,000) for a 'bowl of fine gold . . . having Queen Anne's cipher upon the top of the cover'.[4] Henry had had this melted down after Anne's death, and removed or repurposed most of the other gifts and decorations he had commissioned in her honour.

Also missing from the 1574 inventory are two gilded glass cups decorated with the initials 'HA', a gold spoon topped with a crowned falcon, a basin with 'a falcon in the top' and a large quantity of silver emblazoned with the Rochford arms.[5] What happened to them is not clear, but it is possible that they were destroyed or given away during the reigns of Edward, Mary or even Elizabeth herself. However, a number of paintings associated with Anne did survive in the royal collection and would have adorned her daughter's palaces. The most famous of these was Holbein's *The Ambassadors*, which was conceived shortly before Anne's coronation and laden with references to her queenship. One of the ambassadors is resting his arm close to a pillar dial (a device to determine dates by the sun), which indicates 11 April – the precise date when the court was told that Anne would henceforth be accorded royal honours.[6] Holbein's exquisite miniature, *Solomon and the Queen of Sheba*, is also closely connected with Anne and may have been a gift from her to the king. Completed in around 1534, it is littered with references to the break with Rome and Henry's supremacy over the new Church of England. Both these works still survive today.

It is likely that Holbein painted Anne herself, but such a work has not survived – and neither have any other likenesses taken during her lifetime. The best-known portraits of Anne all date from Elizabeth's reign. It is no coincidence that they were painted to show a strong resemblance between mother and daughter. The most famous, which is now in the collection of the National Portrait Gallery, has recently been dated to the 1580s. Anne's dark eyes and slender neck are strikingly similar to her daughter's, as is her pointed chin – a feature that both women inherited from Anne's father, judging by the depiction on his tomb. Eager to win favour, Elizabeth's courtiers filled their long galleries with posthumously created portraits of her mother, which they displayed alongside those of the queen herself.[7]

Elizabeth encountered other reminders of her mother in the extensive libraries of her palaces. In 1578, a new edition of George Cavendish's *The Life and Death of Cardinal Wolsey* was published.

Among the illustrations was one of Henry VIII and Anne Boleyn in which Anne is dressed very much in the style of her daughter, with a high-necked gown, puffed sleeves and Elizabethan head-dress. Her kirtle is embroidered with the honeysuckles that both Anne and her daughter adopted as their emblem. It seems to have been one of Elizabeth's favourite embellishments for her dresses, given its prevalence in the surviving portraits.

Some of Anne's books still survive today and may have passed to her daughter.[8] The oldest is an exquisitely illuminated Book of Hours from the mid-fifteenth century. It was produced in Bruges for an unnamed English client, but when or how it came into Anne's possession is not clear. She inscribed it: *'Le temps viendra/ je Anne Boleyn'* ('The time will come/I Anne Boleyn') beneath a depiction of the Second Coming and the Resurrection of the Dead. Between the words *'je'* and *'Anne'*, she inserted a small drawing of an armillary sphere, which she used as her emblem before rising to prominence.

A similar work, *The Hours of the Blessed Virgin Mary*, may have been acquired by Anne during her years in France and still survives at Hever Castle. Opposite an illustration of the coronation of the Virgin, Anne inscribed it:

Remember me when you do pray,
That hope doth lead from day to day.
Anne Boleyn.

It is thought that Anne carried this book with her to the scaffold on 19 May 1536.[9] Anne's copy of William Tyndale's translation of the New Testament and a French version of the Bible are in the collections of the British Library.[10] The latter is decorated with 'HA' initials and Tudor roses and is decidedly evangelical in tone. It is likely that both books were in the royal library at the time of Elizabeth's accession and, given her interest in reform and her fluency in French, she probably referred to them often.

A number of books produced specifically for Anne also survived into the reign of her daughter. They include several high-quality French illuminated manuscripts, such as her Epistles and Gospels, each decorated with her falcon device. A particularly fine example is the *Ecclesiaste*, a French transcription and commentary of the Old Testament book of Ecclesiastes.[11] It was produced for Anne during her brief tenure as queen and her crowned silver falcon is on the front cover, along with numerous of her initials and emblems inside the book. Among them is an armillary sphere, which later in the sixteenth century was understood to be a symbol of constancy. This is probably why Anne's daughter made extensive use of the sphere in her portraiture throughout her reign and possibly before she came to the throne. Either at the very beginning of her reign or while she was still a princess, Elizabeth wrote a poem in a psalter opposite a drawing of an armillary sphere. In it, she condemned 'the inward suspicious mind' as being worse than any physical deformity. It is tempting to interpret this as a reference to her father.[12]

As well as inheriting books from her mother, Elizabeth also ordered some of those in her own collection to be decorated with Anne's falcon emblem. One that still survives is embossed with the letters 'ER' supported by a falcon and a phoenix. Among the other precious items that Elizabeth kept from her mother's brief reign were the gold- and silver-bedecked state beds. These were still in her possession in the closing years of her reign, when a German visitor marvelled at their splendour during a tour of Windsor Castle.[13]

The most poignant of all the physical reminders that Elizabeth had of her mother was the 'Chequers Ring', named after the prime minister's country residence where it has been kept for centuries.

This locket ring contains two enamelled portraits: one of Elizabeth that is typical of the style painted when she was in her forties, and the other very likely of her mother. The facial features are Anne's, as is the French hood, and she appears very much as she did in the medal that was struck of her in 1535. Only the hair colour has cast doubt on her identity: it is reddish blonde rather than raven-black, which has led to speculation that the sitter was Katherine Parr. Close though she had been to her last stepmother, Elizabeth had made no move to honour Katherine's memory in the years after her death and it is unlikely that she would have chosen to do so at this point in her life. Neither is the theory that the portrait is of the queen herself in her younger days very convincing. As she entered her forties, Elizabeth would hardly have wished to be reminded of the passing years. Moreover, closer examination reveals darker flecks of enamel on the hair, so the rest may have faded over the years. The ring is also typical of the subtle and personal ways in which Elizabeth paid tribute to Anne throughout her life.

On the underside of the bezel is an enamel phoenix arising from a flaming crown. This has led to conjecture that the ring was given to Elizabeth by Edward Seymour, Earl of Hertford, as the phoenix was a symbol of his family. But considering the Seymours had been Anne Boleyn's mortal enemies, there is reason to doubt this. More likely is that the phoenix was intended to symbolise Anne rising from the flames and triumphing through her daughter, Elizabeth. The phoenix was first specifically associated with Anne in Ulpian Fulwell's *The Flower of Fame*, published in 1575, which included two poems reinforcing her legality as queen and inferring that she lived on in Elizabeth. It was an emblem that the latter frequently employed in her portraits, jewellery and decorative devices. One of the strongest associations between the phoenix and Anne can be found in a banner from a book printed during Elizabeth's reign, in which her 'ER' monogram is supported by a phoenix on one side and a white falcon on the other. Among the New Year gifts she received as queen were a number of bejewelled phoenixes from the close favourites who knew her best. The contemporary politician and diplomat, Bartholomew Clerk, opined: 'Anne's advent was a blessing from God as she was the mother of the Phoenix, Elizabeth.'[14]

The ring has clearly been worn – almost certainly by Elizabeth, given that it would have only fitted someone with fingers as slender as hers. There is a story that it was prised from her finger when she died, although this is not recorded in any reliable sources. She did, though, keep it with her until her death. The size of the ring and the intimacy of the symbols it conveys make it likely that it was commissioned by the queen herself or one of her closest favourites as a very personal memento of her late mother.[15] If it was the latter, then the date of the ring might provide a clue as to the giver. It was probably made around 1575, the year of the entertainments that Robert Dudley staged for his royal mistress at Kenilworth in a spectacular, last-ditch attempt to persuade her to marry him. Dudley's intimacy with the queen would have made him privy to her feelings towards her late mother. An exquisitely crafted ring that paid homage to Anne Boleyn would have been the most persuasive gift imaginable.[16]

A later reminder of Anne can be found in a charter that her daughter granted to the people of Ashbourne in Derbyshire in July 1585, for the founding of a grammar school. Elizabeth had issued numerous charters during her long reign, but this one was special. The exquisite decoration may be the work of the celebrated court artist, Nicholas Hilliard. The centrepiece shows Elizabeth enthroned under a canopy of state, holding the orb and sceptre. She is surrounded by royal arms and emblems, trumpeting her pedigree. At the top of the third folio is a magnificent silver falcon wearing an imperial crown, holding a sceptre and nestling on a tree stump. The message was clear: her right to the throne came from her mother, not just her father. The charter cost £28 12 shillings to produce – almost £6,000 today. It was issued at a time when new Catholic plots in favour of Mary, Queen of Scots were gathering momentum; the queen might have preferred not to draw attention to her scandalous past. But by now, her pride in Anne Boleyn would not be silenced.

CHAPTER 15

'A Queen in heaven'

IN THE SUMMER of 1586, Anthony Babington, a Catholic gentleman who had become acquainted with Mary, Queen of Scots through his service to her guardian, the Earl of Shrewsbury, masterminded a plot to assassinate the English queen and place her Scottish cousin on the throne, assisted by Spanish forces. It soon came to the attention of Elizabeth's spymaster, Sir Francis Walsingham. Shrewdly judging that after almost twenty years of imprisonment, Mary was growing desperate, he arranged for a channel of communication to be established between Mary and the conspirators that he could intercept. Before long, he had enough evidence to have the former Scottish queen charged with treason. Babington and his fellow plotters were rounded up and interrogated. Under torture, they confessed the whole plot and confirmed Mary's complicity. She was tried at Fotheringhay Castle in Northamptonshire, found guilty and sentenced to death.

For years, Elizabeth had resisted intense pressure from her councillors to put her royal cousin to death. The 'bosom serpent' had proved an even more dangerous rival during her captivity in England than she had when Queen of Scots: 'I am not so void of judgement as not to see mine own peril,' Elizabeth told her councillors, 'nor yet so ignorant as not to know it were in nature a foolish course to cherish a sword to cut mine own throat.' Still, she flinched from the idea of ordering the execution of a woman she had never met but who had been a thorn in her side for almost thirty years. 'What will they now say that for the safety of her life a maiden Queen could be content to spill the blood even of her own kinswoman?' she demanded.[1]

Elizabeth was well aware that executing an anointed queen would create a dangerous precedent, so her hesitation was understandable. But there was more to it than that. The only other occasion in the long history of the English monarchy when an anointed queen had been executed was fifty years earlier. The victim then had been her own mother, Anne Boleyn. The prospect of ordering the beheading of another queen – one of her own blood – provoked such horror that Elizabeth almost broke down under the strain. There was no reprieve from her councillors, who plagued her daily. In November 1586, while the queen was seeking refuge at her favourite palace of Richmond, a parliamentary delegation arrived to put yet more pressure on her to sign the execution warrant. 'I am so far from it that for mine own life I would not touch her,' she told them. 'I am right sorry [this] is made so hard, yes, so impossible.'[2]

After sending her advisers on their way with this 'answer answerless', Elizabeth was plunged back into private torment. In the midst of it, a letter arrived from Mary herself. Her intention was to remind her English cousin of their close kinship: she made reference to Henry VII, 'your grandfather and mine'. It might also have been a deliberate attempt to stir painful memories of Anne Boleyn's execution. 'When my enemies have slaked their black thirst for my innocent blood, you will permit my poor desolated servants altogether to carry away my corpse, to bury it in holy ground, with the other Queens of France, my predecessors, especially near the late queen, my mother,' Mary wrote, before begging that she might be permitted to send 'a jewel and a last adieu to my son'.[3] That she would be depriving Scotland's

James VI of his mother in the same brutal way that she had lost hers was too much for Elizabeth to bear. Over the next few weeks, she tried everything to avoid it – even sending secret instructions to Mary's keeper, Sir Amyas Paulet, that he might find a covert way to 'shorten the life' of his captive. He refused to make 'a shipwreck of my conscience', which forced his royal mistress to face the inevitable.[4]

The sympathy that Elizabeth felt towards James was shattered when, in late 1586, he drew a direct comparison between the action she was considering and what her father had done to her mother. He instructed his envoy William Keith to tell the English queen: 'King Henry VIII's reputation was never prejudged but in the beheading of his bedfellow.' He had touched a raw nerve. Elizabeth flew into a rage and, as Keith reported, took such 'chafe as ye would wonder'.[5]

As the crisis deepened, it was her maternal relations to whom Elizabeth turned for advice. Anne Boleyn's cousin, Charles Howard, had risen steadily in her daughter's favour during the previous three decades. His loyalty had been proved numerous times, notably during the Catholic rebellion of 1569, when he had served as general of the horse. He had been knighted three years later and raised to the Order of the Garter in 1575 to replace his traitorous cousin, Thomas Howard, fourth Duke of Norfolk. The crowning glory of his achievements had come in 1585, when Elizabeth had appointed him Lord High Admiral.

Howard had become a regular attendee of the privy council during the Babington conspiracy so was well acquainted with his cousin's dilemma. But, unlike her, he was in no doubt as to the remedy. On 1 February 1587, he had a private conference with Elizabeth and urged 'the great danger she continually lived in'. As proof, he cited reports of new Catholic plots and relayed the rumours that Mary had escaped from her captivity at Fotheringhay.

The queen, who had always appreciated Howard's directness, was 'moved by his lordship to have some more regard to the surety of herself and the state than she seemed to take'. His words broke the deadlock. Elizabeth told him to find her secretary, William Davison, and order him to bring Mary's death warrant to her. Howard wasted no time in carrying out her command. He told Davison that their royal mistress was at last 'fully resolved' and urged that he bring the warrant to be signed, 'that it might be forthwith despatched and deferred no longer'.[6]

That night, Elizabeth was tormented by dreams of Mary's execution. She told Davison that she had 'been so greatly moved' in her dream that she had flown into a passion and railed against him for bringing her the warrant to sign.[7] Little wonder that her councillors sent the warrant to Fotheringhay before she could change her mind. A week later, on 8 February 1587, Mary mounted the scaffold that had been erected in the great hall. When her ladies took off her outer gown, it revealed an under-dress of scarlet, the colour of martyrs. Having proclaimed her status as an anointed queen and referred to her cousin as a fellow sovereign, woman and 'sister', she prepared for death. There was to be no Calais swordsman for this execution. When Mary lowered her head onto the block and gave the signal that she was ready, the assembled throng looked on aghast as the executioner 'struck at her neck' with his axe but missed and instead sliced into the side of her face. 'Lord Jesus, receive my soul,' Mary exclaimed, at which the executioner again hacked at her neck. Only with the third blow was Mary's head finally severed. When the axeman stooped to pick it up, it came away in his hands and he was left holding only Mary's wig. Still the macabre farce was not at an end because her little dog then scurried from where he had been hiding under her dress and 'laid itself down betwixt her head and body, and being besmeared with her blood, was caused to be washed, as were other things whereon any blood was'.[8]

It was the stuff of nightmares and, when Elizabeth heard of it, she was horror-struck. 'Her words failed her,' observed Camden. 'She was in a manner astonished.'[9] For the rest of that evening, she remained in a shocked stupor, unable to speak or to move. The next morning, she flew into a 'heat and passion'. She then set about 'casting the burthen generally upon them all' and threatened to send her entire council to the Tower. In large part, this was a blatant attempt by the queen to distance herself from Mary's death so that she might avoid a backlash from Catholic Europe. But the genuine horror that Elizabeth felt at having sent a queen to the same death as her mother would haunt her for the rest of her days.

Although she denied involvement, Elizabeth knew she could not keep Mary's execution a secret. She entrusted the delicate task of sending news of it to James VI to one of her closest Boleyn relatives: Robert Carey, son of her cousin Henry. In her letter, she referred to 'this kinsman of mine' who she assured James would 'instruct you truly of that which is too irksome for my pen to tell you'.[10] Drawing attention to their kinship was perhaps deliberate: just as Robert Carey's family had recovered from Anne Boleyn's fall and were now high in favour, so James might hope for better times after his mother's execution.

The backlash that Elizabeth feared was swift to materialise. Philip II immediately began planning a huge seaborne invasion, supported by aggrieved Catholics in England. Even though he claimed to be seeking vengeance for Mary, it had long been his ambition to take the English crown. In response, the Elizabethan propaganda machine went into overdrive, asserting her right to the throne and calling on all her subjects to show their loyalty. The message reached the most remote parts of the kingdom. The inhabitants of Tivetshall, a small village in rural Norfolk, expressed their support for the queen by commissioning a huge painted screen in St Margaret's Church, which still survives today. The royal arms are flanked by the queen's initials, with the words: 'O God save our Quene Elizabeth' emblazoned beneath. Directly below them, the white falcon of her mother is proudly displayed. This was Boleyn country and the villagers were eager to remind their sovereign of that.

In May 1588, Philip's mighty Armada set sail from Spain. Not for more than five hundred years had England faced such a potent risk of invasion. Rumours that the Spanish fleet would be bolstered by ships from France and the Netherlands threw the privy council into alarm. But the queen herself had a strong aversion to war and was slow to act. Again, her Howard cousin persuaded her. As Lord High Admiral, he was in command of the English navy and well placed to judge the urgent action that was needed. It is a sign of their closeness that he employed language that few other of her advisers would have dared to use: 'For the love of Jesus Christ, Madam, awake thoroughly, and see the villainous treasons round about you, against your Majesty and your realm, and draw your forces round about you, like a mighty prince, to defend you.'[11]

Thanks to Howard's efforts and those of his navy – not to mention the favourable intervention of the weather – by early August 1588 the Armada had been all but vanquished. It was one of the most celebrated victories in England's history and, ever mistress of public relations, Elizabeth was quick to make the most of it. She commissioned an array of celebratory portraits and medals, and delivered a famous speech to her troops at Tilbury, by which time the danger had passed. But she was a good deal slower to pay the wages of the men who had secured the victory for her. By late August her navy was ridden with sickness and desperately short of victuals. Howard begged: 'I had rather open the Queen's Majesty's purse something to relieve them.'[12] This time, though, his words fell on deaf ears.

The darker side of the Armada victory has largely been obscured by the dazzling image of its heroine: Gloriana, God's anointed Virgin Queen. And yet, at the time there were a number of dissenting voices. The scandal of Mary, Queen of Scots' execution was slow to subside, and in the years that followed, rumours began to circulate about her English nemesis. The hostile Catholic writer Nicholas Sander, whose most influential book was published two years before Mary's death, was responsible for one of the most popular: that Anne Boleyn had been Henry VIII's daughter as well as his wife, the result of his clandestine affair with her mother. The old rumours about Elizabeth's parentage were also revived and the Scottish author Adam Blackwood not only corroborated Sander's tale but declared that she was the incestuous daughter of Anne Boleyn by her brother George. He concluded: 'You cannot, Elizabeth, as you wish, maintain an honest life, unless you seek to differ from the race of your mother, who was the shame of her mother and whore of her father, and who was the horrible lover of her own brother.' Cardinal William Allen took up the theme and declared Anne 'an infamous courtesan' whose relationship with Henry VIII – Elizabeth's 'supposed father' – was 'incestuous copulation'.[13] Such tales had no basis in truth, but they were still damaging to the reputation of a queen who had never quite erased the stain of her mother's past.

A little over three weeks after the defeat of the Armada, Elizabeth lost the man who had been her closest favourite and confidant for almost fifty years. Robert Dudley, Earl of Leicester, had served her faithfully – in affairs of government, if not those of the heart – since the beginning of the reign and played a pivotal role in the campaign against the Armada. As soon as the threat had receded, he travelled north to Buxton in Derbyshire to take the healing spring waters. The fifty-six-year-old courtier had been suffering from poor health for some time, although the cause is unclear and has been variously ascribed to malaria and stomach cancer. Nevertheless, his end – when it came – was sudden. The earl only made it as far as Oxfordshire and rested at Rycote, the home of Henry and Margery Norris, where he and the queen had spent many happy times. It was from there ('your old lodging at Rycot') that he wrote to her for the last time. The letter was brief: he thanked the queen for some medicine that she had sent him and stressed that her own health was 'the chiefest thing in the world I do pray for'. He ended: 'I humbly kiss your foot' and signed it 'Your most faithful and obedient servant'. Leicester died on 4 September. The grief-stricken queen kept the note, which she inscribed 'his last lettar', in a locked casket among her most treasured possessions until her own death in 1603.[14]

If Leicester's death had stirred affectionate memories of a place connected with Elizabeth's mother, this was not enough to make her look more kindly upon his widow, her maternal kin. The earl had made Lettice an executor of his fortune, which soon proved more a burden than a privilege. In the years that followed, she was beset by a series of costly legal battles over her late husband's estates. As executor, the countess was also obliged to ensure that Leicester's debts were settled. These were substantial, totalling some £50,000 (equivalent to around £8.5 million today), of which £25,000 was owed to the crown. When Lettice petitioned the queen to release her from these debts, Elizabeth seized her chance for revenge by ordering a detailed examination of Leicester's estates so that she could recover every penny that was owed to her. During the months that followed, she pursued her old rival relentlessly, forcing Lettice to sacrifice a large part of her jointure, including Leicester House, as well as a number of her jewels, in order to settle the debt.[15]

Throughout these troubled later years of Elizabeth's reign, her Boleyn relatives continued to dominate both her private and public worlds. By 1589, her cousin Katherine Howard (née Carey) had become the senior gentlewoman of the privy chamber, although her authority over its other members had already been noted by the Spanish ambassador ten years earlier. As other favourites died off, Katherine and her family became ever more entrenched at the heart of the court. Katherine's younger sister Philadelphia, Lady Scrope, was appointed a lady of the bedchamber, as were two of her daughters. One of these was named after the queen, who was her godmother, and in later years her daughter (another Elizabeth) also joined her service. Katherine's father, husband and brother all served as Lord Chamberlain. Her loyalty to her royal cousin is demonstrated by the fact that, in contrast to other influential members of court, she never exploited her position for financial gain and was not an active broker of patronage.

From the beginning of the 1590s, loss became a dominant theme in Elizabeth's life. The decade began with the death of the queen's beloved old nursemaid and attendant, Blanche Parry. She had barely left the queen's side since Anne Boleyn had chosen her to attend her daughter in 1533, when Elizabeth was just a baby. Her unflinching loyalty and dedicated service to 'my dear Sovereign lady and mistress' had become the benchmark against which all of the queen's other ladies were measured – and few could match it. Throughout Elizabeth's life, Blanche had been a rare and vital source of constancy and stability, helping her to weather the storms of disgrace, abandonment, imprisonment, betrayal and treason.

Blanche had also provided a precious link with the past. By the 1580s, she was one of the only people in the queen's life who could remember her mother and who had shared Elizabeth's private reminiscences of her childhood. Tradition has it that the queen was with her old nursemaid when she died on 12 February 1590 and was in 'great sorrow'.[16] Although Blanche had not held any titles, Elizabeth ordered that she be given a funeral befitting a baroness. It was held at St Margaret's Church, Westminster, where a beautiful marble effigy was later erected.

In September 1592, the queen's retired Champion (a prestigious office with responsibility for Accession Day tilts), Sir Henry Lee, organised an elaborate entertainment for his royal mistress close to his house at Ditchley in Oxfordshire. As part of this, he commissioned the famous Ditchley Portrait, a magnificent full-length study of Elizabeth, bedecked in a sumptuous white gown and standing on a map of the world. Storms rage behind her while the sun shines before her, which may be an allusion to Lee's recent disgrace for his affair with one of the queen's ladies – although it is also a fitting representation of Elizabeth's turbulent life before becoming queen. Close to her left ear, she wears a jewel in the form of an armillary sphere – the earliest known symbol used by her mother. Lee perhaps ordered that this be included as a means of securing his forgiveness. He displayed the same symbol on his sleeves when sitting for an earlier portrait.[17]

Elizabeth also had reminders of Anne during her private hours. Like her mother, she took great delight in music. She had an excellent singing voice and a natural aptitude for dancing. Even well into her sixties, she was still performing highly energetic dances such as the volta. Elizabeth also inherited Anne's skill at the lute and virginals (an early keyboard) and liked to play music 'when she was solitary to shun melancholy'.[18] The virginals was one of her favourite instruments. A beautifully gilded and decorated set still survives. Directly above the keyboard is Anne's crowned falcon with the royal coat of arms nearby. It has been suggested that the instrument originally belonged to Anne and was inherited by her daughter.[19] If that was the case, then perhaps

Elizabeth had the virginals repaired or redecorated later in her reign, since they bear the date 1594.

It is possible that in these, the later years of her life, Elizabeth commissioned a biography of her mother. Its author was George Wyatt. His grandfather, the courtier-poet Sir Thomas Wyatt, had made little secret of his admiration for Anne Boleyn: indeed, it had landed him a spell in the Tower, along with her other suspected lovers, and he had only been saved by his close association with Thomas Cromwell. After leading a rebellion against Queen Mary, Thomas's son and namesake had been executed. As a convicted traitor, his title and lands had been forfeit to the crown, including the family home, Allington Castle. But these had been restored to the Wyatts by Elizabeth when she became queen. The traitor's son and heir, George, who was born a few days before the rebellion, inherited his family's literary tradition, although none of his writings were published.

During the later years of Elizabeth's reign, possibly in response to the vicious calumny put about by hostile Catholic writers such as Nicholas Sander, George Wyatt began work on a biography of Anne and would devote the entire latter part of his life to it (he died in 1624). He was well placed to write it, having 'gathered many notes touching this lady' from members of his family, as well as some of Anne's closest female associates.[20] Wyatt more than hinted that Elizabeth had commissioned it. He wrote that he had been 'entreated by *some who might command me* [Wyatt's italics] to further this endeavour' and that the biography had been undertaken 'at the request of him that hath been by authority set on work in this so important business . . . for the singular gifts of God in him of learning, wisdom, integrity and virtue'. It is possible that Wyatt was referring to the queen in the masculine gender, as Elizabeth herself did on numerous occasions. But it has also been conjectured that he was referring to

Henry Carey, who, as her closest kin, had a vested interest in rehabilitating the Boleyns. Wyatt had also been encouraged by John Whitgift, then Archbishop of Canterbury, who had become a close friend of the queen since his appointment in 1583 and would attend her on her deathbed. In addition to his biography, Wyatt also included Anne Boleyn in his 'History of the English Reformation', hailing her as 'Elect of God', and may have been responsible for a vindication of her relations with his grandfather.[21] Perhaps it was only towards the end of her life that Elizabeth felt able to set the record straight about her mother through her support of Wyatt's writings.

Another writer who leapt to the defence of the queen's mother in the latter part of Elizabeth's reign was the philosopher and statesman, Francis Bacon. His play, *The Tragedy of Anne Boleyn*, which he described as 'an incense to her sweet memory', left the audience in no doubt as to where his sympathies lay. But he judged it prudent to write the more controversial aspects in code, such as Henry VIII's disappointment in Elizabeth's sex, the fickle nature that led him to having Anne condemned, the injustice of her trial and her cruel death.[22] These parts would only be deciphered centuries later. While the queen welcomed any defence of her 'dearest mother', she would not sanction any criticism of her father. Even though he wrote it years after Elizabeth's death, William Shakespeare was careful to avoid any such controversy in his play, *Henry VIII*, and focused instead on Henry's love for Anne Boleyn and her many virtues. He did, though, include a thinly veiled criticism of the king's first marriage in his most famous play, *Hamlet*, written between 1599 and 1601, in which the villain marries his late brother's widow.

Elizabeth herself may have penned a tacit reference to her legitimacy in a translation of the Roman philosopher Boethius's most famous work, *De Consolatione Philosophiae* (*The Consolation of Philosophy*), in 1593. Boethius wrote it while imprisoned for treason and awaiting execution. This inspired the theme of his text, which reflected on the fact that evil could still exist in a world governed by God, and that true virtue comes from within. It was a theme that resonated with the queen and her late mother, both of whom had been blighted by false accusations. One of the most telling lines of Elizabeth's translation is:

> If your first spring and author,
> God you view,
> No man bastard be.[23]

Even now, aged sixty and in the thirty-fifth year of her reign, Elizabeth still felt the need to assert her legitimacy. Five years later, she embarked upon a translation of Plutarch's warning against being too curious about familial origins. She may have had in mind the slanders that her Catholic adversaries were spreading about her incestuous beginnings when she wrote the line: 'Compelled to hear, yet hear I must.'[24]

In July 1596, Elizabeth lost one of her closest Boleyn relatives: Henry Carey, Baron Hunsdon. He had continued to enjoy his royal cousin's bounty during almost forty years of service, and since 1577 he had been at the centre of power as a privy councillor. Even on his deathbed, the queen offered to create him Earl of Wiltshire, the title of his uncle and her grandfather, Thomas Boleyn. His refusal was typical of the frank, plain-speaking style that had made him one of Elizabeth's most trusted advisers: 'Madam, as you did not count me worthy of this honour in life, then I shall account myself not worthy of it in death.' Elizabeth paid for his funeral in Westminster Abbey, where his sister Katherine lay buried. To honour his memory, the queen granted many of Henry's lands and offices to his eldest son, Sir George

Carey, who had already risen to the positions of Lord Chamberlain and captain of the gentlemen pensioners.

As the 1590s progressed, Elizabeth lost other treasured links to her mother. In 1599, Henry Norris's wife Margery died, grief-stricken after five of her six sons had died in military service to the queen. Two years earlier, Elizabeth had written to console her 'Old Crow' upon the death of her third son John in Ireland. 'Harm not yourself for bootless help,' she had urged, 'but show a good example to comfort your dolorous yoke-fellow [husband]. Nature can have stirred no more dolorous affection in you as a Mother for a dear Son, than a gratefulness and memory of his service past, hath wrought in Us his Sovereign.'[25] On Margery's death, there was a court of wards inquiry into her property and the queen personally intervened to write off £2,000 of Margery's debt to relieve her widower Henry. He followed his wife to the grave eighteen months later. A lavish monument was erected in his honour and that of his wife and their six sons at Westminster Abbey.[26]

The queen's grief at the loss of those who had been connected with her mother did not soften her attitude towards one Boleyn relative, however. She was still deeply embittered against Lettice Knollys. But in 1598, Lettice's son by her first marriage, Robert Devereux, Earl of Essex, who had become a close favourite of the queen, persuaded Elizabeth to 'hearken to terms of pacification'.[27] A meeting was arranged on 1 March at the home of a mutual acquaintance. Motivated more by eagerness to return to court than a genuine desire to be reconciled with her royal cousin, Lettice brought 'a fair jewel of £300' to present to her royal mistress. But at the last minute, Elizabeth pulled out. A furious Essex went immediately to demand an explanation but, for once, found his way to the privy chamber barred. Eventually, the queen invited Lettice to court and everyone watched with bated breath as the two women embraced. It was brief, perfunctory and entirely insincere. When Lettice, who was 'very contented' by the encounter, tried to push home her advantage by expressing a wish to repeat it, her request was summarily dismissed. Within days, Elizabeth was referring to the countess with 'some wonted unkind words', and made it clear that she would never again grant her an audience.[28]

The following year, Elizabeth made her first visit to Penshurst Place in Kent, the magnificent former home of the dukes of Buckingham. Her mother's childhood home, Hever Castle, lay just four miles away, so it is likely that she visited there too. After Anne of Cleves' death, Hever had passed to the Waldegrave family, whose staunch Catholicism had landed them in trouble during the reigns of Edward and Elizabeth. This has been used to explain the fact that there is no record of Elizabeth visiting Hever as queen, but recent research by the curator there has revealed that the Waldegraves never actually lived in the castle and that it was rented out. This makes the prospect that Elizabeth did walk in her mother's footsteps all the more tantalising. Such a scene was later imagined in a watercolour painting by Walter Henry Sweet.[29] The queen made several more visits to Penshurst during the next three years.

Elizabeth's visit to Kent had provided a welcome distraction from the cares of state. The same year, the Earl of Essex disgraced himself by defying her orders while serving in Ireland. When he returned to England without permission, he was placed under house arrest at York House. In vain, his mother sent messages to Elizabeth, begging for an audience so that she might plead her son's case. She even sent a 'most curious fine gown' worth £100. Having failed to work any positive effect on the queen, Lettice made the situation worse by moving to a house that overlooked Essex's prison so that she might catch a glimpse of her precious son. When Elizabeth heard that mother and son had 'saluted each other out of a window', she was incensed.[30]

Although Essex was eventually released and regained some of the queen's former affection, he soon realised that his enemies had made the most of his absence and that both his income and influence at court had been greatly diminished. The following year, he staged a reckless and hopelessly disorganised rebellion. Among its participants was his stepfather Sir Christopher Blount, a low-ranking soldier whom his mother Lettice had married just six months after the Earl of Leicester's death. He and Essex's other followers were no match for the royal forces and their uprising was swiftly crushed. It is doubtful that Essex had ever intended Elizabeth's overthrow, merely a full return to her favour, but his rivals were swift to capitalise on his foolhardy protest. Both Essex and his stepfather were convicted of high treason and sentenced to death. By now, Lettice had come to realise that if she petitioned her royal cousin, it was more likely to harm than help the cause of her husband and son. She could only hope that the latter's former favour with the queen would be enough to spare his life. But there was no reprieve. On 25 February 1601, Essex and Blount were beheaded. Elizabeth's only concession was that her disgraced favourite should be afforded the privilege of a private execution within the walls of the Tower, close to where her mother had been put to death. The same courtesy was not extended to Lettice's husband.

Elizabeth might have triumphed over her old rival, but it was an empty victory. She had robbed Lettice of a cherished son but in so doing had lost her last great favourite, the man who had helped recapture the glories of her youth, when she had bewitched a court filled with eager suitors. His betrayal left her reclusive and fearful. 'These troubles waste her much', reported Sir John Harington. 'She walks much in her privy chamber . . . the dangers are over,

and yet she always keeps a sword by her table.'[31] According to
another account, not long after Essex's death, the queen called
for a looking glass for the first time in twenty years and, upon
seeing her face 'lean and full of wrinkles', she 'fell presently into
exclaiming against those which had so much commended her,
and took it so offensively, that some which before had flattered
her, durst not come into her sight'.[32]

One of the last paintings of Elizabeth was the celebrated
Rainbow Portrait, which may have been commissioned by Sir
Robert Cecil for her visit to his home in December 1602.[33] Even
though she was then approaching seventy years of age, the queen
appears as youthful and radiant as ever. The painting is laden
with symbolism, some of which relates to her mother. The
bodice of her dress is embroidered with spring flowers – including
honeysuckle. Her left sleeve is decorated with a large serpent
(a symbol of wisdom) from whose mouth hangs a heart. Just
above its head is an armillary sphere. The portrait was a last,
glorious assertion of Elizabeth's queenship – and, more subtly,
of the loyalty to her late mother that had endured throughout
her long life.

Elizabeth had been physically robust for most of her life, taking
brisk early-morning walks in the gardens of her palaces, eating
only sparingly and out-dancing her ladies even when she was well
into her sixties. But now her health began to falter. She barely
stirred out of doors and was reported to be 'extreme oppressed'
with a deep melancholy. As ever, she turned to her Boleyn relatives
for comfort. Robert Carey tried to lift her spirits by telling her
that she appeared in perfect health. 'No, Robin, I am not well,'
she replied, before confiding 'that her heart had been sad and
heavy for ten or twelve days, and in her discourse she fetched not
so few as forty or fifty great sighs'. In vain, Carey tried to cheer
her: 'I used the best words I could to persuade her from this

melancholy humour, but I found by her it was too deep rooted in her heart, and hardly to be removed.'[34]

By the beginning of 1603, it was obvious to those closest to the queen that she did not have long to live. In January, she moved from Whitehall to Richmond Palace, her 'warm box', to which she could 'best trust her sickly old age'.[35] One hundred and thirty miles away, her troublesome relative, George Boleyn, was also facing his end. On 12 January, he drew up a will in which he named the queen among his executors. In typically choleric style, he explained that this was because 'her majesty gave me all that ever I have and [her] subjects gave me nothing and therefore know no cause wherefore I should be beholden to any of them'. Neither did he make any individual bequests but he left all his movable goods to be distributed among his servants.[36] By 25 January, the embittered and resentful Boleyn was dead. He was buried in Lichfield Cathedral, where he had served for the previous twenty-six years.

As she had throughout her life, Elizabeth kept her maternal kin close as death approached. Among them was Philadelphia Scrope, daughter of Henry and Katherine Carey, who had served as lady of the bedchamber for the previous ten years. Elizabeth Southwell, the young granddaughter of Charles and Katherine Howard (now Earl and Countess of Nottingham), was also in attendance and later wrote an account of the queen's final days. Katherine herself was not there because by now she, too, was at the end of her life. When news reached Elizabeth that her faithful servant had died at the Howard family's London residence, Arundel House, on 25 February, her grief spiralled to irreversible depths and was stronger even than that showed by Katherine's widower, Charles. 'The Queen loved the Countess well, and hath much lamented her death, remaining ever since in deep melancholy that she must die herself, and complains much of many infirmities wherewith she seems suddenly to be overtaken,' reported one eyewitness. Neglectful of her own health, Elizabeth 'rests ill at nights, forbears to use the air in the day, and abstains more than usual from her meat, resisting physic, and is suspicious of some about her as ill-affected'. Giovanni Scaramelli, the Venetian envoy to England, agreed: 'The Queen for many days has not left her chamber . . . they say that the reason for this is her sorrow for the death of the Countess.'[37]

Memories of another death now returned as Elizabeth's mind wandered ever further back over her life. The familiar guilt over Mary, Queen of Scots' execution made her cry out in torment. Robert Carey described how she 'shed many tears and sighs, manifesting her innocence that she never gave consent to the death of that Queen'.[38] Thenceforth, Elizabeth lost any desire to go on living. She refused to eat, take any medicine or go to bed,' but fell into an almost trance-like state, 'holding her finger almost continually in her mouth, with her eyes open and fixed upon the ground, where she sat on cushions without rising or resting herself, and was greatly emaciated by her long watching and fasting'. Ever mistress of her own fate, it seems that she had simply decided to die. 'The Queen grew worse, because she would be so, none about her being able to persuade her to go to bed,' reported her exasperated cousin, Robert Carey. Another visitor to Richmond concurred: 'It seems she might have lived if she would have used meanes; but she would not be persuaded, and princes must not be forced.'[39]

At length, the queen's recently widowed cousin, Charles Howard, was sent for. He had remained one of Elizabeth's most trusted advisers since his pivotal role in defeating the Armada of 1588 and had helped to repel several other invasion attempts – as well as the Essex rebellion in 1601. The queen's anxious attendants rightly judged that Howard would succeed where others had failed. Shortly after coming into Elizabeth's presence, he persuaded her to go to bed.

But there was still an urgent matter that needed to be dealt with before the queen could slip into welcome oblivion. Although she had made a dazzling virtue of her virginity, securing the love of her people and a place in history by creating an iconic image for herself as the Virgin Queen, it had come at a price. For several years now, the court and council had been able to talk of little else but who would take the throne after Elizabeth's death, as Camden observed: 'The question of the succession every day rudely sounded in their ears.'[40] The most likely candidate was the queen's closest blood relative, James VI of Scotland. He was the great-great-grandson of Elizabeth's grandfather, Henry VII, and had succeeded to the Scottish throne at just thirteen months old, upon the enforced abdication of his mother, Mary, Queen of Scots. Now aged thirty-six, he was a committed Protestant, which in Elizabeth's eyes was some compensation for his being the son of the woman who had plagued her for almost thirty years.

Aware that as soon as she named her successor, all eyes would turn to them and she herself would be all but forgotten, Elizabeth had steadfastly refused to settle the matter. But as time wore on and it had become increasingly obvious that James would succeed, she had felt her influence begin to slip away. 'The court was very much neglected, and in effect the people were generally weary of an old woman's government,' a contemporary noted. 'They adored him [James] as the sun rising, and neglected her as now ready to set.'[41] Even Elizabeth's close kin now had an eye to the future, not the past. After seeing the queen so ill, Robert Carey wrote to tell the King of Scots that the crown of England would soon be his and vowed: 'I would be the first man that should bring him news of it.'[42]

To avoid the turbulence of a contested succession or even civil war, it was imperative that Elizabeth formally name her heir before she breathed her last. With her life slipping rapidly away, her anxious councillors gathered around the queen's bed to press the matter upon her once more. For the last time, it was her Boleyn cousin, Charles Howard, who succeeded where others had failed. Answering his plea, the queen replied that it should be 'our cousin of Scotland'.[43]

Her final duty discharged, the queen signalled that the Archbishop of Canterbury, John Whitgift, should attend her. He knelt by her side and 'continued long in prayer, 'till the old man's knees were weary'. But when he made to rise and depart, Elizabeth made a sign with her hand. Philadelphia, Lady Scrope, who understood her royal cousin better than most, told Whitgift that the queen desired him to continue. He duly sank back to his knees and prayed for another half an hour.

On 24 March, between two and three o'clock in the morning, Elizabeth 'departed this life, mildly, like a lamb, easily like a ripe apple from the tree'.[44] Her Boleyn relatives eased the passing from one reign – one dynasty – to the next. According to tradition, Lady Scrope opened the window of the bedchamber and dropped a sapphire ring to her brother, Robert Carey, who was waiting below.[45] The ring had been given to her by James VI, who had instructed her to send it to him as a sign that the Tudor queen was dead and that he was the first Stuart king of England. As Carey reflected, with his 'near kinswoman' dead: 'Now was I to begin a new world.'[46]

Elizabeth's story had started with the Boleyns and it ended with them too.

EPILOGUE

'Surprised her sex'

O N THE DAY of Anne Boleyn's death, Archbishop Cranmer had declared: 'She who has been the Queen of England upon earth will to-day become a Queen in heaven.' The same sentiment was repeated in an elegy to her daughter sixty-six years later: 'She who was on earth a Goddess, a Virgin and a Royal maiden is now in heaven Royal, A Virgin and a Goddess.'[1] Both women had evoked the Virgin Mary in the imagery of their queenship. Now, in death, they were immortalised by that same image.

The Boleyn coat of arms was proudly displayed throughout Elizabeth's funeral procession. Later, Anne's falcon badge was added to her daughter's magnificent tomb in Westminster Abbey. To the very end, Elizabeth had honoured her mother's scaffold plea to 'meddle' in her cause – and, as always, had 'judged the best'. It is interesting to speculate whether, if Elizabeth had never come to the throne, Anne's rehabilitation would ever have been attempted. Perhaps Anne would have had to wait for modern scholarship, with its emphasis on reimagining history's villains (witness Richard III and Thomas Cromwell), to set the record straight.

One of the most celebrated screen portrayals of Anne Boleyn is *Anne of the Thousand Days* (1969), starring Richard Burton as Henry VIII and Geneviève Bujold as his ill-fated second wife. In a particularly memorable scene, as the heroine faces death, she declares to her estranged husband: 'Elizabeth shall be a greater queen than any king of yours! She shall rule a greater England than you could ever have built! Yes – MY Elizabeth SHALL BE QUEEN! And my blood will have been well spent!'[2] The scene is pure fiction: Anne did not see Henry again after her arrest and even a woman of her shrewdness and ambition could not have predicted that her daughter – now illegitimate – would ever inherit the throne of England.

But if Anne had survived to see her daughter crowned queen, she would have gloried in her success: in seeing Elizabeth bring to fruition the plans that she herself had conceived. Anne's relationship with Henry had sparked a revolution in England's religious life, ushering in the Reformation, the break with Rome and the establishment of a new Church of England, over which the monarch reigned supreme. Her commitment to reform had been for more than just personal gain, however, and the same religious ideas that she promoted had been taken forward by her daughter, who firmly – and permanently – established Protestantism as the official religion of the kingdom. It is still written into the royal succession that the crown can only be inherited by a Protestant.[3]

The turbulence and uncertainty that Elizabeth had endured after her mother's execution had taught her the wisdom of pragmatism and compromise. These traits, more than any other, had enabled her to resolve the deep divisions created by her father's reformation and exacerbated by the reigns of her siblings. In so doing, she had established greater peace and stability than England had enjoyed since the advent of the Tudor dynasty. With peace came prosperity and the emergence of England as a world power, epitomised by the exploits of Elizabeth's adventurers, the flourishing of trade and the vanquishing of her overseas rivals – notably

Philip II and his Armada. It might not have been the untarnished 'Golden Age' that Elizabethan propaganda and later, rose-tinted histories claimed, but it was still an impressive achievement for a woman whom most of Catholic Europe had dismissed as 'the illegitimate child of . . . a public strumpet'.[4]

Elizabeth's sex had been problematic for her, disastrous for her father and had sealed her mother's doom. It is ironic, then, that it had ultimately proved her greatest triumph. She had ascended the throne at a time when it was widely considered 'monstrous' that a woman should 'bear rule'. But by the end of her long reign, England had fallen in love with queens. Elizabeth's first biographer, William Camden, claimed that she had 'surprised her sex'.[5] The implication was that she had triumphed in spite of being a woman, when in fact she triumphed because of it. She had wielded her feminine traits to brilliant effect in order to deftly control a court filled with ambitious and power-hungry men. In this, she had been very much her mother's daughter: for a time, Anne had kept a king and his court in thrall in just the same way. But her daughter had learned from her example and avoided the pitfalls of marriage and childbirth, making a glorious virtue of her virgin state and becoming a legend in her own lifetime. She had defied convention – just as Anne had broken the mould of a meek and compliant queen consort. Elizabeth had been the living embodiment of her mother's legacy and, as queen, she had constantly striven to avenge Anne's death – and, more positively, to celebrate her achievements.

The cheers that greeted James VI as he made his way south to claim the English throne soon petered out when his new subjects realised what an inadequate replacement he was. It was clear that the only trait he shared with his illustrious predecessor was that he had barely known his mother – who, like Anne Boleyn, had suffered a violent end. The scornful Venetian ambassador echoed the general opinion when he complained that the new king lacked the 'great majesty' and 'solemnities' of his Tudor predecessor.[6] His accession heralded the prospect of uniting England and Scotland for the first time in their history, but his efforts towards this were roundly rejected and it would be more than a hundred years before the Act of Union was finally passed. In the dying days of her reign, Elizabeth's courtiers had neglected her in their eagerness to pay court to her successor; now they longed for the days of 'Good Queen Bess' to return. She had proved that a 'weak and feeble woman' could rule just as effectively as a man – if not more so. Little wonder that when, later that century, the so-called 'Glorious Revolution' gave Britain its first joint monarchs, it was Mary who was welcomed with far greater enthusiasm than her husband William. The same popularity was enjoyed by Mary's sister and successor Anne and exceeded by that of Victoria and Elizabeth II, all of whom had cause to be grateful to this Tudor trailblazer.

By resolving to remain a Virgin Queen, Elizabeth I had brought her father's dynasty to an end. But her mother's bloodline would endure. Elizabeth II was a direct descendant of Anne Boleyn's sister Mary, and her grandson William, Prince of Wales (who is first in line to the throne) is descended from Mary on both his father's side and that of his mother, the late Diana, Princess of Wales. It seems that in the story of the Boleyns and the British monarchy, there are a few more chapters yet to be written.

ACKNOWLEDGEMENTS

On the scaffold, Anne Boleyn invited anyone who might 'meddle' in her cause to 'judge the best'. Nobody has done more so than the two people to whom this book is dedicated. Owen Emmerson, Historian and Assistant Curator at Hever Castle, and James Peacock, Founder and Manager of the Anne Boleyn Society and Palace Host at Hampton Court, have been unfailingly generous in sharing their extensive knowledge and insights of Anne and I will be forever in their debt. I am also extremely grateful to Owen for granting me permission to include the beautiful watercolour of an imagined visit by Elizabeth I to her mother's childhood home which he recently acquired on behalf of Hever Castle. I would also like to thank Owen's colleague Kate McCaffrey, for her fascinating research into Anne's book of hours. Owen and Kate's joint publication, *Becoming Anne*, was an invaluable source for my research, as was *The Boleyns of Hever*, which Owen co-authored with Claire Ridgway of TheAnneBoleynFiles.com, ElizabethIFiles and The Tudor Society.

As ever, I owe a huge debt of gratitude to Alison Weir. This book was her inspiration. The idea for it may have originated with a series of joint events we did after the publication of Alison's seminal book, *The Lady in the Tower*, and my *Elizabeth's Women* back in 2009. Provocatively entitled 'The Whore and the Virgin', the events enabled us to explore these two extraordinary women's interweaving stories, the profound impact that Anne had on her daughter and that both had on the history of England. I don't think either of us will forget being introduced as 'The Whore and the Virgin' by one event host. It brought the house down.

Despite *Anne Boleyn & Elizabeth I* being the fourteenth book that my wonderful agent, Julian Alexander, has steered me through, his commitment, support and wisdom have never wavered and I will never be able to thank him enough. It has also been a delight to work with Julian's new assistant, Sarah Stamp, whose enthusiasm and efficiency have made my life so much easier. I have been extremely fortunate to have the support and expertise of the incomparable teams at Hodder & Stoughton in the UK and Grove Atlantic in the USA. Huge thanks go to my editors, Rupert Lancaster and George Gibson, for helping to shape the book and for championing it so enthusiastically. I would also like to thank the Assistant Editors, Ciara Mongey and Emily Burns for their exceptional eye for detail, their patience and helpfulness. Juliet Brightmore has, as ever, unearthed some wonderful pictures to bring the text to life. It has been a great reassurance to have the impeccable work of Nick Fawcett as copy editor, Jacqui Lewis as proof reader and Geraldine Beare, who compiled the index. My thanks are also due to Rebecca Mundy, Alice Morley and Kaitlin Astrella, whose creativity and energy have promoted my work on both sides of the Atlantic.

I am extremely grateful to Paul Fitzsimmons, an expert in Tudor antiques, for his wonderful discoveries – in particular Anne's carved oak falcon, the leopard head and the exquisite chair that may have been made for her in the French court. It is thanks to the historian and Anne Boleyn expert, Sandi Vasoli, that I was introduced to Paul and his extensive collection. I am also indebted to Sandi for her joint presentation with James Peacock on Anne and Elizabeth, and for her book about the letter which may have been written by Anne during her imprisonment in the Tower of London.

Among the many other experts whose work has been invaluable, I would like to pay particular thanks to my friends and fellow historians Nicola Tallis and Sarah Gristwood, as well as to Charlotte Bolland, Senior Curator, Research and 16th Century Collections, at the National Portrait Gallery, for her advice on the Elizabeth I 'serpent' portrait, and JoAnn DellaNeva for sending me her excellent and scholarly work on Lancelot de Carle's poem about Anne Boleyn's fall. I am very fortunate to have such knowledgeable colleagues at Historic Royal Palaces. My thanks go to Sebastian Edwards, Deputy Chief Curator, for sharing his research on Anne's recently-discovered falcon, a tapestry made in her honour and her extensive collection of books. I am also indebted to Dr Alden Gregory for his fascinating article, published in *Tudor Places*, on Anne's apartments in the Tower. Although I discovered his research after my book had been completed, I would like to thank Jack Beesley, whose BA dissertation on Anne Boleyn's memory in the reign of Elizabeth I forms the basis of a soon-to-be-published article in the *Royal Studies Journal*.

Following in the footsteps of Anne and her daughter Elizabeth took me to some fascinating places, from the British Library and The National Archives in London to my familiar stomping grounds at Hampton Court and the Tower. I am extremely grateful to Jean and Paul Macintyre for their wonderful hospitality in Norfolk. This included joining my husband and I on a visit to a very cold, blustery and remote St Margaret's, Tivetshall, and helping me hunt down the Boleyn chapel in Norwich Cathedral. Jean very kindly provided photographs of the house of Anne's grandfather, William Boleyn, on King Street in Norwich. My thanks also go to Lucy Petrie of Gresham College in London, which owns an exquisite linen tablecloth made during Elizabeth's reign in which her mother's falcon emblem is proudly displayed. It was a huge privilege to see this newly-conserved treasure at Jane Lightfoot Textiles and I am very grateful to Sarah Stevenson and her colleagues for making this possible.

Anne Boleyn and Elizabeth I attract a global on line following, and I would like to thank the following for bringing their stories to light and for so kindly spreading the word about my own research: Natalie Grueninger (onthetudortrail.com), Sarah Morris (thetudor-travelguide.com) and Adam Pennington (thetudorchest.com). I am also very grateful to the podcasters Carol Ann Lloyd (Royals, Rebels and Romantics) and Deb Hunter (All Things Tudor).

I would not be able to write my books without the support of my family and friends. It is something I have always been lucky enough to have but that I will never for granted.

NOTES

Introduction

1 *CSPV*, Vol. VI, Part ii, No. 884, p. 1059; Weir, A., *The Lady in the Tower: The Fall of Anne Boleyn* (London, 2009), p. 305.

CHAPTER 1: *'Fettered with chains of gold'*

1 This still survives today. Standing prominently in the middle aisle of the church, it shows Geoffrey Boleyn and his wife Alice in fashionable attire, with the inscription 'God be merciful to us sinners' above them.

2 The total sum was £1,246, equivalent to around £778,000 today.

3 Wyatt, T., 'Of the Courtier's Life'.

4 *LP*, Vol. XI, No. 17. The claim made by the English Catholic priest Nicholas Sander, writing in 1585, that Anne was the result of an adulterous affair between Thomas Boleyn's wife and Henry VIII can be discounted, not least because Henry was a child at the time of Anne's birth. He later refuted the suggestion that he and Elizabeth had been lovers ('Never with the mother!'). Sander, N., *Rise and Growth of the Anglican Schism*, ed. D. Lewis (London, 1877), pp. 23–4; *LP*, Vol. XII, Part ii, No. 952.

5 When Mary's grandson, George Carey, second Baron Hunsdon, petitioned Elizabeth I for the Irish Earldom of Ormond in 1597, he referred to Thomas Boleyn's 'eldest daughter, Mary'. *CSPD: Elizabeth, 1595–97*, p. 135. However, Robert Cecil advised him not to pursue the matter for several reasons, including the fact that Mary was not the eldest.

6 Loades, D. M. (ed.), *The Papers of George Wyatt*, Camden Society, 4th series, Vol. V (London, 1968), p. 29.

7 Paget, H., 'The Youth of Anne Boleyn', *Bulletin of the Institute of Historical Research*, Vol. LIV (London, 1981), pp. 164–5.

8 Paget, 'Youth of Anne Boleyn', p. 166. Anne's original letter still survives in the library of Corpus Christi College, Cambridge.

9 Christine de Pizan, *The Book of the City of Ladies and Other Writings*, ed. Rebecca Kingston and Sophie Bourgault (Hackett Publishing Company, Incorporated, 2018). ProQuest Ebook Central, p. 68.

10 De Carles, quoted in Ascoli, G., *La Grande-Bretagne devant L'Opinion Française* (Paris, 1927), lines 55–8.

11 Carley, J. P., *The Books of King Henry VIII and his Wives* (London, 2004), p. 124.

12 De Carles, in Ascoli, lines 53–4.

13 The term derives from the letter of protestation by six German princes in 1529 against the Roman Catholic Church's condemnation of Martin Luther.

14 Dowling, M., 'Anne Boleyn and Reform', *The Journal of Ecclesiastical History*, Vol. 35, No. 1 (Cambridge, January 1984), p. 32.

15 Ibid., p. 33.

16 Gristwood, S., *Game of Queens: The Women Who Made Sixteenth-Century Europe* (London, 2016), p. 68.

17 Paul Fitzsimmons, who bought Anne Boleyn's falcon at auction, is the owner of the chair. Detailed research to determine its provenance is underway at the time of going to press.

18 Cavendish, G., *The Life of Cardinal Wolsey* (London, 1827), pp. 29–34.

19 Hall, E., *The Union of the Two Noble Families of Lancaster and York, 1550* (reproduced by Scolar Press, Menston, 1970), fo. lccccii.

20 Loades (ed.), *Papers of George Wyatt*, p. 185.

21 *CSPV*, Vol. IV, Nos. 823, 824; Robinson, H. (ed.), *Original Letters relative to the English Reformation*, 2 vols (Cambridge, 1846–7), Vol. II, p. 553; De Carles, in Ascoli, lines 62–8.

22 Sander, *Anglican Schism*, p. 25.

23 Wyatt, G., 'Extracts from the Life of the Virtuous, Christian and

Renowned Queen Anne Boleyn', in Singer, S. W. (ed.), Cavendish, G., *Life of Cardinal Wolsey*, pp. 35, 424, 441. A handwritten manuscript survives in a collection of Wyatt family papers: BL Add MS 62135 fos. 48–65.

24 Hall, *Lancaster and York*, fo. Crlvi(r).

25 Ridley, J. (ed.), *The Love Letters of Henry VIII* (Oxford, 1988), p. 41.

26 Wyatt, in Singer (ed.), *Life of Cardinal Wolsey*, p. 428.

27 Ridley, *Love Letters*, p. 41.

28 Ibid., pp. 35, 65.

29 BL Additional MS 19398 f. 44.

30 Robinson, H. (ed.), *Original Letters Relative to the English Reformation*, 2 vols (Cambridge, 1846–7), Vol. II, p. 553; Brewer, J. S., *The Reign of Henry VIII*, 2 vols (London, 1968), Vol. II, p. 172n.

31 *LP*, Vol. IX, p. 288.

32 *CSPV*, Vol. IV, No. 682.

33 Brewer, J. S., *The Reign of Henry VIII*, 2 vols (London, 1968), Vol. II, p. 486.

34 *LP*, Vol. V, Part i, p. 11.

35 *LP*, Vol. VI, Part i, p. 150.

36 Dowling, 'Anne Boleyn and Reform', pp. 35–6.

37 Ibid, p. 33.

38 *Acts and Monuments*, Vol. V, p. 605.

39 *Bodleian Library*, MS Don. C.42, Latymer, W., *Treatyse on Anne Boleyn*, fos. 31.v, 32; Dowling, 'Anne Boleyn and Reform', p. 33.

40 Coast, D., 'William Tyndale, Henry VIII and The Obedience of a Christian Man', *The Historical Journal*, Vol. LXIV, No. 4 (Cambridge, September 2021), pp. 823–43; Dowling, 'Anne Boleyn and Reform', p. 36.

41 Weir, A., *The Six Wives of Henry VIII* (London, 2007), p. 320.

42 Dowling, 'Anne Boleyn and Reform', p. 42.

43 Dowling, M. (ed.), William Latymer, 'Cronickille of Anne Bulleyne', *Camden Miscellany*, Vol. XXX (London, 1990), p. 63.

44 Dowling, 'Anne Boleyn and Reform', p. 45.

45 Carley, *Books of King Henry VIII and his Wives*, pp. 128–9; Bodleian Library MS Don.C42 fos. 21–33; Dowling, 'Anne Boleyn and Reform', p. 45; *CSPF 1558–1559*, No. 1303.

46 Garret was burned for heresy in 1540. It is not clear whether Anne had been pleading for his life in her letter to Wolsey or that of Garret's rector, Thomas Forman, who had been implicated in Garret's book dealing.

47 Sloane MS 1207 fos. 1r–4r. See also Dowling, 'Anne Boleyn and Reform', p. 30. For other examples of Anne patronising radical religious reformers, see Carley, *Books of King Henry VIII and his Wives*, pp. 131–2.

48 *LP*, Vol. VII, Part ii, p. 251; *CSPS*, Vol. V, Part ii, No. 85; Dowling, 'Anne Boleyn and Reform', p. 45.

49 Wyatt, in Singer (ed.), *Life of Cardinal Wolsey*, pp. 429–30.

50 Hall, *Lancaster and York*, fo. CCiiii(r).

51 BL Hargrave MS 497 fo. 32.

52 *CSPV*, Vol. IV, No. 802.

53 BL Harley MS M303 fo. 1.

54 Ibid.

55 Weir, *Lady in the Tower*, p. 11.

56 DellaNeva, J., *The Story of the Death of Anne Boleyn: A Poem by Lancelot de Carle* (Tempe, 2021), p. 167.

CHAPTER 2: 'A virgin is now born'

1 *LP Henry VIII*, Vol. VI, No. 235.

2 Hall, *Lancaster and York*, fo. CCr.

3 BL Cotton MS Titus B I fo. 161.

4 *CSPV*, Vol. IV, No. 870; *LP*, Vol. VI, No. 531.

5 Hall, *Lancaster and York*, fo. CCr(r).

6 BL Egerton MS 985 fos. 49–59r 'Coronation of the most noble Princess Queen Anne'. See also Harley MS 543 fos. 119–28.

7 The other was Edward IV's queen, Elizabeth Woodville, an equally controversial choice as consort.

8 BL Egerton MS 985 fos. 49–59r 'Coronation of the most noble Princess Queen Anne'.

9 *LP Henry VIII*, Vol. VI, No. 563.

10 Nothing visible remains of the royal apartments today. They were demolished during the reign of Charles II, by which time they had fallen into disrepair. I am grateful to Dr Alden Gregory, Buildings Curator at Historic Royal Palaces, for sharing his research on the now lost Tudor royal apartments with me.

11 The falcon was often painted in silver, with a gold crown and sceptre, standing on a gold trunk out of which sprouted red and white roses and the words '*Mihi et mea*' ('Me and mine' or 'me and my love'). Pinches, J. H. and R. V., *The Royal Heraldry of England* (London, 1974), p. 146.

12 I am grateful to Sebastian Edwards, Head of Collections at Historic Royal Palaces, for drawing my attention to a reference in the accounts of the Great Wardrobe to a tapestry showing 'the falcon with fetterlock' (Edward IV's emblem), which the royal arras-makers were paid to repair in 1535–6. TNA E 315 fo. 455.

13 Hackett, H., *Virgin Mother, Maiden Queen: Elizabeth I and the Cult of the Virgin Mary* (London, 1995), p. 31.

14 Quoted in Arber, E., *An English Garner: Ingatherings from our history and literature*, 8 vols (London, 1877–96).

15 BL MS Royal 18 A.lxiv – Leland, J. and Udall, N., *Versis and ditties made at the coronation of queen Anne.*

16 Hall, *Lancaster and York*, fo. CCxiiii.

17 BL MS Royal 18 A.lxiv – Leland, J. and Udall, N., *Versis and ditties made at the coronation of queen Anne.*

18 Hume, M. A. S. (ed.), *Chronicle of King Henry VIII of England: Being a Contemporary Record of Some of the Principal Events of the Reigns of Henry VIII and Edward VI. Written in Spanish by an Unknown Hand* (London, 1889), p. 14.

19 Walker, J. M., *Dissing Elizabeth: Negative Representations of Gloriana* (Durham, 1998), p. 82.

20 Hall, *Lancaster and York*, fo. CCxiiii(r); Hackett, *Virgin Mother, Maiden Queen*, p. 30

21 *LP*, Vol. VI, Part i, p. 295.

22 Ibid., p. 300.

23 *Lisle Letters*, Vol. I, p. 477.

24 Wyatt, *Life of Anne Boleigne*, p. 19.

25 *LP*, Vol. VI, Part ii, pp. 436, 446; *CSPS, 1531–33*, p. 788; *LP*, Vol. VI, No. 1069; Loades (ed.), *Papers of George Wyatt*.

26 Nichols, F. M., *The Hall of Lawford Hall: Records of an Essex House and of its Proprietors from the Saxon Times to Henry VIII* (London, 1891), p. 443; *Lisle Letters*, Vol. I, p. 518.

27 BL Egerton MS 985 fos. 33–33r. See also *Calendar of Letters, Despatches and State Papers relating to the negotiations between England and Spain, preserved in the Archives of Simancas and Elsewhere (CSPS), Mary I 1554–8*, XIII, p. 166.

28 Colvin, H. M., *The History of the King's Works*, 6 vols (1963–82), Vol. IV (ii), p. 105.

29 Hayward, M. and Ward, P., *The Inventory of King Henry VIII: Textiles and Dress*, Vol. II (London, 2012), p. 149.

30 Hall, E., *Chronicle, Containing the History of England, During the Reign of Henry IV and the Succeeding Monarchs* (London, 1809), p. 805.

31 BL Egerton MS 985 fos. 33–33r.

32 Weir, A., *Henry VIII: King and Court* (London, 2001), p. 137.

33 Harley MS 283 fo. 75§.

34 *LP Henry VIII*, Vol. VI, No. 1070. Dinteville was one of the sitters in Holbein's celebrated painting, *The Ambassadors*.

35 *LP Henry VIII*, Vol. VI, No. 1599.

36 *LP*, Vol. VI, No. 1065; Borman, T., *Elizabeth's Women: The Hidden Story of the Virgin Queen* (Random House, 2009), p. 16.

37 Hall, *Chronicle*, p. 805.

38 BL Add MS 62135 fo. 58r.

39 The first queen of England – albeit an uncrowned one – was Matilda, the daughter and sole surviving heir of Henry I, who died in 1135. Her claim was immediately disputed by her cousin, Stephen, which led to years of civil war before the throne passed to Matilda's son, Henry II.

40 Strickland, A., *The Life of Queen Elizabeth* (London, 1910), Vol. II, p. 651.

41 BM Harley MS 283 fo. 75.

42 Weir, *Six Wives*, p. 258.

43 Hume, *Spanish Chronicle*, p. 42.

44 *LP*, Vol. VII, Part i, p. 465.

45 *LP*, Vol. VI, No. 1112.

46 Hall, *Chronicle*, pp. 807–8.

47 *LP*, Vol. VI, No. 1112.

48 de Carles, quoted in Ascoli, lines 183–5.

49 Hall, *Chronicle*, pp. 807–8.

50 Ibid., p. 808. See also BL Egerton MS 985 fos. 33–33r; Harley MS 543 fos. 128–129r.

51 *LP*, Vol. VI, No. 1125.

52 *LP*, Vol. VII, Part i, p. 360.

53 *LP*, Vol. VI, No. 1125.

CHAPTER 3: *'No other Princess in England'*

1 Ives, E., *The Life and Death of Anne Boleyn* (Oxford, 2005), p. 189.

2 *CSPV*, Vol. IV, No. 824; DellaNeva, *Death of Anne Boleyn*, p. 169.

3 Elizabeth I, *Collected Works*, p. 34.

4 Hume, *Spanish Chronicle*, p. 42.

5 The park was full of oak trees and, legend has it, Elizabeth was sitting in the shade of one of them when she received the news that she was queen in November 1558. Queen Victoria and Prince Albert visited the tree in 1846 and were presented with a branch and an acorn from it. Sadly, the tree no longer survives: its remains were removed in 1978 and a replacement oak was planted by Queen Elizabeth II in 1985.

6 Borman, *Elizabeth's Women*, p. 22.

7 Her third husband, David Souche (or Zoche), may have died in either 1526 or 1536. The fact that she was generally known by the name of her second husband, Sir Thomas Bryan, suggests the earlier date.

8 Powel, D., *Historie of Cambria* (1584), preface.

9 Strype, J., *Ecclesiastical Memorials, Relating chiefly to Religion, and the*

Reformation of it . . . *under King Henry VIII, King Edward VI and Queen Mary I*, 3 vols (Oxford, 1822), Vol. I, Part i, p. 224.

10 Ibid., pp. 491–2, 500.

11 *Lisle Letters*, Vol. II, p. 28.

12 Strype, *Memorials*, Vol. I, Part i, pp. 511, 556.

13 Ibid., p. 617.

14 Ibid., Part i, p. 84.

15 Loades, D. M., *Mary Tudor. The Tragical History of the first Queen of England* (Richmond, 2006), p. 37.

16 Heath, J. B., 'An Account of Materials Furnished for the use of Queen Anne Boleyn, and the Princess Elizabeth, by William Loke, The King's Mercer, between the 20th January 1535 and the 27th April, 1536', *Miscellanies of the Philobiblon Society*, Vol. VII (London, 1862–3).

17 Heath, 'Materials Furnished for Queen Anne Boleyn and the Princess Elizabeth'.

18 *CSPV*, 1603–1607, Vol. X (London, 1900), No. 91.

19 At Hunsdon in 1535. *Parker Correspondence*, p. ix.

20 Bodleian Library MS C.Don.42 fos. 20–33; Latymer, 'Cronickille of Anne Bulleyne', p. 63.

21 *CSPV*, Vol. V, No. 934, p. 539; Ives, *Anne Boleyn*, p. 272; Dowling, M., *Humanism in the age of Henry VIII* (London, 1986), pp. 233–4.

22 *LP*, Vol. VII, Part i, p. 36.

23 *LP*, Vol. VI, Part ii, p. 629.

24 *LP*, Vol. VII, Part i, p. 69.

25 Ibid., p. 31.

26 *LP*, Vol. VII, No. 497.

27 *LP*, Vol. VII, Part i, pp. 31–2.

28 Ibid., p. 68.

29 Ibid., pp. 31, 323.

30 Weir, *Six Wives*, p. 261.

31 Succession to the Crown Act 1533, 25 Hen 8 c 22.

32 *CSPS 1534–5*, Vol. V, Part i, p. 72.

33 *LP*, Vol. VII, Part i, p. 214.

34 Weir, *Six Wives*, p. 264.

35 *Lisle Letters*, Vol. II, pp. 128, 139; *LP*, Vol. VII, No. 509.

36 *LP*, Vol. VII, Nos. 114, 958.

37 See Dewhurst, J., 'The Alleged Miscarriages of Catherine of Aragon and Anne Boleyn', *Medical History*, Vol. XXVIII (Chalfont St Giles, 1984), pp. 55–6.

38 *LP*, Vol. VII, No. 1193. It is possible that Chapuys was referring to the pregnancy that ended in July, rather than another one that happened shortly afterwards. Anne may have suffered at least one other miscarriage in 1534, but the evidence is contradictory.

39 *LP*, Vol. VII, Part i, pp. 84, 142; IX, p. 197; Porter, L., *Mary Tudor: The First Queen* (London, 2007), pp. 96–7.

40 *LP*, Vol. IX, p. 424.

41 Ibid., p. 463.

42 *CSPS*, IV, Part ii, No. 1165.

43 *LP*, Vol. VIII, No. 174.

44 *CSPS 1534–5*, Vol. V, Part i, p. 573.

45 *LP*, Vol. VIII, p. 193.

46 *LP*, Vol. VII, Part ii, p. 495; VIII, p. 58.

47 *LP*, Vol. VIII, No. 440.

48 *LP*, Vol. VII Part i, p. 204; Hume, *Spanish Chronicle*, p. 42; Ives, *Anne Boleyn*, p. 248.

49 *LP*, Vol. IX, pp. 189, 568.

50 *LP Henry VIII*, Vol. XV, No. 954.

51 *CSPS*, Vol. V, Part i, p. 484; Part ii, p. 81.

52 Weir, *Six Wives*, pp. 272–3; Hibbert, C., *Elizabeth I: A Personal History of The Virgin Queen* (London, 2001), p. 15.

53 *LP*, Vol. VII, Part ii, p. 485.

54 *LP*, Vol. X, No. 901; Starkey, D., *Six Wives: The Queens of Henry VIII* (London, 2003), p. 584.

55 Weir, *Six Wives*, p. 345; *LP*, Vol. X, p. 450.

56 Ibid., p. 293; *LP*, Vol. X, No. 351.

CHAPTER 4: '*Of corrupt seed*'

1 *LP*, Vol. X, No. 141.

2 Ibid., No. 199.

3 Ibid., No. 200. The theory that Henry sustained a brain injury that caused his increasingly erratic and tyrannical behaviour holds little weight. The only account that claims he was knocked unconscious was written by someone who was in Paris at the time of the accident. Moreover, the character traits that he displayed in the years that followed had always been there, albeit less prominently.

4 Wyatt, *Life of Anne Boleigne*, p. 19.

5 *LP*, Vol. X, No. 282; Wriothesley, C., *A Chronicle of England During the Reigns of the Tudors*, 2 vols (London, 1875, 1877), Vol. II, p. 33.

6 *LP*, Vol. X, No. 351.

7 Ibid.

8 Ibid.

9 *CSPS 1536–8*, Vol V, Part ii, p. 84.

10 TNA SP 1/103 fos. 322–7; *LP Henry VIII*, Vol. X, No. 913.

11 A total of 376 monasteries were suppressed in the first phase of the dissolution, which focused on the smaller establishments. The amount raised from the sale of the jewels, plate, lead and other valuables that were seized was estimated at £100,000 (equivalent to more than £32 million today). The annual incomes of the houses, meanwhile, brought the crown a further £32,000 (£10.3 million).

12 *LP Henry VIII*, Vol. X, No. 699.

13 Skip was interrogated but soon released and the episode did not impede his subsequent career. He rose to become Bishop of Hereford in 1539, a position that he retained until his death in 1552.

14 Cox, J.E. (ed), *Works of Archbishop Cranmer* (Cambridge, 1844), Vol. II, p. 314.

15 *CSPS*, Vol. V part II, p. 137.

16 *CSPF Elizabeth 1558–9*, No. 1303.

17 Hall, *Chronicle*, p. 819.

18 *LP*, Vol. X, No. 793.

19 This was confirmed by Afua Hirsch, a former barrister, whom I interviewed for the documentary, *The Fall of Anne Boleyn* (Channel 5, 2020).

20 Weir, A., *The Life of Elizabeth* (New York, 1998), p. 51; Cowen Orlin, L., *Locating Privacy in Tudor London* (Oxford, 2007), p. 231.

21 *LP*, Vol. X, nos. 908, 965.

22 *Lisle Letters*, Vol. IV, p. 46.

23 *CSPF Elizabeth* 1558–9, No. 1303.

24 Wyatt, in Singer (ed.), *Life of Cardinal Wolsey*, p. 452; Weir, *Six Wives*, p. 317.

25 Ibid., pp. 451–60.

26 Stowe MS 151 fos. 1–2. For a detailed analysis of this letter see Vasoli, S., *Anne Boleyn's Letter from the Tower: A New Assessment* (MadeGlobal Publishing 2015).

27 *LP*, Vol. X, pp. 361–2; TNA KB 8/9.

28 Wriothesley, *Chronicle*, p. 137–8; Wyatt, *Life of Anne Boleigne*, p. 23.

29 Hume, *Spanish Chronicle*, p. 65.

30 *CSPS*, Vol. V, Part ii, p. 126; *LP*, Vol. X, No. 908.

31 *CSPS*, Vol. V, Part ii, p. 126; *LP*, Vol. X, No. 908.

32 Marcus, L. S., Mueller, J. and Rose, M. B. (eds), *Elizabeth I: Collected Works*, p. 313.

33 Weir, *Lady in the Tower*, pp. 209–11.

34 *LP*, Vol. X, p. 381.

35 Ibid., No. 908.

36 Ibid., p. 333.

37 Weir, *Six Wives*, p. 330.

38 Wriothesley, *Chronicle* Vol. I, p. 41.

39 Wyatt, in Singer (ed.), *Life of Cardinal Wolsey*, pp. 464–5.

40 *LP*, Vol. X, No. 909.

41 Dowling, 'Anne Boleyn and Reform', p. 34.

42 Weir, *Six Wives*, p. 331.

43 *LP*, Vol. X, No. 908.

44 TNA C193/3 fo. 80.

45 Reported by one of Lady Lisle's correspondents. *Lisle Letters*, Vol. III, p. 365.

46 Hall, *Chronicle*, p. 819. A transcript of Anne's scaffold speech also survives among the Wyatt papers: BL Add MS 62135 fos. 63r–64.

47 *Lisle Letters*, Vol. III, p. 366.

48 DellaNeva, *Death of Anne Boleyn*, p. 295.

49 Aylmer, J., *An harborowe for faithfull and trewe subiectes* (Strassburg, 1559), sig. F iv.

CHAPTER 5: *'Storms and tempests'*

1 Hall, *Chronicle*, p. 819.

2 *Lisle Letters*, Vol. III, No. 713.

3 Plowden, A, *The Young Elizabeth* (Cheltenham, 2011), p. 55.

4 *LP*, Vol. II, No. 1250.

5 Sander, N., *Rise and Growth of the Anglican Schism*, ed. Lewis, D. (London, 1877), pp. 25–6, 33. George Wyatt, who refuted many of Sander's claims, concurred that that there was 'some little show of a nail' on the side of one of her fingers (p. 25).

6 *CSPF Foreign, 1558–1559*, No. 1303; *LP*, Vol. X, No. 908.

7 Aylmer, J., *An harborowe for faithfull and trewe subiectes* (Strassburg, 1559), sig.N3v.

8 *CSPV*, Vol. V, No. 934, p. 535.

9 Borman, *Elizabeth's Women*, p. 45.

10 *LP*, Vol. XI, p. 130.

11 Weir, *Lady in the Tower*, p. 301.

12 HMC *Rutland* I, p. 310.

13 *LP*, X, p. 403.

14 *LP*, Vol. XI, p. 96.

15 *LP*, Vol. X, p. 374.

16 Ibid., p. 452.

17 Ibid., p. 504.

18 Hall, *Chronicle*, p. 819; *Statutes of the Realm*, Vol. III.

19 Ibid.; Weir, *Lady in the Tower*, p. 286; Boehrer, B. T., *Monarchy and*

Incest in Renaissance England: Literature, Culture, Kinship and Kingship (Philadelphia, 1992), p. 44.

20 After the dissolution of Thetford Priory, FitzRoy's remains were interred in St Michael's Church, Framlingham, Suffolk.

21 *LP*, Vol. X, No. 909.

22 Sander, *Anglican Schism*, p. 231; Weir, A., *The Children of Henry VIII* (New York, 1996), p. 215.

23 Weir, *Lady in the Tower*, p. 299.

24 *CSPF Foreign, 1558–1559*, No. 1303.

25 *LP*, Vol. XIII, Part ii, No. 544.

26 Strype, *Memorials*, Vol. I, Part i, p. 436; Wiesener, L., *The Youth of Queen Elizabeth, 1533–1558*, 2 vols (London, 1879), Vol. I, p. vi.

27 BL Cotton Otho X fo. 234r.

28 Ibid..

29 Ibid..

30 *LP, Vol. XIII*, Part ii, No. 280.

31 Jenkins, E., *Elizabeth the Great* (London, 1958), pp. 95–6.

32 Taylor-Smither, L.J. 'Elizabeth I: A Psychological Profile', *Sixteenth Century Journal*, Vol. XV No.1 (Kirksville, 1984), p. 53.

CHAPTER 6: *'A child toward'*

1 *LP*, Vol. XI, p. 55.

2 Ibid., p. 346.

3 Hall, *Chronicle*, p. 825.

4 Egerton MS 985 fo. 36.

5 Hall, *Chronicle*, p. 825.

6 Wood, M.A.E., *Letters of Royal and Illustrious Ladies of Great Britain* 3 volumes (London, 1846), Vol. III, p. 112.

7 Ibid.

8 BL Cotton Vespasian MS F III, fo. 48; Marcus, Mueller. and Rose, *Elizabeth I: Collected Works*, p. 34.

9 Collins, A. J. (ed.), *Jewels and Plate of Queen Elizabeth I: The Inventory of 1574* (London, 1955), p. 199. John Astley's mother, Anne Wood, was the sister of Elizabeth, who married Sir James Boleyn, elder brother of Thomas Boleyn, Queen Anne's father.

10 *Parker Correspondence*, p. 483.

11 *Lisle Letters*, Vol. V, No. 1086.

12 Warnicke, R. M., *The Marrying of Anne of Cleves: Royal Protocol in Early Modern England* (Cambridge, 2000), p. 408.

13 Strickland, A., *Lives of the Queens of England* (London, 1851), Vol. III, p. 59.

14 Public Act, 32 Henry VIII, c.38: An Act concerning Pre-contracts of Marriages, and touching Degrees of Consanguinity. See also Boehrer, *Monarchy and Incest*, p. 44.

15 Strickland, *Life of Elizabeth*, p. 13.

16 Weir, A., *Children of England: the heirs of King Henry VIII* (London, 1996), p. 9.

CHAPTER 7: *'No words of Boleyn'*

1 Weir, *Six Wives*, p. 427.

2 Recent research has proved that Anne of Cleves spent more time at Hever than was previously thought. Emmerson, O. and Ridgway, C., *The Boleyns of Hever Castle* (MadeGlobal Publishing, 2021), pp. 110–11.

3 Weir, *Six Wives*, p. 557

4 Carley, *Books of King Henry VIII and his Wives*, p. 124

5 Shell, M., *Elizabeth's Glass* (Lincoln, 1993), p. 3

6 My italics.

7 Prescott, A. L., 'The Pearl of the Valois and Elizabeth I', in M. P. Hannay (ed.), *Silent But for the Word: Tudor Women as Patrons, Translators, and Writers of Religious Works* (Kent, Ohio, 1985), pp. 69–70.

8 Perry, M., *The Word of a Prince: A Life of Elizabeth I from Contemporary Documents* (Woodbridge, 1990), pp. 32–4. The original is now in the British Museum: BM Cotton MS Nero C X fo. 13.

9 LP, Vol. XIX, Part i, No. 780; Vol. XVIII, Part i, No. 364.

10 It has been suggested that this was added later, when Elizabeth was queen. An inventory records that the picture hung in her presence chamber at Whitehall Palace. However, there is no evidence of overpainting. See Clarke, S. and Collins, L., *Gloriana: Elizabeth I and the Art of Queenship* (Cheltenham, 2022), p. 35.

11 In 1547, Elizabeth sent a portrait to her brother, Edward VI, but, contrary to what has often been asserted, it was probably not this one.

12 Hentzner, P., *Travels in England during the Reign of Queen Elizabeth* (London, 1889), p. 47.

13 Norfolk's execution was scheduled for 29 January, but he was saved by the king's own death the day before.

14 Bell, S. G., *The Lost Tapestries of the City of Ladies: Christine de Pizan's Renaissance Legacy* (Berkeley and Los Angeles, 2004), p. 36; Pizan, Christine de, *The Book of the City of Ladies and Other Writings*, ed. Bourgault, S. and Kingston, R. (Indianapolis and Cambridge, 2018), p. 52.

15 Starkey, D. (ed.), *The Inventory of King Henry VIII: The Transcript* (London, 1988), p. 381 (fo. 440v).

16 Weir, *Six Wives*, p. 544.

17 Martienssen, A.K., *Queen Katherine Parr* (London, 1973), p. 233.

18 Robinson, H. (ed.), *Original Letters Relative to the English Reformation*, 2 vols (Cambridge, 1846–7), Vol. I, p. 76.

19 Haynes, S., *A Collection of the State Papers Relating to the Affairs in the Reigns of King Henry VIII, King Edward VI, Queen Mary and Queen Elizabeth, From the Year 1542 to 1570* (London, 1740), sig. Ccv.

20 BL Lansdowne 1236 fo. 35.

21 Haynes, *State Papers*, p. 108.

22 Aylmer, J., *An harborowe for faithfull and trewe subiectes* (Strassburg, 1559), sig.N1; Robinson, H. (ed.), *Original Letters Relative to the English Reformation*, 2 vols (Cambridge, 1846–7), Vol. I, pp. 278–9.

23 Strype, *Memorials*, Vol. II (London, 1822), pp. 195–6.

24 Strangford, Viscount (ed.), 'The Household Expenses of the Princess

Elizabeth during her residence at Hatfield, October 1, 1551, to September 30, 1552', *The Camden Miscellany*, Vol. II (London, 1853), pp. 30, 41.

25 Strangford, 'Household Expenses', pp. 35–6.

26 Starkey, D., *Elizabeth: Apprenticeship* (London, 2001), p. 110.

27 Nichols, J. G., *The Chronicle of Queen Jane and of Two Years of Queen Mary*, Camden Society, no. XLVIII (London, 1850), p. 93; Wriothesley, *Chronicle*, Vol. II, p. 88.

28 McCulloch, D. (ed.), 'The Vita Mariae Angliae Reginae of Robert Wingfield of Brantham', *Camden Miscellany*, Vol. XXVIII, Camden Society, 4th series, Vol. XXIX (London, 1984), p. 247.

CHAPTER 8: *'The school of affliction'*

1 Somerset, A., *Elizabeth I* (London, 1991), p. 71.

2 *CSPV*, Vol. V, No. 934, p. 539.

3 Ibid.

4 *CSPS Mary I 1553–4*, XI, p. 169.

5 Plowden, *Tudor Women*, p. 137.

6 Perry, *Word of a Prince*, p. 85.

7 *CSPV*, Vol. VI ii, No. 884, p. 1058.

8 *CSPV*, Vol. IV, No. 924.

9 *CSPV*, Vol. VI, Part ii, No. 884, p. 1059.

10 *CSPS Mary I 1553–4*, XI, p. 411.

11 Naunton, *Fragmenta Regalia*, in Hentzner, *Travels*, p. 99.

12 Known as the 'Tide Letter', it still survives among the collections of The National Archives: SP 11/4/2 fo. 3–3v.

13 Wriothesley, *Chronicle* II, p. 113.

14 Nichols, *Chronicle of Queen Jane and Queen Mary*, pp. 70–1.

15 Ibid., p. 71.

16 *CSPS Mary I 1554*, XII, p. 140; Weir, *Children of Henry VIII*, p. 260.

17 Strickland, *Queens*, Vol. III, pp. 501–2.

18 Foxe, *Acts and Monuments*, VIII, p. 613.

19 Ibid., p. 615.

20 Ibid., p. 614; Marcus, Mueller. and Rose, *Elizabeth I: Collected Works*, p. 96.

21 Manning, C. R., 'State Papers relating to the custody of the Princess Elizabeth at Woodstock, in 1554 . . .', *Norfolk Archaeology*, Vol. IV (1855), p. 159.

22 Foxe, *Acts and Monuments*, VIII, pp. 617–18.

23 During his imprisonment in the Salt Tower, Castiglione affirmed his loyalty to Elizabeth by carving her initial inside a love heart onto the wall. This can still be seen today. Both he and Kat Astley were subsequently released.

24 Perry, *Word of a Prince*, p. 86. The original letter is in the British Library, Lansdowne MS 94 fo. 21.

25 Perry, *Word of a Prince*, p. 887.

26 *CSPV*, Vol. VI, Part ii, No. 884, p. 1058.

27 MacCulloch, 'Vita Mariae Reginae', p. 275.

28 Camden, W., *The Historie of the Most Renowned and Victorious Princesse Elizabeth, Late Queene of England* (London, 1630), p. 8.

29 Loades, *Mary Tudor*, p. 143, quoting John Foxe.

30 Nichols, J. G., *The Progresses and Public Processions of Queen Elizabeth*, 3 vols (London, 1823), Vol. I, pp. 23–5.

31 *CSPV*, Vol. VI, Part iii, No. 1274.

32 Rodríguez-Salgado, M. J. and Adams, S. (eds), 'The Count of Feria's Dispatch to Philip II of 14 November 1558', *Camden Miscellany*, 4th series, Vol. XXVIII (London, 1984), p. 335.

CHAPTER 9: *'The sore which was with age over-skinned'*

1 Knox, J., *First Blast of the Trumpet Against the Monstrous Regiment of Women*, first published 1558 (New York, 1972), pp. 9–10.

2 Sander, *Anglican Schism*, p. 241; Naunton, *Fragmenta Regalia*, in Hentzner, *Travels*, p. 98.

3 Kings MS 396 – Genealogical of Elizabeth I.

4 Marcus, Mueller and Rose, *Elizabeth I: Collected Works*, p. 95; Haynes, *State Papers*, p. 98.

5 Strype, J., *Annals of the Reformation and Establishment of Religion and . . . other occurrences in the Church of England; during the first twelve years of Queen Elizabeths . . . Reign*, 4 vols (Oxford, 1824), Vol. I, Part I, pp. 14–15.

6 Wriothesley, *Chronicle*, Vol. II, p. 142.

7 Anglo, S., *Images of Tudor Kingship* (London, 1992), p. 36.

8 Law, E., *The History of Hampton Court Palace*, 3 vols (London, 1885–91), Vol. I, p. 170. John Heath was responsible for painting and gilding the falcons at Hampton Court. I am indebted to Sebastian Edwards, Head of Collections at Historic Royal Palaces, for sharing his research on the falcon badge with me.

9 Duncan, S. and Schutte, V. (eds), *The Birth of a Queen: Essays on the Quincentenary of Mary I* (New York, 2016), p. 80.

10 Geoffrey Abbott, a former Yeoman Warder at the Tower, claimed that during Elizabeth's reign the vault in which Anne had been buried was opened and its contents viewed. There is no contemporary evidence for this, however, and Anne's remains had in any case been laid to rest before the altar, rather than in a vault. Weir, *Lady in the Tower*, p. 324.

11 Sander, *Anglican Schism*, pp. 230–1.

12 *Statutes of the Realm*, Vol. IV; Duncan and Schutte, *Birth of a Queen*, pp. 80–1.

13 Brown, R. L. and Bentinck, G. C. (eds), *Calendar of State Papers and Manuscripts, Relating to English Affairs*, Vol. VII: 1558–1580 (Cambridge, 2013), pp. viii–ix.

14 Hill Cole, M., 'Maternal Memory: Elizabeth Tudor's Anne Boleyn', in D. Stump, L. Shenk and C. Levin (eds), *Elizabeth and the Sovereign Arts* (Tempe, 2011), p. 11.

15 BL Stowe MS 555 fo. 3; Harley MS 1650 fo. 2; Collins (ed.), *Jewels and Plate*, p. 14; Hill Cole, 'Maternal Memory', pp. 9–10.

16 Warkentin, G. (ed.), *The Queen's Majesty's Passage & Related Documents* (Toronto, 2004), p. 107.

17 Brown and Bentinck (eds), *Calendar of State Papers*, p. 13; Strong, R., *Coronation: A History of Kingship and the British Monarchy* (London, 2005), p. 223.

18 Anglo, *Images of Tudor Kingship*, pp. 87–9.

19 TNA SP70/7 fos. I–II; *CSPF 1558–9*, No. 1303 (transcript).

20 Pratt, J. (ed.), *The Acts and Monuments of John Foxe*, 8 vols (London, [1877?]), Vol. V, pp. 136–7, 175.

21 Aylmer, sig.B4v.

22 Bridges, J., *The Supremacie of Christian Princes* (London, 1573), p. 853; Holinshed, R., *Chronicles* (London, 1577), p. 1565.

23 Bodleian Library MS C.Don.42 fos. 20–33; Dowling, M. (ed.), William Latymer, 'Cronickille of Anne Bulleyne', *Camden Miscellany*, Vol. XXX (London, 1990), pp. 23–65.

24 *Parker Correspondence*, pp. 59, 70, 391, 400. Parker's loyalty to Anne was such that he had a panel portrait of her at his home. This was apparently listed among his possessions at the time of his death in 1575.

25 Dowling, 'Anne Boleyn and Reform', p. 34.

CHAPTER 10: *'Of her own blood and lineage'*

1 Naunton, *Fragmenta Regalia*, in Hentzner, *Travels*, p. 145. Williams's impressive tomb, which bears his effigy, still stands in the middle of the chancel.

2 Naunton, *Fragmenta Regalia*, in Hentzner, *Travels*, pp. 145–6.

3 Daalder, J. (ed.), Wyatt, T., *Collected Poems* (London, 1975), p. cxlix.

4 Naunton, *Fragmenta Regalia*, in Hentzner, *Travels*, p. 160.

5 See, for example, Harrison, G. B., *The Letters of Queen Elizabeth* (London, 1935), p. 83; *CSPD, Addenda, 1566–79*, pp. 245–6.

6 *LP*, Vol. VIII, No. 567.

7 Naunton, *Fragmenta Regalia*, in Hentzner, *Travels*, p. 158.

8 Ibid., p. 129.

9 Lawson, J. A. (ed.), *The Elizabethan New Year's Gift Exchanges 1559–1603* (Oxford, 2013), pp. 40, 48 (59.131, 59.350).

10 Naunton, *Fragmenta Regalia*, in Hentzner, *Travels*, p. 39

11 Williams, N., *All the Queen's Men: Elizabeth I and Her Courtiers* (London, 1972), p. 51.

12 Adams, S., 'Eliza enthroned? The court and its politics', in C. Haigh (ed.), *The Reign of Elizabeth I* (London, 1984), p. 64.

13 TNA LC2/4/3 fo. 53.

14 Newton, T., *An epitaphe upon the worthy and honorable lady, the Lady Knowles* (1569).

15 Weir, A., *Mary Boleyn: 'The Great and Infamous Whore'* (London, 2011), p. 246; Lawson, *New Year's Gift Exchanges*, p. 115 (65.225).

16 Knollys, W., 'Papers relating to Mary, Queen of Scots', *Philobiblon Society Miscellanies*, Vol. XIV (London, 1872–6), p. 65.

17 One of the books in which Katherine recorded the gifts given to the queen at New Year still survives in the British Library: Sloane MS 814.

18 Charles Howard's sister Douglas was appointed a maid of honour but later fell from favour when she had an affair with the queen's great favourite, Robert Dudley, and bore him a son.

19 TNA C115/M19/7543.

20 TNA C115/M18/7511.

21 Mary did not long outlive Elizabeth. The exact date and place of her death are not known, but she was buried at Holme Lacy in Herefordshire on 15 August 1603.

CHAPTER 11: *'A French partisan'*

1 Boehrer, *Monarchy and Incest*, p. 46.

2 Mary's late father, James V of Scotland, was the son of Henry VIII's eldest sister, Margaret Tudor. The fact that Henry VIII had excluded this branch of his family from the succession came to matter less when two of his immediate successors reigned for just a short time, leaving his younger daughter Elizabeth as the sole survivor of the Tudor dynasty.

3 The whole incident is chronicled in *CSPF Elizabeth 1561–2*, pp. 244, 303–4, 309, 311, 329, 344, 356, 361.

4 Dowling, 'Anne Boleyn and Reform', p. 33; *CSPS*, Vol. XI, p. 393.

5 Haigh, *Elizabeth*, p. 22.

6 *CSPS Elizabeth 1558–67*, I, p. 45.

7 Klarwill, Von V., *Queen Elizabeth and Some Foreigners* (London, 1928), pp. 113–15.

8 Newton, T., *An epitaphe upon the worthy and honorable lady, the Lady Knowles* (1569).

9 Knollys, 'Papers relating to Mary, Queen of Scots', p. 60.

10 Ibid., pp. 65.

11 HMC, *Calendar of the manuscripts of the most hon. the marquis of Salisbury* (London, 1883), Vol. I, p. 400.

12 Wright, T., *Queen Elizabeth and her Times, A Series of Original Letters, Selected from the Inedited Private Correspondence of the Lord Treasurer Burghley, the Earl of Leicester, the Secretaries Walsingham and Smith, Sir Christopher Hatton, etc*, 2 vols (London, 1838), Vol. I, p. 308.

13 Ibid., pp. 308–9.

14 Weir, *Mary Boleyn*, p. 248.

CHAPTER 12: 'Angry with any love'

1 *CSPS Mary I 1553–4*, XI, p. 393.

2 Naunton, *Fragmenta Regalia*, in Hentzner, *Travels*, pp. 100–1.

3 Adams, *Feria's Despatch*, p. 331.

4 Boyle, J. (ed.), *Memoirs of the Life of Robert Carey . . . Written by Himself* (London, 1759), p. 73n.

5 Adams, *Feria's Despatch*, p. 331.

6 Boyle, J. (ed), *Memoirs of the Life of Robert Carey. . .Written by Himself* (London, 1759), p. 74.

7 Harington, Sir J., *Nugae Antiquae: Being a Miscellaneous Collection of Original Papers in Prose and Verse: Written in the Reigns of Henry VIII, Queen Mary, Elizabeth, King James, etc* (London, 1779), p. 125.

8 Naunton, *Fragmenta Regalia*, in Hentzner, *Travels*, p. 106.

9 Haigh, *Elizabeth*, p. 20.

10 Somerset, *Elizabeth*, p. 90; Plowden, *Tudor Women*, p. 154.

11 Pryor, F., *Elizabeth I: her life in letters* (California, 2003), p. 31; HMC *Salisbury* I, p. 158.

12 Francis Steuart, A. (ed), *Sir James Melville. Memoirs of His Own Life, 1549–93* (London, 1929), p. 94; *CSPV*, Vol. VII, No. 748; Levin, C., *The Heart and Stomach of a King: Elizabeth I and the Politics of Sex and Power* (Philadelphia, 1994), p. 172.

13 Weir, *Elizabeth*, p. 46.

14 *CSPS*, III, p. 252; Somerset, *Elizabeth*, p. 96.

15 Marcus, Mueller and Rose, *Elizabeth I: Collected Works*, p. 170.

16 Weir, *Lady in the Tower*, p. 303.

17 Mueller, J. and Marcus, L. S. (eds), *Elizabeth I: Autograph Compositions and Foreign Language Originals* (Chicago, 2003), p. 35.

18 Collins, A. (ed), *Letters and Memorials of State, in the reigns of Queen Mary, Queen Elizabeth, etc. . . Written and collected by Sir Henry Sidney, etc* 2 volumes *(London*, 1746), Vol. II, pp. 200–3.

19 Harington, *Nugae Antiquae*, p. 124.

20 Bodleian Library MS C.Don.42 fos. 20–33; Dowling, M. (ed.), William Latymer, 'Cronickille of Anne Bulleyne', *Camden Miscellany*, Vol. XXX (London, 1990), p. 62.

21 *CSPF Elizabeth 1586–88*, p. 86.

22 Murdin, *State Papers*, p. 558. In 1584, the incident was relayed by Mary, Queen of Scots, in her notorious 'scandal letter' to Elizabeth. Her source was Bess of Hardwick, who, together with her husband, was responsible for Mary's imprisonment for a time. The Queen of Scots claimed that Bess had told her: 'She would never return to Court to attend you [Elizabeth], for anything in the world, because she was afraid of you when you were in a rage, such as when you broke her cousin Scudamore's finger, pretending to all the court that it was caused by a fallen chandelier.' Ibid.

23 Ives, *Anne Boleyn* (2005), pp. 334–5.

24 Murdin, W., *A Collection of State Papers Relating to Affairs in the Reign*

of Queen Elizabeth, 1571–96 . . . Left by William Cecil Lord Burghley . . . at Hatfield House (London, 1759), p. 558; *CSP Scotland 1584–5* VII, p. 5; C. Erickson, *The First Elizabeth* (London, 1999), p. 262; Somerset, *Elizabeth*, p. 101; Johnson, P., *Elizabeth I: A Study in Power and Intellect* (London, 1974), p. 115; Weir, *Elizabeth*, pp. 48–9.

25 Gristwood, S., *Elizabeth and Leicester* (London, 2007), pp. 132–3.

26 The 'Bisley Boy' legend states that in 1542, the future Elizabeth I (then aged nine) was sent to Overcourt House in the Cotswold village of Bisley to escape the plague in London. While there, she sickened with a fever and died. Knowing that Henry VIII was on his way to visit his daughter, her panic-stricken governess searched the village in vain for a girl who resembled Elizabeth closely enough to fool the king. The only child of the right age and hair colour was a boy, so in desperation she dressed him in the princess's clothes and the deception was complete.

27 Levin, *Heart and Stomach of a King*, pp. 82–3; Laing, D. (ed), *Notes of Ben Jonson's Conversations with William Drummond of Hawthornden* Volume I (London, 1842), p. 23.

28 Arthur Dudley's account implicated Kat Astley and her husband, who were said to have spirited the child away from Hampton Court as soon as he was born and had hushed up the affair ever since. There is no other evidence to corroborate the story, but it suited Philip's interests to make sure that it was repeated far and wide. For that reason, it was given more credence than it perhaps deserved.

29 Murdin, *State Papers*, p. 558; *CSP Scotland 1584–5*, Vol. VII, p. 5; C. Erickson, *The First Elizabeth* (London, 1999), p. 262; Somerset, *Elizabeth*, p. 101; Johnson, *Power and Intellect*, p. 115; Weir, *Elizabeth*, pp. 48–9; *Jonson's Conversations*, p. 23; Jenkins, *Elizabeth the Great*, p. 123; HMC *Salisbury* II, p. 245; Marcus, Mueller and Rose, *Collected Works*, p. 157.

30 Harington, *Nugae Antiquae*, pp. 123–4.

31 Frye, S., *Elizabeth I. The Competition for Representation* (New York & Oxford University Press, 1993), p. 12.

32 Marcus, Mueller and Rose, *Collected Works*, p. 168; Heisch, 'Patriarchy', p. 50.

CHAPTER 13: *'Nearness of blood'*

1 Marcus, Mueller and Rose, *Collected Works*, p. 118.

2 Weir, *Elizabeth*, p. 201.

3 Prior, F., *Elizabeth I: Her Life in Letters* (Berkeley, 2003), p. 65.

4 Dowling, 'Anne Boleyn and Reform', p. 34; Hill Cole, 'Maternal Memory', p. 7.

5 TNA KB 27/1241/2.

6 Mitchell, D. M., 'Table linen associated with Queen Elizabeth's visit to Gresham's Exchange', in A. Saunders (ed.), *The Royal Exchange*, London Topographical Society, Vol. CLII (London, 1997), pp. 50–6. Mitchell argues that this linen was based on patterns woven in haste for Elizabeth's coronation, which were in turn inspired by those commissioned by Henry VIII for Anne Boleyn's use. Hayward, *Inventory of Henry VIII*, Vol. II, p. 218.

7 Of this, only a napkin survives; it is now in the Victoria and Albert Museum, London.

8 *Parker Correspondence*, pp. 414, 420.

9 Hill Cole, 'Maternal Memory', pp. 11–12.

10 Ibid., p. 12.

11 The valance is now in The Burrell Collection, Glasgow. Hayward, *Inventory of Henry VIII*, pp. 152–3. For another example of the honeysuckle emblem, see 'The Ecclesiaste' book once owned by Anne, now at Alnwick Castle. Also Starkey, D. (ed.), *The Inventory of King Henry VIII: The Transcript*, Vol. I (London, 1988), nos. 9225, 9226.

12 Another theory is that Leicester himself had admitted his betrayal to the queen as early as April 1579. The Spanish ambassador reported that she had cancelled an audience with him at short notice and gone with great haste to Leicester's house, where she

had stayed until 10 o'clock at night. A few days later, Leicester had left court for Buxton, ostensibly to take the waters, but he stayed away an unusually long time. Tallis, N., *Elizabeth's Rival: The Tumultuous Tale of Lettice Knollys, Countess of Leicester* (London, 2017), p. 177; Wilson, D., *Sweet Robin: a biography of Robert Dudley, Earl of Leicester, 1533–1588* (London, 1981), p. 229; Weir, *Elizabeth*, pp. 312–13.

13 Nichols, *Progresses*, Vol. I, pp. 527–8; Vol. II, p. 276; Somerset, *Ladies in Waiting*, p. 318

14 *CSPD Elizabeth 1580–1625* Addenda, p. 137.

15 *CSPD Elizabeth, 1581–1590*, p. 114.

16 *CSPS Elizabeth 1580–6*, III, p. 426.

17 *CSPD Elizabeth 1580–1625*, Addenda, p. 137.

18 Bruce, J (ed), *The Correspondence of Robert Dudley, Earl of Leycester, During his Government of the Low Countries, in the years 1585 and 1586* Camden Society XXVII (London, 1844), pp. 112, 144; Tallis, *Elizabeth's Rival*, p. 179.

CHAPTER 14: 'The time will come'

1 Williams, N., *All the Queen's Men: Elizabeth I and her Courtiers* (London, 1972), p. 180.

2 BL Stowe MS 555 fo. 99; Harley MS 1650 fo. 98; *LP Henry VIII*, Vol. VII, No. 9.

3 The clock is still part of the Royal Collection.

4 Collins, *Jewels and Plate*, p. 197n.

5 Starkey, *Inventory of Henry VIII*, Vol. I, Nos. 178, 703, 723, 1887–1890, 10920; Ives, *Anne Boleyn*, pp. 232–3. It is not clear whether the Rochford arms related to Anne or her brother George, whose goods were forfeited after his execution in 1536.

6 For a full analysis of the symbolism in the painting, see Ives, *Anne Boleyn*, pp. 234–5.

7 Recent research by the National Portrait Gallery has uncovered an

intriguing find. An X-ray of a portrait of Elizabeth holding some roses revealed not only that in the original painting she was holding a snake but that behind her was the face of a woman. The woman's dark eyes and French hood prompted a flurry of speculation that she was Anne Boleyn. However, the headdress dates to the 1570s or 1580s, and she wears a ruff that was fashionable many years after Anne's demise. Dendrochronological analysis suggests that the panel on which it was painted was first used between 1572 and 1582. Sadly, therefore, while the identity of the original sitter remains a mystery, it is unlikely to be Elizabeth's mother. I am indebted to Dr Charlotte Bolland, Senior Curator, Research and 16th Century Collections, at the National Portrait Gallery, for sharing her insights into the painting with me.

8 In *The Books of King Henry VIII and his Wives*, p. 124, James P. Carley states that there are nine or so surviving books that can be associated with Anne.

9 Kate McCaffrey, Assistant Curator at Hever Castle, has undertaken detailed research into Anne's books of hours: https://www.themorgan.org/blog/book-fit-two-queens.

10 BL C23 a8; Royal MS 19 D III.

11 This is now in the collection of the Duke of Northumberland at Alnwick Castle: Percy MS 465 fo. 231.

12 Doran, S. (ed.), *Elizabeth: The Exhibition at the National Maritime Museum* (London, 2003), p. 201; Ives, *Anne Boleyn*, p. 244; Strong, R., *Gloriana: The Portraits of Queen Elizabeth I* (London, 1987), pp. 138–9.

13 Hentzner, *Travels in England*, p. 72.

14 Sloane MS 814 fos. 8, 14; *A Catalogue of the Principal Works of Art at Chequers* (London, 1923), p. 80; Hill Cole, 'Maternal Memory', p. 6.

15 Immediately after Elizabeth's death, her successor, James I, gave it to the first Lord Home as a reward for his services.

16 Hill Cole, 'Maternal Memory', p. 13n.

CHAPTER 15: 'A Queen in heaven'

1 Perry, *Word of a Prince*, p. 274; Johnson, *Power and Intellect*, p. 291.

2 Marcus, Mueller and Rose, *Collected Works*, pp. 186–8, 199–202; Perry, *Word of a Prince*, pp. 272–3; Johnson, *Power and Intellect*, p. 291.

3 Strickland, *Life of Elizabeth*, p. 476.

4 Fraser, A., *Mary, Queen of Scots* (London, 1994), p. 529.

5 Walker, *Dissing Elizabeth*, p. 87.

6 Kenny, R. W., *Elizabeth's Admiral: The Political Career of Charles Howard, Earl of Nottingham, 1536–1624* (London, 1970), pp. 104–6.

7 BM Cotton MS Titus C VII fo. 50v.

8 Longford, E. (ed), *The Oxford Book of Royal Anecdotes* (Oxford University Press, 1989), p.244. The dog died soon afterwards, apparently from pining for his dead mistress.

9 Camden, *Elizabeth*, p. 115.

10 Marcus, Mueller and Rose, *Collected Works*, p. 296.

11 Laughton, J. K., *State Papers Relating to the Defeat of the Spanish Armada, Anno 1588*, 2 vols (London, 1894), Vol. I, pp. 225–6.

12 Laughton, J. K., *State Papers Relating to the Defeat of the Spanish Armada, Anno 1588*, 2 vols (London, 1894), Vol. II, pp. 138–42.

13 Boehrer, *Monarchy and Incest*, pp. 47–8; Weir, *Lady in the Tower*, p. 314.

14 The letter is now in the collections of The National Archives. SP 12/215 fo. 114.

15 *CSPD Elizabeth 1591–4*, p. 386; *1601–03*, pp. 22–3; *HMC Bath V*, pp. 221–3.

16 Borman, *Elizabeth's Women*, p. 347.

17 George Clifford, third Earl of Cumberland, who succeeded Lee as Champion, also wore a garment decorated with spheres in his portrait of c.1590. See Strong, *Gloriana*, pp. 140–1.

18 Watkins, S., *In Public and in Private: Elizabeth I and her World* (London, c.1998), p. 50.

19 Ives, *Anne Boleyn*, p. 257.

20 Weir, *Lady in the Tower*, pp. 309–11, 343–4.

21 Loades (ed.), *Papers of George Wyatt*, p. 24; Weir, *Lady in the Tower*, p. 308.

22 Bacon, F., *The Tragedy of Anne Boleyn* (c.1588); Weir, *Lady in the Tower*, pp. 316–17.

23 TNA SP 12/289.

24 Shell, *Elizabeth's Glass*, pp. 17, 19.

25 Harrison, *Letters*, p. 268; Pasmore, S., *The Life and Times of Queen Elizabeth I at Richmond Palace* (Richmond Local History Society, 2003), p. 56.

26 It still stands today, in the chapel of St Andrew, off the north transept.

27 Birch, T., *Memoirs of the Reign of Queen Elizabeth from the year 1581 till her Death*, 2 vols (London, 1754), Vol. II, p. 362.

28 Historical Manuscripts Commission, *Report on the Manuscripts of Lord De L'Isle & Dudley, preserved at Penshurst Place* (London, 1925), Vol. II, pp. 328–30; Tallis, *Elizabeth's Rival*, p. 279; Somerset, *Ladies in Waiting*, p. 88; Perry, *Word of a Prince*, p. 304.

29 I am extremely grateful to Dr Owen Emmerson, who recently acquired this painting for Hever and generously supplied a copy for the illustration section of this book. He also shared his research about the Waldegraves with me, for which I am indebted.

30 HMC *De L'Isle and Dudley*, Vol. II, pp. 442–4.

31 Harington, *Nugae Antiquae*, p. 90.

32 Nichols, *Progresses*, Vol. III, p. 612; Merton, C., 'The Women Who Served Queen Mary and Queen Elizabeth: Ladies, Gentlewomen and Maids of the Privy Chamber, 1553–1603' (Cambridge PhD thesis, 1992), p. 90.

33 The portrait has remained in the Cecil family ever since and still hangs at Hatfield House.

34 Harington, p. 96; Carey, *Memoirs*, pp. 136–8.

35 Bassnett, S., *Elizabeth I: A Feminist Perspective* (Oxford & New York, 1988), p. 258.

36 TNA PROB 11/101, fol. 1r.

37 *CSPD Elizabeth 1601–3*, pp. 298, 301; *CSPV*, Vol. IX, No. 1159. See also HMC *Salisbury* XII, p. 670.

38 Carey, *Memoirs*, p. 137.

39 Merton, p. 90; Birch, *Memoirs*, Vol. II, pp. 506–7; Carey, *Memoirs*, pp. 139–40; Pasmore, p. 65.

40 *CSPD Elizabeth 1580–1625*, Addenda, p. 407.

41 Weir, *Elizabeth*, p. 470; Camden, *Elizabeth*, p. 222.

42 Carey, *Memoirs*, pp. 139–40.

43 Kenny, *Elizabeth's Admiral*, p. 257. Another account claims that Elizabeth was beyond speech by this point and merely raised her hand to her head when the King of Scots' name was mentioned, to signal her assent. Carey, *Memoirs*, pp. 140–1.

44 Bruce, J. (ed.), *The Diary of John Manningham*, Camden Society (London, 1868), entry for 23 March 1603.

45 Carey himself gave a different account and claimed that it was only after some wrangling with the council that he was finally permitted to ride north with the news – and the ring. Carey, *Memoirs*, pp. 144–52.

46 Ibid., p. 152.

EPILOGUE: *'Surprised her sex'*

1 Hackett, *Virgin Mother, Maiden Queen*, pp. 214, 216.

2 *Anne of the Thousand Days* (Universal Pictures / The Rank Organisation, 1969). See also: Emmerson, O. and Ridgway, C., *The Boleyns of Hever Castle* (MadeGlobal Publishing, 2021), p. 110.

3 This became law with the Act of Settlement in 1701. Most of its provisions are still in place today, although the disqualification arising from marriage to a Roman Catholic was removed in 2015.

4 *CSPV*, Vol. VI, Part ii, No. 884, p. 1058.

5 Camden, *Elizabeth*, quoted in Haigh, *Elizabeth*, p. 22.

6 Stewart, A., *The Cradle King: A Life of James VI & I* (London, 2003), pp. 171–2.

ABBREVIATIONS

BL   British Library

CSPD   *Calendar of State Papers, Domestic Series*

CSPF   *Calendar of State Papers, Foreign Series*

CSPS   *Calendar of State Papers, Spain*

CSPV   *Calendar of State Papers, Venetian*

HMC   Historical Manuscripts Commission

LP   *Letters and Papers, Foreign and Domestic, Henry VIII*

TNA   The National Archives

When citing original sources, I have modernised the spelling for ease of reference.

BIBLIOGRAPHY

1. Archival Sources

Alnwick Castle Archives

Percy MS 465 fo. 231 – Anne Boleyn's French manuscript, *Ecclesiaste*, decorated with her falcon emblem

Bodleian Library

Bodleian Library MS C.Don.42 fos. 20–33 – William Latymer's 'Cronickille of Anne Bulleyne'

British Library

Additional MS 4293 – Miscellaneous warrants, papers, etc., collected by Birch, 1536–1765

Additional MS 35830 – State Papers (Hardwick), 1553–1561

Additional MS 40662 – Carles, L. de, *Histoire de Anne Boleyn Jadis Royne d'Angleterre*

Additional MS 62135 fos. 48–65 – A collection of documents by and relating to members of the Wyatt family. Includes a handwritten manuscript copy of *The life of the virtuous, Christian and renowned Queen Anne Boleyn* by George Wyatt and a transcript of Anne Boleyn's scaffold speech (fos. 63r–64)

Additional MS 71009 – Descriptions of Tudor Court ceremonies, including 'The Coronation of Queen Anne' (fos. 57r–60)

Cotton MS Titus B I fo. 161 – Acts necessary to be made at the Parliament of 1533, which confirmed the king's marriage with Anne Boleyn

Cotton MS Titus C VII fo. 50v – Davison's account of his part in Mary, Queen of Scots' execution, 1587

Cotton MS Otho C X fos. 232r–232v – Anne Boleyn's letter to Henry VIII from the Tower, 6 May 1536; fo. 234r–234v – Lady Margaret Bryan to Cromwell, requesting new clothes for Elizabeth and how she is to be styled [1536]

Cotton MS Vespasian C XIV – Miscellaneous papers from the reign of Elizabeth I

Cox, JE (ed), *Works of Archbishop Cranmer*, 2 vols. (Cambridge, 1844)

Egerton MS 985 fos. 33–33r – 'How the Queen's Chamber Shall Be Apparelled' for a birth; fos. 49–59r – 'Coronation of the most noble Princess Queen Anne'

Egerton MS 3320 – Elizabeth I's Coronation Drawings, 14–15 January 1559

Hargrave MS 497 – Papers relating to Coronations, Funerals, Investitures, etc. In particular: Investiture of Anne Boleyn as Marquess of Pembroke (fos. 32–32r); The Proceedings at Queen Elizabeth's Funeral (fos. 36–39r)

Harley MS 283 fo. 75 – Letter from Anne Boleyn announcing the birth of a 'princess', September 1533

Harley MS 303 fo. 1 – Letters Patent confirming Anne Boleyn as Marquess of Pembroke

Harley MS 543 – the coronation of Anne Boleyn (fos. 119–28); the christening of Princess Elizabeth (fos. 128–9r)

Harley MS 6561 – Jacques Lefèvre d'Étaples, translated for Anne Boleyn by 'her moost lovyng and fryndely brother', George Boleyn [before 1533]

Kings MS 396 – Genealogical tree of Elizabeth I

Lansdowne 1236 fo. 35 – Elizabeth demands the release of her kinsman, John Astley, during the Seymour scandal of 1549, and praises his wife Kat for raising her

Royal MS 7 C XVI – Household Accounts of King Henry VIII, etc.

Royal MS 16 E XIII – Frontispiece and title-page of *Le Pasteur évangélique* showing Anne Boleyn's falcon badge

Royal MS 18 A. lxiv – Leland, J. and Udall, N., *Versis and ditties made at the coronation of queen Anne*

Sloane MS 814 – New Year's gifts received by Elizabeth I between 1572 and 1587

Sloane MS 1207 fos. 1r–4r – Letter from the evangelical, Thomas Alwaye, to Anne Boleyn [c.1530], petitioning her for help

Stowe MS 151 fos. 1–2 – Transcript of Anne Boleyn's letter to the king written from the Tower on 6 May 1536 and found within Cromwell's papers

The National Archives

C115/M18/7511 – Charles Cornwallis to Lady Mary Scudamore (née Shelton), 1599

C115/M19/7543 – Thomas Radcliffe, Earl of Essex to Lady Mary Scudamore (née Shelton), 9 October 1576

C193/3 fo. 80 – Warrant issued by Henry VIII to Sir William Kingston, detailing the arrangements for Anne Boleyn's execution

KB 27/1241/2 – Plea roll of the Court of Queen's Bench showing Elizabeth enthroned beneath her mother's motto, *Semper Eadem*

LC2/4/3 fo. 53 – Blanche Parry's living allowance at court following Elizabeth I's accession

PROB 11/101 fo. 1r – The will of George Boleyn, Dean of Lichfield, 12 January 1603

SP 1/103 fos. 322–7 – 'The Queen's reckoning': list of Anne Boleyn's expenses at the time of her death, 1536

SP 11/4/2 fos. 3–3v – The 'Tide Letter', 1554

SP 12/215 fo. 114 – Robert Dudley's last letter to Elizabeth I

SP 12/289 fo. 48 – Elizabeth I's translation of Boethius's *The Consolation of Philosophy*

SP 70/7 fos. 1–11 – Alexander Ales's letter to Elizabeth I, with an account of her mother's downfall and execution, 1559

2. Printed Primary Sources

Arber, E. (ed.), *John Knox, First Blast of the Trumpet against the Monstrous Regiment of Women* (London, 1878)

Aylmer, J., *An harborowe for faithfull and trewe subiectes* (London, 1559)

Birch, T., *Memoirs of the Reign of Queen Elizabeth from the year 1581 till her Death*, 2 volumes (London, 1754)

Bourgault, S. and Kingston, R. (eds), Christine de Pizan, *The Book of the City of Ladies and Other Writings* (Indianapolis and Cambridge, 2018)

Boyle, J. (ed.), *Memoirs of the Life of Robert Carey . . . Written by Himself* (London, 1759)

Bridges, J., *The Supremacie of Christian Princes* (London, 1573)

Brown, R. (ed.), *Calendar of State Papers and Manuscripts, Relating to English Affairs, Existing in the Archives and Collections of Venice, and in other Libraries of Northern Italy*, Vols IV–IX (London, 1871–97)

Brown, R. L. and Bentinck, G. C. (eds), *Calendar of State Papers and Manuscripts, Relating to English Affairs, 1558–1580* Vol. VII (Cambridge, 2013)

Bruce, J. (ed.), *Annals of the First Four Years of the Reign of Queen Elizabeth by Sir John Hayward, Knt*, Camden Society Old Series VII (London, 1840)

Bruce, J (ed), *The Correspondence of Robert Dudley, Earl of Leycester, During his Government of the Low Countries, in the years 1585 and 1586* Camden Society XXVII (London, 1844)

Bruce, J. (ed.), *Correspondence of Matthew Parker* (Cambridge, 1853)

Byrne, M. St Clare (ed.), *The Lisle Letters*, 6 vols (Chicago, 1981)

Camden, W., *The Historie of the Most Renowned and Victorious Princesse Elizabeth, Late Queene of England* (London, 1630)

Collins, A. (ed.), *Letters and Memorials of State, in the reigns of Queen Mary, Queen Elizabeth, etc . . . Written and collected by Sir Henry Sidney, etc*, 2 volumes (London, 1746)

Dowling, M. (ed.), William Latymer, 'Cronickille of Anne Bulleyne', *Camden Miscellany*, Vol. XXX (London, 1990), pp. 23–65

Ellis, H. (ed.), *Original Letters Illustrative of English History, Including Numerous Royal Letters*, 3rd series, Volumes II–IV (London, 1846)

Foxe, J., *Acts and Monuments of These Latter and Perillous Dayes* (London, 1563)

Francis Steuart, A. (ed.), *Sir James Melville. Memoirs of His Own Life, 1549–93* (London, 1929)

Grafton's Chronicle; or, History of England . . . From the Year 1189, to 1558, Inclusive, Vol. II (London, 1809)

Hall, E., *Chronicle, Containing the History of England, During the Reign of Henry IV and the Succeeding Monarchs* (London, 1809)

Harington, Sir J., *Nugae Antiquae: Being a Miscellaneous Collection of Original Papers in Prose and Verse: Written in the Reigns of Henry VIII, Queen Mary, Elizabeth, King James, etc* (London, 1779),

Harrison, G. B. and Jones, R. A., *Andre Hurault de Maisse, A Journal of all that was accomplished by Monsieur de Maisse, ambassador in England from King Henri IV to Queen Elizabeth, 1597* (London, 1931)

Harrison, G. B., *The Letters of Queen Elizabeth* (London, 1935)

Haynes, A., *Collection of State Papers Relating to Affairs in the Reigns of King Henry VIII, King Edward VI, Queen Mary and Queen Elizabeth, From the Year 1542 to 1570 . . . Left by William Cecil, Lord Burghley . . . at Hatfield House* (London, 1740)

Haynes, S., A *Collection of the State Papers Relating to the Affairs in the Reigns of King Henry VIII, King Edward VI, Queen Mary and Queen Elizabeth, From the Year 1542 to 1570* (London, 1740)

Hentzner, P., *Travels in England during the Reign of Queen Elizabeth. With Fragmenta Regalia; Or, Observations on Queen Elizabeth's Times and Favourites By Sir Robert Naunton* (London, 1889)

Historical Manuscripts Commission, *Calendar of the Manuscripts of the Marquis of Salisbury, Preserved at Hatfield House, Herts*, Volumes I–XV (London, 1883–1930)

Historical Manuscripts Commission, *Report on the Manuscripts of Lord De L'Isle & Dudley, preserved at Penshurst Place*, Volumes I and II (London, 1925)

Historical Manuscripts Commission, *Calendar of the Manuscripts of the*

Most Honourable the Marquess of Bath, preserved at Longleat, Wiltshire, 1533–1659, Volume V (London, 1980)

Hume, M. A. S. (ed.), *Calendar of Letters and State Papers relating to English Affairs, preserved principally in the Archives of Simancas, Elizabeth I*, 4 vols (London, 1892–9)

Hume, M. A. S. et al. (eds), *Calendar of Letters, Despatches, and State Papers, relating to the Negotiations between England and Spain, preserved in the Archives at Simancas and Elsewhere, 1547–1558* (London, 1912–54)

Hume, M. A. S. (ed.), *Chronicle of King Henry VIII of England: Being a Contemporary Record of Some of the Principal Events of the Reigns of Henry VIII and Edward VI. Written in Spanish by an Unknown Hand* (London, 1889)

Ives, E. (ed.), *Letters and Accounts of William Brereton of Malpas*, Record Society of Lancashire and Cheshire, Vol. CXVI (Chester, 1978)

Jordan, W. K. (ed.), *Chronicle and Papers of Edward VI* (London, 1966)

Knollys, W, 'Papers relating to Mary, Queen of Scots', *Philobiblon Society Miscellanies*, Vol. XIV (London, 1872–6), pp. 14–69

Laing, D. (ed), *Notes of Ben Jonson's Conversations with William Drummond of Hawthornden* Volume I (London, 1842)

Laughton, J. K., *State Papers Relating to the Defeat of the Spanish Armada*, Navy Records Society, Vol. I (London, 1894)

Lemon, R., et al. (eds), *Calendar of State Papers, Domestic Series, of the Reigns of Edward VI, Mary, Elizabeth, (James I) 1547–1580 (1581–1625)*, 12 vols (London, 1856–72)

Manning, C. R., 'State Papers relating to the custody of the Princess Elizabeth at Woodstock, in 1554', *Norfolk Archaeology*, Vol. IV (1855), pp. 133–226

Marcus, L. S., Mueller, J. and Rose, M. B. (eds), *Elizabeth I: Collected Works* (Chicago and London, 2002)

Martienssen, A.K., *Queen Katherine Parr* (London, 1973)

McClure, N. E., *The Letters and Epigrams of Sir John Harington* (London, 1930)

Mueller, J. and Marcus, L. S. (eds), *Elizabeth I: Autograph Compositions and Foreign Language Originals* (Chicago, 2003)

Mulcaster, R., *The Quene's Majestie's passage through the citie of London to westminster the day before her coronacion* (London, 1559)

Murdin, W., *A Collection of State Papers Relating to Affairs in the Reign of Queen Elizabeth, 1571–96 . . . Left by William Cecil Lord Burghley . . . at Hatfield House* (London, 1759)

Newton, T., *An epitaphe upon the worthy and honorable lady, the Lady Knowles* (1569)

Nichols, J. G., *The Chronicle of Queen Jane and of Two Years of Queen Mary*, Camden Society, no. XLVIII (London, 1850)

Nichols, J. G. (ed.), *The Diary of Henry Machyn: Citizen and Merchant-Taylor of London, from AD 1550 to AD 1563* (London, 1848)

Nichols, J. G., *The Progresses and Public Processions of Queen Elizabeth*, 3 vols (London, 1823)

Pasmore, S., *The Life and Times of Queen Elizabeth I at Richmond Palace* (Richmond Local History Society, 2003)

Pratt, J. (ed.), *The Acts and Monuments of John Foxe*, 8 vols (London, [1877?])

Pryor, F., *Elizabeth I: her life in letters* (California, 2003)

Ridley, J. (ed.), *The Love Letters of Henry VIII* (Oxford, 1988)

Rigg, J. M. (ed.), *Calendar of State Papers, Relating to English Affairs, Preserved Principally at Rome, in the Vatican Archives and Library, 1558–71 and 1572–78*, 2 vols (London, 1916 and 1926)

Robinson, H. (ed.), *Original Letters Relative to the English Reformation*, 2 vols (Cambridge, 1846–7)

Rodríguez-Salgado, M. J. and Adams, S. (eds), 'The Count of Feria's Dispatch to Philip II of 14 November 1558', *Camden Miscellany*, 4th series, Vol. XXVIII (London, 1984), pp. 302–44

Rye, W. B. (ed.), *England as seen by Foreigners in the days of Elizabeth and James the First* (London, 1865)

Sander, N., *Rise and Growth of the Anglican Schism*, ed. Lewis, D. (London, 1877)

Singer, S. W. (ed.), Cavendish, G., *The Life of Cardinal Wolsey*, including Wyatt, G., *Some Particulars of the Life of Queen Anne Boleigne* (London, 1827)

The Statutes of the Realm. Printed By Command of His Majesty King George the Third. In pursuance of an Address of the House of Commons of Great Britain. From Original Records and Authentic Manuscripts, 11 vols (London, 1810–28)

Stevenson, J. et al. (eds), *Calendar of State Papers, Foreign Series, of the Reign of Elizabeth I, 1558–1591* (London, 1863–1969)

Strangford, Viscount (ed.), 'The Household Expenses of the Princess Elizabeth during her residence at Hatfield, October 1, 1551, to September 30, 1552', *The Camden Miscellany*, Vol. II (London, 1853)

Strype, J., *Ecclesiastical Memorials, Relating chiefly to Religion, and the Reformation of it . . . under King Henry VIII, King Edward VI and Queen Mary I*, 3 vols (Oxford, 1822)

Strype, J., *Annals of the Reformation and Establishment of Religion and . . . other occurrences in the Church of England; during the first twelve years of Queen Elizabeths . . . Reign*, 4 vols (Oxford, 1824)

Taylor-Smither, LJ, 'Elizabeth I: A Psychological Profile', *Sixteenth Century Journal*, Vol. XV No.1 (Kirksville, 1984)4 vols (Oxford, 1824)

Thomas, W., *The pilgrim: a dialogue of the life and actions of King Henry the Eighth*, ed. Froude, J.A. (London, 1861)

Wood, M. A. E., *Letters of Royal and Illustrious Ladies of Great Britain*, 3 vols (London, 1846)

Wright, T., *Queen Elizabeth and her Times, A Series of Original Letters, Selected from the Inedited Private Correspondence of the Lord Treasurer Burghley, the Earl of Leicester, the Secretaries Walsingham and Smith, Sir Christopher Hatton, etc*, 2 vols (London, 1838)

Wriothesley, C., *A Chronicle of England During the Reigns of the Tudors*, 2 vols (London, 1875, 1877)

Wyatt, G., *Extracts from The Life of the Virtuous, Christian, and Renowned Queen Anne Boleigne* (London, 1817)

3. Secondary Sources

Anglo, S., *Images of Tudor Kingship* (London, 1992)

Arber, E., *An English Garner: Ingatherings from our history and literature*, 8 vols (London, 1877–96)

Archer, J. E., Goldring, E. and Knight, S., *The Progresses, Pageants and Entertainments of Queen Elizabeth I* (Oxford, 2007)

Arnold, J., *'Lost from Her Majesties back': items of clothing and jewels lost or given away by Queen Elizabeth I between 1561–1585, entered in one of the day books kept for the records of the Wardrobes of Robes* (Costume Society, 1980)

Arnold, J., *Queen Elizabeth's Wardrobe Unlock'd* (Leeds, 1988)

Ascoli, G., *La Grande-Bretagne devant L'Opinion Française* (Paris, 1927)

Bassnett, S., *Elizabeth I: A Feminist Perspective* (Oxford & New York, 1988)

Bell, S. G., *The Lost Tapestries of the City of Ladies: Christine de Pizan's Renaissance Legacy* (Berkeley and Los Angeles, 2004)

Bernard, G. W., *Anne Boleyn: Fatal Attractions* (New Haven and London, 2010)

Boehrer, B. T., *Monarchy and Incest in Renaissance England: Literature, Culture, Kinship, and Kingship* (Philadelphia, 1992)

Bolland, C. (ed.), *The Tudors: Passion, Power and Politics* (London, 2022)

Bolland, C. and Cooper, T., *The Real Tudors: Kings and Queens Rediscovered* (London, 2015)

Borman, T., *Elizabeth's Women: The Hidden Story of the Virgin Queen* (Random House, 2009)

Brewer, J. S., *The Reign of Henry VIII*, 2 vols (London, 1968)

Broomhall, S. (ed.), *Women and Power at the French Court, 1483–1563* (Amsterdam, 2018)

Bruce, J. (ed.), *The Diary of John Manningham*, Camden Society (London, 1868)

Carley, J. P., *The Books of King Henry VIII and his Wives* (London, 2004)

A Catalogue of the Principal Works of Art at Chequers (London, 1923)

Clarke, S. and Collins, L., *Gloriana: Elizabeth I and the Art of Queenship* (Cheltenham, 2022)

Coast, D., 'William Tyndale, Henry VIII and The Obedience of a Christian Man', *The Historical Journal*, Vol. LXIV, no. 4 (Cambridge, September 2021), pp. 823–43

Collins, A. J. (ed.), *Jewels and Plate of Queen Elizabeth I: The Inventory of 1574* (London, 1955)

Colvin, H. M., *The History of the King's Works*, 6 vols (London, 1963–82)

Cooper, T. (ed.), *Elizabeth I & Her People* (London, 2014)

Cooper, T. (ed.), *Tudors to Windsors* (London, 2018)

DellaNeva, J., *The Story of the Death of Anne Boleyn: A Poem by Lancelot de Carle* (Tempe, 2021)

Dewhurst, J., 'The Alleged Miscarriages of Catherine of Aragon and Anne Boleyn', *Medical History*, Vol. XXVIII (Chalfont St Giles, 1984), pp. 49–56

Doran, S. (ed.), *Elizabeth: The Exhibition at the National Maritime Museum* (London, 2003)

Doran, S. (ed.), *Henry VIII: Man and Monarch* (London, 2009)

Doran, S. (ed.), *Elizabeth and Mary: Royal Cousins, Rival Queens* (London, 2021)

Dovey, Z., *An Elizabethan Progress: The Queen's Journey into East Anglia, 1578* (Stroud, 1996)

Dowling, M, *Humanism in the age of Henry VIII* (London, 1986)

Dowling, M., 'Anne Boleyn and Reform', *The Journal of Ecclesiastical History*, Vol. 35, No. 1 (Cambridge, January 1984), pp. 30–46

Duncan, S. and Schutte, V. (eds), *The Birth of a Queen: Essays on the Quincentenary of Mary I* (New York, 2016)

Dunn, S., *Elizabeth and Mary: Cousins, Rivals, Queens* (New York, 2004)

Emmerson, O. and McCaffrey, K., *Becoming Anne* (Norwich, 2022)

Emmerson, O. and Ridgway, C., *The Boleyns of Hever Castle* (MadeGlobal Publishing, 2021)

Fraser, A., *Mary, Queen of Scots* (London, 1994)

Fraser, A., *The Six Wives of Henry VIII* (London, 1996)

Friedmann, P., *Anne Boleyn* (Stroud, 2013)

Frye, S., *Elizabeth I. The Competition for Representation* (New York and Oxford University Press, 1993)

Gregory, A., 'Anne Boleyn and the Tower of London', *Tudor Places* magazine (April 2022)

Gristwood, S., *Elizabeth and Leicester* (London, 2007)

Gristwood, S., *Game of Queens: The Women Who Made Sixteenth-Century Europe* (London, 2016)

Gristwood, S., *The Tudors in Love: The Courtly Code Behind the Last Medieval Dynasty* (London, 2021)

Hackett, H., *Virgin Mother, Maiden Queen: Elizabeth I and the Cult of the Virgin Mary* (Basingstoke, 1995)

Haugaard, W., 'Elizabeth Tudor's Book of Devotions: A Neglected Clue to the Queen's Life and Character', *Sixteenth-Century Journal*, Vol. XII (1981), pp. 79–105

Hayward, M. (ed.), *Dress at the Court of Henry VIII* (Leeds, 2007)

Hayward, M. and Ward, P., *The Inventory of King Henry VIII: Textiles and Dress*, Vol. II (London, 2012)

Heath, J. B., 'An Account of Materials Furnished for the use of Queen Anne Boleyn, and the Princess Elizabeth, by William Loke, The King's Mercer, between the 20th January 1535 and the 27th April, 1536', *Miscellanies of the Philobiblon Society*, Volume VII (London, 1862–3)

Hibbert, C., *Elizabeth I: A Personal History of The Virgin Queen* (London, 2001)

Hill Cole, M., 'Maternal Memory: Elizabeth Tudor's Anne Boleyn', in D. Stump, L. Shenk and C. Levin (eds), *Elizabeth and the Sovereign Arts* (Tempe, 2011)

Hoak, D. (ed.), *Tudor Political Culture* (Cambridge, 1995)

Hunt, A., *The Drama of Coronation: Medieval Ceremony in Early Modern England* (Cambridge, 2008)

Ives, E., *The Life and Death of Anne Boleyn* (Oxford, 2005)

Ives, E. W., 'Anne Boleyn and the Early Reformation in England: The Contemporary Evidence', *Historical Journal*, Vol. XXXVII, No. 2 (Cambridge, June 1994), pp. 389–400

Johnson, P., *Elizabeth I: A Study in Power and Intellect* (London, 1974)

Kenny, R. W., *Elizabeth's Admiral: The Political Career of Charles Howard, Earl of Nottingham, 1536–1624* (London, 1970)

Law, E., *The History of Hampton Court Palace*, 3 vols (London, 1885–91)

Lawson, J. A. (ed.), *The Elizabethan New Year's Gift Exchanges 1559–1603* (Oxford, 2013)

Levin, C., *The Heart and Stomach of a King: Elizabeth I and the Politics of Sex and Power* (Philadelphia, 1994)

Licence, A., *In Bed with the Tudors: The Sex Lives of a Dynasty from Elizabeth of York to Elizabeth I* (Stroud, 2013)

Loades, D. M., *Elizabeth I: The Golden Reign of Gloriana* (London and New York, 2003)

Loades, D. M., *The Tudor Court* (Oxford, 2003)

Loades, D. M., *Mary Tudor. The Tragical History of the first Queen of England* (Richmond, 2006)

Loades, D. M., *Henry VIII* (Stroud, 2011)

Loades, D. M. (ed.), *The Papers of George Wyatt*, Camden Society, 4th series, Vol. V (London, 1968)

Longford, E. (ed), *The Oxford Book of Royal Anecdotes* (Oxford University Press, 1989)

MacCaffrey, W. T., *Elizabeth I* (London, 1993)

Mackay, L., *Inside the Tudor Court: Henry VIII and his Six Wives through the Eyes of the Spanish Ambassador* (Stroud, 2015)

Mackay, L., *Among the Wolves of Court: The Untold Story of Thomas and George Boleyn* (London, 2021)

McCulloch, D. (ed.), 'The Vita Mariae Angliae Reginae of Robert Wingfield of Brantham', *Camden Miscellany*, Vol. XXVIII, Camden Society, 4th series, Vol. XXIX (London, 1984)

McIntosh, J. L., *From Heads of Household to Heads of State: The Preaccession Households of Mary and Elizabeth Tudor, 1516–1558* (New York, 2009)

Merton, C., 'The Women Who Served Queen Mary and Queen Elizabeth: Ladies, Gentlewomen and Maids of the Privy Chamber, 1553–1603' (Cambridge PhD thesis, 1992)

Mitchell, D. M., 'Table linen associated with Queen Elizabeth's visit to Gresham's Exchange', in A. Saunders (ed.), *The Royal Exchange*, London Topographical Society, Vol. CLII (London, 1997), pp. 50–6

Nichols, F. M., *The Hall of Lawford Hall: Records of an Essex House and of its Proprietors from the Saxon Times to Henry VIII* (London, 1891)

Norton, E, *The Anne Boleyn Papers* (Stroud, 2013)

Paget, H., 'The Youth of Anne Boleyn', *Bulletin of the Institute of Historical Research*, Vol. LIV, No. 130 (London, November 1981), pp. 162–70

Perry, M., *The Word of a Prince: A Life of Elizabeth I from Contemporary Documents* (Woodbridge, 1990)

Pinches, J. H. and R. V., *The Royal Heraldry of England* (London, 1974)

Plowden, A, *The Young Elizabeth* (Cheltenham, 2011)

Porter, L., *Mary Tudor: The First Queen* (London, 2007)

Prescott, A. L., 'The Pearl of the Valois and Elizabeth I', in Hannay, M. P. (ed.), *Silent But for the Word: Tudor Women as Patrons, Translators, and Writers of Religious Works* (Kent, Ohio, 1985), pp. 61–76

Princely Magnificence: Court Jewels of the Renaissance (London, 1981)

Prior, F., *Elizabeth I: Her Life in Letters* (Berkeley, 2003)

Reilly, E. G. S., *Historical Anecdotes of the Families of the Boleynes, Careys, Mordaunts, Hamiltons and Jocelyns* (Newry, 1839)

Richards, J. M., *Elizabeth I* (London and New York, 2012)

Richardson, R. E., *Mistress Blanche: Queen Elizabeth I's Confidante* (Herefordshire, 2007)

Ridley, J., *Elizabeth I: The Shrewdness of Virtue* (New York, 1988)

Shell, M., *Elizabeth's Glass* (Lincoln, Nebraska and London, 1993)

Smith, L. B., *Henry VIII: The Mask of Royalty* (St Albans, 1973)

Smither, L. J., 'Elizabeth I: A Psychological Profile', *Sixteenth-Century Journal*, Vol. XV, No.1 (London, 1984), pp. 47–72

Somerset, A., *Elizabeth I* (London, 1991)

Somerset Fry, P., *Chequers: The Country Home of Britain's Prime Ministers* (London, 1977)

Starkey, D., *Elizabeth: Apprenticeship* (London, 2001)

Starkey, D., *The Reign of Henry VIII: Personalities and Politics* (London, 2002)

Starkey, D., *Six Wives: The Queens of Henry VIII* (London, 2003)

Starkey, D. (ed.), *The English Court: From the Wars of the Roses to the Civil War* (Longman, 1987)

Starkey, D. (ed.), *The Inventory of King Henry VIII: The Transcript*, Vol. I (London, 1988)

Strickland, A., *Lives of the Queens of England* (London, 1851)

Strickland, A., *The Life of Queen Elizabeth* (London, 1910)

Strong, R., *The Cult of Elizabeth: Elizabethan Portraiture and Pageantry* (London, 1987)

Strong, R., *Gloriana: The Portraits of Queen Elizabeth I* (London, 1987)

Tallis, N., *Elizabeth's Rival: The Tumultuous Tale of Lettice Knollys, Countess of Leicester* (London, 2017)

Vasoli, S., *Anne Boleyn's Letter from the Tower: A New Assessment* (MadeGlobal Publishing 2015)

Walker, J. M., *Dissing Elizabeth: Negative Representations of Gloriana* (Durham, 1998)

Warkentin, G. (ed.), *The Queen's Majesty's Passage & Related Documents* (Toronto, 2004)

Warnicke, R. M., *The Rise and Fall of Anne Boleyn: Family Politics at the Court of Henry VIII* (Cambridge, 1989)

Warnicke, R. M., *The Marrying of Anne of Cleves: Royal Protocol in Early Modern England* (Cambridge, 2000)

Watkins, S., *In Public and in Private: Elizabeth I and her World* (London, c.1998)

Watkins, S. B., *Lady Katherine Knollys: The Unacknowledged Daughter of Henry VIII* (Winchester, 2015)

Weir, A., *Children of England: the heirs of King Henry VIII* (London, 1996)

Weir, A., *Elizabeth the Queen* (London, 1999)

Weir, A., *Henry VIII: King and Court* (London, 2001)

Weir, A., *The Six Wives of Henry VIII* (London, 2007)

Weir, A., *The Lady in the Tower: The Fall of Anne Boleyn* (London, 2009)

Weir, A., *Mary Boleyn: 'The Great and Infamous Whore'* (London, 2011)

Wiesener, L., *The Youth of Queen Elizabeth, 1533–1558*, 2 vols (London, 1879)

Williams, N., *All the Queen's Men: Elizabeth I and her Courtiers* (London, 1972)

Wilson, D., *In the Lion's Court: Power, Ambition and Sudden Death in the Reign of Henry VIII* (London, 2002)

Wilson, D., *Sweet Robin: a biography of Robert Dudley, Earl of Leicester, 1533–1588* (London, 1981)

Wood, M.A.E., *Letters of Royal and Illustrious Ladies of Great Britain* 3 volumes (London, 1846)

PICTURE ACKNOWLEDGEMENTS

Alamy Stock Photo: 2 above left/Science History Images, 2 centre right/Heritage Image Partnership Ltd, 5 above left/Artefact, 7 above right/CBN, 8 above left/Ian Dagnall, 11 below left/Buff Henry Photography, 13 above left/Heritage Image Partnership Ltd, 14 centre left/Art Collection 2, 14 below right/GL Archive, 15 above right, 16 above left/The Picture Art Collection. The Bodleian Libraries, University of Oxford: 8 below left (MS.Cherry 36, front board), 10 above right (MS.Douce 363 fol 76r). Courtesy Tracy Borman: 3 above. Bridgeman Images: 16 above right. ©British Library Board. All rights reserved/Bridgeman Images: 4 below, 9 centre right. With thanks to Owen Emmerson, Castle Historian and Assistant Curator, Hever Castle: 15 below. ©Mark Fiennes Archive. All rights reserved 2023/Bridgeman Images: 5 above right. Courtesy Paul Fitzsimmons/Marhamchurch Antiques, Devon: 2 below left, 11 above left, 13 centre right. ©CSG CIC Glasgow Museums Collection/Gifted by Sir William and Lady Burrell to the City of Glasgow, 1944/Bridgeman Images: 10 above left. Gresham College, London: 13 below. Hatfield House, Hertfordshire/Bridgeman Images: 16 below. Hever Castle & Gardens, Kent: 1, 3 below, 4 centre right, 10 below right. Photo ©Historic Royal Palaces/Bridgeman Images: 6 below. ©Lambeth Palace Library/Bridgeman Images: 14 above right. The National Archives, UK: 5 centre right and below (SP1/103 ff 322-7), 9 above left (KB27/1241/2). The Archives of the Duke of Northumberland at Alnwick Castle, DNP: 9 below left (MS 465, ff 32r). Private Collection: 7 centre. Courtesy Dr Peter Rowan: 11 above right and centre. Royal Collection Trust/© His Majesty King Charles III, 2023/Bridgeman Images: 4 above left, 8 centre right. Collection SCHUNCK, municipality Heerlen (NL): 6 above/photo Klaus Tummers. The Parish Church of St John the Baptist, Cirencester: 12 above left and above right. Victoria and Albert Museum, London: 12 centre and below right. Yale Center for British Art, Paul Mellon Collection: 7 below.

INDEX